D1744038

# LIMINAL WHITENESS IN EARLY US FICTION

www.edinburghuniversitypress.com/series/incal

# LIMINAL WHITENESS IN EARLY US FICTION

Hannah Lauren Murray

EDINBURGH
University Press

Edinburgh University Press is one of the leading university presses in
the UK. We publish academic books and journals in our selected subject
areas across the humanities and social sciences, combining cutting-edge
scholarship with high editorial and production values to produce academic
works of lasting importance. For more information visit our website:
edinburghuniversitypress.com

© Hannah Lauren Murray, 2021

Edinburgh University Press Ltd
The Tun – Holyrood Road, 12(2f) Jackson's Entry, Edinburgh EH8 8PJ

Typeset in 10/12.5 Adobe Sabon by
IDSUK (DataConnection) Ltd, and
printed and bound by CPI Group (UK) Ltd,
Croydon, CR0 4YY

A CIP record for this book is available from the British Library

ISBN 978 1 4744 8173 1 (hardback)
ISBN 978 1 4744 8175 5 (webready PDF)
ISBN 978 1 4744 8176 2 (epub)

The right of Hannah Lauren Murray to be identified as the author of this
work has been asserted in accordance with the Copyright, Designs and
Patents Act 1988, and the Copyright and Related Rights Regulations 2003
(SI No. 2498).

# CONTENTS

# ACKNOWLEDGEMENTS

This book originated in a seminar on Ernest Valdemar's blackened tongue in 2010 at the University of Leeds. For that discussion, and her continued encouragement, support and honesty, I thank Bridget Bennett. At the University of Nottingham, my work benefited enormously from the encyclopaedic knowledge, incisive questions and lightning-quick email responses of Matthew Pethers and Graham Thompson. I am particularly grateful to Matthew for suggesting I read a little-known novel called *Sheppard Lee*. Tom Bishop, Alex Bryne, Lorenzo Costaguta, Michelle Green, Daniel King, Alice Lilly, Rosemary Pearce, Rachel Williams and Olivia Wright served as excellent lunchtime companions and readers. At King's College London, Michael Collins was (and continues to be) an encouraging and supportive mentor, and Vicky Carroll a true friend. My colleagues at the University of Liverpool warmly welcomed me in September 2019 and I thank them for their friendliness and collaboration, both in person and on the other side of a Microsoft Teams screen.

Awards from the Arts and Humanities Research Council UK and the University of Nottingham School of Cultures, Languages and Area Studies funded this research. A generous Fulbright American Studies Research Grant in 2015 funded my archival work on Robert Montgomery Bird at the Kislak Library, University of Pennsylvania, and I thank John Pollack for his support while at Penn. At Edinburgh University Press, my series editors Chris Hanlon, Sarah Robbins and Andrew Taylor have been fantastic in their enthusiasm for the project, and I thank my press editors Ersev Ersoy and Michelle Houston for their support with the publishing process. The two anonymous readers took great care in responding to the work and supplied generous constructive suggestions. Thanks also to Lucy Arnold, Bridget Bennett, Jimmy Packham and Stephanie Palmer for facilitating discussion of my work as a visiting speaker and to Dara Downey at *The Irish Journal of Gothic and Horror Studies* for her edits of an article that forms part of Chapter 4.

I was fortunate to join the British Association of Nineteenth-Century Americanists soon after its inception and it has served as an excellent scholarly home. The Melville and Brockden Brown societies have been incredibly friendly and warm in their support of early career scholars. On both sides of the Atlantic I have received encouragement, advice, feedback and drinks from several colleagues within the nineteenth century research community not mentioned above: J. Michelle Coghlan, Hilary Emmett, Duncan Faherty, Tomos Hughes, Wyn Kelley, Katie McGettigan, Ben Pickford, Matthew Salway, Ed Sugden, Tom Wright and Xine Yao. Since I have known her, Hester Blum has been a model of intellectual generosity and enthusiasm.

My parents Patricia and Philip, and my sister Ella, have encouraged and supported me in all my academic endeavours, even when it has not been clear exactly what an American literature researcher does all day. Thanks to Chuck, Elizabeth and the whole Ziegler menagerie for the sunshine and boundless joy. Tim, your unwavering support and belief in me – especially when my own faith faltered – has sustained me.

# A NOTE ON LANGUAGE

In this book I capitalise White and Whiteness. I leave the terms in lower case if they appear so in quoted material. I am conscious that capitalised White/ness appears in the language of White supremacist groups that elevate Whiteness as a superior racial identity. My argument in *Liminal Whiteness* is not only evidently against this ideology, it situates how this ideology develops in early US fiction through episodes of liminality and precarity. Capitalisation of White/ness focuses attention on Whiteness as a significant social construct deserving of critique, rather than a default position that today maintains its power through invisibility.

# INTRODUCTION: INEXPLICABLE VOICES – LIMINAL WHITENESS IN THE EARLY UNITED STATES

This is a book about dead White men. To put it more precisely, this is a book about what happens when White men become deathly in fiction. Voices from the dead, dying and supernatural pervade early US fiction. Readers repeatedly encounter speaking visions and ghosts, talking corpses, quasi-supernatural speakers such as ventriloquists and spiritualist mediums, enchanted beings and spectral figures. In this book I identify 'liminal Whiteness' in works from Charles Brockden Brown to Frank J. Webb. Their dead, dying and otherworldly White characters, who exist on the threshold between the physical and spiritual worlds, transform into socially dead non-White groups in ways that amplify the possibility of White exclusion and dispossession. These figures, speaking when and where they should not, utter powerful articulations of White anxiety in the early United States.

Critical work in the past three decades has identified and investigated the haunting presence of non-White groups in American literature. Toni Morrison influentially suggests in *Playing in the Dark* (1992) that an African American 'shadow' or ghost can be detected in White-authored texts, even when 'texts are not "about" Africanist presences or characters or narrative or idiom'. In Morrison's view, symbolic and literal representations of the racially oppressed are 'the vehicle by which the American self knows itself'.[1] But few have asked what happens when this racial otherness appears in a White and often male body. In this book, I examine the possibility that across the works of Brown, Washington Irving, James Fenimore Cooper, Robert Montgomery Bird, Edgar

Allan Poe, Nathaniel Hawthorne, Herman Melville and Webb, to quote Renée Bergland, White, male and middle-class Americans 'contain . . . the female, the dark-skinned, the alienated worker, and the geographically marginal'.[2] By articulating fears of marginalisation, exclusion and loss for White citizens, the liminal figure disturbs prescriptions of racial belonging and increasingly essentialist ideas of White identity in the early US. At the same time, by 'containing' threats of dispossession and replacement within the bodies of White men, authors attempt to exorcise anxieties about shifting ideals of citizenship, social position and racial mobility in the early United States.

From Brown to Webb, scenes of death, dying and the supernatural offer the possibility for White citizens – characters and readers – to imagine the living death and dispossession experienced by the non-White noncitizen. Transforming the White man into a less-than-White and spectral figure is a potent way to speculate potential loss. Russ Castronovo, in *Necro Citizenship* (2001), argues for the ambivalent position of the dead or spectral body in nineteenth-century America. The dead are marginalised entities and are no longer able to claim the rights of the living citizen, mirroring many socially dead groups in the early United States. The non-White or non-male body both signal 'darker patterns of dis*corp*oration' or the exclusion from the community and the body politic, and they offer counterpoints to how good White (male) citizens should behave. For example, antebellum conduct guides use slavery figuratively to warn young White men against masturbation; men must escape 'slavery to the self' and to the private body in order to become self-restrained and respectable citizens.[3] The socially dead and the dead body are perceived as unchanging and unable to participate in their community, but at the same time deceased White men offer living citizens models of behaviour through memorialisation and commemoration. They are held up as an idealised form of state identity because death represents the 'abstract body' of 'democratic selfhood' that has been stripped of individual living and material desires, and replaced with spiritual and political ideals.[4] In other words, the individual subject must experience a metaphoric death, casting aside any identity associated with gender, race, ethnicity, religion, sexuality or class, in order to become a well-behaved citizen. To enjoy political representation, the individual must subscribe to set behaviours expected of the citizen, behaviours that ground Whiteness itself, which in this book I outline as: industry, rationality, respectability, sociality and – ironic for a political condition that demands conformity – autonomy.

This abstracted and purportedly disembodied citizenship has bodily specificity; by elevating deceased figures such as the Founding Fathers, the ideal citizen's body came to be seen as White, male, heterosexual, able-bodied, Protestant and middle class. Think of Glendinning Sr in Melville's *Pierre* (1852), who appears in gleaming and 'unclouded, snow-white' mausoleum marble, preserved as the 'personification of perfect human goodness and virtue'. In the transformation of White men into white marble, the statue is a static, unchanging model of respectable patriarchy. Commemorated as a loving and responsible husband and father, Glendinning's death blinds his family to the 'specks and flaws' of his individual transgressions.[5] *Liminal Whiteness in Early US Fiction* addresses what happens when the statue of the dead White man starts to crumble and when the White male fails to demonstrate or loses these expected values. Through his examples of those who lack civic rights – groups from which citizens should transcend and differentiate themselves – Castronovo asks: 'How does the subject's death generate the conditions for the citizen's birth?'[6] In this book, I show that many early US authors are preoccupied with how citizens are themselves at risk of returning to subjects by imagining the transformation of White men into liminal spectres.

## CRITICAL AND LIMINAL WHITENESS

In this book, Whiteness operates as a shifting social category that expands or contracts in different contexts, thereby including or excluding different groups of people and placing individuals along its borders or limens. I approach Whiteness under the lens of critical Whiteness studies, which employs three modes of the 'critical': to draw attention to Whiteness as a site of critique, to criticise structures of Whiteness in an antiracist framework, and to be critical – both necessary and urgent – to our understanding of how Whiteness operates and dominates today. This scholarly tradition stretches back to W. E. B. DuBois writing 'The Souls of White Folks' in 1920, in which he claims to 'see these souls undressed and from the back and side. I see the working of their entrails. I know their thoughts and they know that I know.'[7] For DuBois, African Americans' proximity to and lived experience of White supremacy enables them to perceive how race operates and to navigate the social conditions that produce racial inequality. We could go even further back to examine how African American writers depict the effect of chattel slavery and racial hierarchies on White men and women, which I turn to in my final chapter on Webb's *The Garies and their Friends* (1857). The initial aim of critical Whiteness studies, put forward by writers such as DuBois, James Baldwin, Audre Lorde and bell hooks, has been to invert the expectation that Whiteness – and male Whiteness specifically – is the invisible yet expected default position in society against which all other groups stand out, particularly Black people.[8] But Whiteness is not an absence of identity and this default abstraction is a form of identity politics, leading to assumptions of dominance over non-White nonmale groups. To appear as unmarked – Melville's white marble father – when all other bodies are marked (by race, gender, sexuality) is still a distinct category. George Yancy isolates Whiteness in *Look, a White!* (2012), arguing that making Whiteness visible 'returns to white people the problem of whiteness' so they can understand social and material conditions that produce Whiteness as an identity, conditions already visible to – and understood by – people of colour.[9]

As critical Whiteness studies has developed, scholarship has expanded beyond a Black/White binary to examine how Whiteness operates along geographical borders and in relation to indigeneity, and its intersections with class, ethnicity, nationality and gender to form intra-White hierarchies in which people can be more or less White.[10] Whiteness is not an innate biological condition, but a social construct: not simply phenotype, but 'a way of "doing" identity'.[11] In other words, Whiteness is a practice of personal values and behaviours that have come to be identified and maintained as White. As Sara Ahmed discusses, Whiteness is phenomenological – it is a way of being in the world, 'an orientation that puts certain things within reach'. Specific ways of being that she terms 'styles, capacities, aspirations, techniques, habits' become White; for example, the assumption that White people are at home in professional spaces, as Ahmed illustrates through her experience of the university.[12] Whiteness promises a sense of ownership over the self and by extension, access to spaces. In an early US context, which I discuss shortly, Whiteness meant not being a piece of property, but it nevertheless became a property in itself that White Americans could use to assert their social dominance over people of colour and enjoy exclusive social rights.[13]

Whiteness brings together those who perform desired values such as autonomy, industry, rationality, respectability and sociality, and marks out those who appear to deviate from or fail to demonstrate them. The cohesive power and protection of Whiteness is a 'straightening device' that compels bodies 'line up' to show and share expected behaviours – to be like everyone else who appears White.[14] Ahmed's way of thinking about Whiteness guides this book – Whiteness is a lived experience consisting of relations between people who move in the world in the same way and the marking out of those who do not. If Whiteness is an identity that operates beyond skin colour alone, then it is open to be malleable and shifting – in the nineteenth century, people could be considered not White even if they were 'Caucasian'. Whiteness is not a flat, monolithic state but is instead 'variegated': Germans, the Irish, Italians, Eastern Europeans and Jews gradually became White through changing attitudes that non-Anglo populations could possess White-coded values, whereas poor rural White groups have been described as 'white trash' and 'not quite right' for lacking respectability or industriousness.[15] As a result, these groups have lost their Whiteness, pushed closer to the descriptors of people of colour. Critical Whiteness studies has often focused on the construction and maintenance of Whiteness, but has paid less attention to the reverse, that if Whiteness can be established or bestowed on groups, then its loss or removal can be threatened. In this book, a constellation of White figures – not just those on the peripheries of society but also fully enfranchised, educated and professional Anglo-American men – experience the loss of Whiteness through a perceived failure or refusal to meet White identity expectations. Ahmed argues that if a body cannot perform these behaviours it loses its capabilities and access: 'When someone's whiteness is in dispute, then they come under "stress", which in turn threatens body motility, or what the body "can do".'[16] In early US fiction, White figures who lose or fail to show these values lose their motility and *mortality* in becoming what I term 'liminally White'.

Although carrying general connotations of in-betweenness, looking at liminality's anthropology-specific roots shows its aptness for discussing how Whiteness is lost or gained in the early US. Arnold van Gennep's *Rites of Passage* (1908) conceives liminality as a transformative process in which an individual experiences the death of one stage of life and the birth of a new stage. In van Gennep's study of African and Asian tribes, this process occurs during key events in an individual's life – adulthood, marriage, childbirth and death – and is evident in 'preliminal rites (rites of separation), liminal rites (rites of transition), and postliminal rites (rites of incorporation)'.[17] Victor W. Turner's research in the 1960s and 1970s reinvigorated the concept to focus on van Gennep's 'liminal rites', by defining liminality as a temporary 'interstructural situation' in which someone transitions between the 'relatively fixed or stable condition[s]' of 'legal status, profession, office or calling, rank or degree'. Turner associates the liminal with 'such general oppositions as life and death, male and female, food and excrement, simultaneously, since they are at once dying from or dead to their former status and life, and being born and growing into new ones'. Liminality is characterised by the 'blurring and merging' of these oppositions or 'distinctions'.[18] A change in social status is marked by blurring or merging of categorical distinctions, of which race is one. Joseph Roach's work on New Orleans, for example, establishes the carnival as a liminal zone, in which the theatrical crossing of racial boundaries by Mardi Gras Indians mirrors the lawlessness and timelessness found at the moment of death.[19]

In the Ndembu rites that Turner observed in his fieldwork, those in transition often 'have no status, property, insignia, secular clothing indicating rank or role, [or] position in a kinship system'.[20] They experience a temporary social death during which their ties to family and community are severed and they have no claim to possessions or position. To be liminal means to be marginalised and to lose status, to hope for a return or reclamation. In this book I conceive of liminal Whiteness as a process of transformation, but more specifically as an experience of precarity and demotion that is crystallised on the borders between life and death, between the physical and spiritual. I am less interested in hybridity or in-betweenness, but rather the experience of being less-than. Fiction of the early United States features White characters continually in flux along and falling outside the borders of citizenship, personhood and Whiteness itself.

A range of literary scholarship has considered texts that represent liminal figures, spaces and moments. These studies are led by Turner's work to focus on the 'ambivalence and uncertainty' of liminality, and acknowledge that writers often 'shun complete incorporation' found in post-liminal states.[21] Literary liminality explores the 'undoing, dissolution, [and] decompositions' of Turner's liminal process, without the resolution of growth and progress found in the post-liminal state.[22] In the deliberately ambiguous and uncertain texts in this book, the liminal moment speculates permanent social exclusion and precarity, with the threat of Whiteness and citizenship not reclaimed or returned. Each author grapples with containing liminal Whiteness by either setting up a neat yet unconvincing post-liminal resolution of return and renewal, for example body-hopping Sheppard Lee's reclamation of his own body and land, or by removing liminal figures from the commons through death or disappearance, such as Bartleby's spectral wasting away. The liminal is a mode where characters inhabit alternative subject positions, and writers explore and exorcise the threat of discorporation, at a time when full citizenship was in flux and vulnerable to social, legal and economic change.

The majority of literary liminality studies attend to marginal or minor literature to theorise the experience of writing from the thresholds of society. While this book does not seek to diminish this scholarship, it instead takes up Isabel Soto's call that 'liminality as a threshold or critical tool need not be limited to marginal or marginalised literatures'.[23] For the majority of this book, the several canonical White male authors I discuss, who write from a position of social dominance, use the language of liminal Whiteness to imagine the potential loss of rights for White men. To echo Peter Coviello's words, returning to these White male authors and texts is a deliberate 'archival strategy, one that means to foreground, and then bring into sharper focus, some of the consequences, the lived intricacy' of Whiteness and citizenship and fears of their loss as felt by those who possess both.[24] In concentrating on this set of writers, we see how discourses of White male citizenship and White supremacy are consciously constructed by those who benefit the most from them and yet are anxious about the possibility of precarious White citizenship. As I discuss later, reading for Whiteness – and specifically liminal Whiteness – in White male texts is a recuperative act because the self-representation of White male citizenship's values is woven into both quotidian and fantastical encounters. I respond to Yancy's claim to turn the problems of Whiteness to White people, by not only recognising Whiteness as a critical site, and returning the gaze to Whiteness, but to also claim that White authors grapple with fears of social precarity through the language of liminality, the imagined loss of Whiteness and life itself. Fears of no longer being White permeate early US fiction and provide a genealogy for contemporary White anxieties of being marginalised and minoritised, which still finds a voice in the language of exclusion and death. Whiteness and male Whiteness has its own identity politics rooted in perceived victimhood as a result of increased rights for White women, people of colour, the LGBTQ+ community. As I discuss in the following pages, liminal

Whiteness means inhabiting a state of being below the full rights of citizenship that were afforded to able White men in the early United States.

## LIMINAL WHITENESS IN THE EARLY UNITED STATES

In the early United States, the identity expectations of Whiteness are inextricable from the conscious creation and delineation of citizenship: Whiteness and citizenship collapse into one. After the Revolution, America entered a liminal period of citizen-defining, as people suddenly transitioned from colonial subjects to independent self-governing citizens. Early national historian and congressman David Ramsay encapsulated this transformation, commenting in 1789 that 'a nation was born in day. Nearly three millions of people who had been subjects, became citizens.' Ramsay recognised that not everyone living in the US could be a citizen, stating that 'Negroes are inhabitants, but not citizens' because they were not enfranchised.[25] Processes for becoming an American citizen were written into the Naturalization Acts of 1790 onwards, which guaranteed citizenship after two years' residency to White immigrants who could prove 'good character' through a clean criminal record and a public declaration of exclusive US affiliation.[26] Amendments during the decade reinscribed citizenship as White only; by 1798, the path to citizenship was open to White aliens after an extended fourteen-year period of residency.[27] But without a constitutional framework specifying what citizenship looks like for those born in the US – beyond law-abiding national allegiance – its origins are 'speculative' and take form through extra-legal and cultural discussion.[28] As David Ricci outlines, a good citizen carries out legal, political and social responsibilities by obeying the laws of their country, participating in state activities (such as voting) and exercising their virtues in society. This cultural ideology of 'virtue' manifests as a set of expected qualities and behaviours that in the early US included autonomy, industry, rationality, respectability and sociality.[29] These personal and civic qualities were not explicitly stated in legal texts, yet character became increasingly indistinguishable from Whiteness, specifically Anglo-Saxon Protestant Whiteness. In the Naturalization Acts only a 'free white person' was assumed to have the capability to prove 'good character', but the tethering of Whiteness to citizenship extended beyond naturalisation. Race became the dominant language for framing and discussing citizenship because of the assumption of different groups' capability to perform these personal and civic values.

To be a 'citizen' carries two meanings – Ramsay's definition of a free and autonomous person who has undergone transformation from colonial subject, but also an able, White, male, propertied group who possess full legal, political and social rights, as outlined by Ricci. I choose to focus almost entirely on White male characters because they are the most enfranchised group, who paradoxically embody an abstracted citizenship yet repeatedly communicate fears of losing this entitlement and being treated as dependent, lazy, irrational, disreputable, unsociable. This group were required to fulfil all legal, political and social expectations of citizenship (the five values in the above paragraph) because they were considered capable of doing so. By contrast, those outside of the category of 'able white men' existed on the 'borders of belonging' in early US society.[30] Native Americans, African Americans, White women, recent immigrants, the disabled, the itinerant and the institutionalised all existed on a sliding scale of states below full legal, social and political citizenship, from White women expected to display civic virtues yet receiving limited freedom and suffrage, to enslaved African Americans viewed as human property incapable of understanding or participating in civilised society – both states that I discuss in comparison to White male citizenship throughout the book. For example, the novels of Brown centre young White men navigating and negotiating citizenship in the growing American city and along the frontier. In contrast, non Anglo-American populations – African Americans free or enslaved, Native Americans and some European immigrants – exist as marginalised figures, appearing as shadowy or even invisible characters with no development or interior life. When I discuss White women in Chapter 1 – Clara Wieland and Constantia Davis – it is through the lens of rationality, a defeminising quality that women were encouraged to develop in order to ward off sexual predators, choose husbands and raise wise sons. Women were seen as inherently irrational and had to be partially androgenised to meet the social expectations of citizenship. Specifically, White male civic expectations centred on autonomy and claiming an inalienable property-in-oneself, ensuring by definition an independent, self-possessed individual who could sell their labour and own property, as opposed to the dependency experienced by disenfranchised and propertyless White women and people of colour.

The discourse of capability to perform civic values in the early US was predicated on a tradition of racial hierarchies constructed on assumptions of racial character. American natural historians classed 'African' and 'Indian' groups as ill tempered, incapable of complex thoughts, cruel, lazy, childish and brutish, and therefore unable to self-govern and ill-suited for citizenship, at first through the environmental theories of Benjamin Rush and Samuel Stanhope Smith, and later the polygenism of Samuel George Morton, George Gliddon and Josiah Nott. At the same time, blackface minstrelsy and grotesque racial caricature, such as Edward Williams Clay's *Life in Philadelphia* (1828–9), mocked Black pretensions of genteel 'White' behaviour in order to ridicule the civic ambitions of free African Americans. Where this book ends, with *The Confidence-Man* in 1857, the Dred Scott decision had legally formalised these cultural beliefs by barring African Americans from national citizenship. Chief Justice Roger Taney explicitly stated that the constitution had never intended 'all the rights and privileges and immunities' of US citizenship for Africans transported in bondage, nor their descendants, as they were considered 'a subordinate and inferior class of beings' incapable of achieving autonomy and accessing political and legal freedoms.[31] In the same year that Melville writes of a White man who completely exploits his autonomy to the point where his own character is untethered from race, class or nationality, the Supreme Court confirmed that African Americans could not have this freedom.

Early US anxieties over social status were rooted in perceptions of race; creating a White identity bolstered claims on properties and rights of citizenship. In response to fears of increased rights for African Americans, over the course of the first half of the nineteenth century Whiteness became an '*enforced* identification, an identification from which one increasingly could not demur' and which was employed by politicians, professionals, writers and workers to unite White Americans.[32] The language of Whiteness – discussions of autonomy, industry, rationality, respectability, sociality and their synonyms – articulates anxieties that one could no longer be treated like a White person. These discussions of Whiteness are inseparable from concerns over class position. In *The Wages of Whiteness* (1991), David Roediger argues that the White working classes strove, through the language of labour, to distinguish themselves as self-possessed citizens above African Americans, and therefore deserving of full legal, social and economic rights from lawmakers and employers. These anxieties were not exclusive to the working classes. For example, Dana Nelson's *National Manhood* (1998) identifies a mid-century national project to formalise rational White middle-class masculine identity through an increasing professionalisation dependent on classification, objectification and management of 'Other' (not White or not male) bodies.[33]

The cultural work of early US fiction not only articulates White – and often male and middle-class – civic values but imagines what can happen if those identity expectations are not fulfilled. From Brown to Webb, texts offer moments where the voice of the liminal White character questions and challenges ideals of White citizenship. In a period when Whiteness became both formalised and formative to individual and communal identity, liminal Whiteness destabilises Whiteness and disturbs this 'enforced identification' by challenging or threatening ideals of Whiteness. In their association with non-White groups denied citizenship and social freedom, these liminal White figures suggest the possibility of White men losing hold of a valued social position.

The liminal figure is not necessarily an outsider, but often an educated, moneyed or professional figure. Characters throughout the works of Brown to Webb fit into the wide-ranging label of 'middle class' by possessing a certain amount of economic and cultural capital, a combination of education, profession, taste and wealth. The concept of being middle class is difficult to define in an American context since, as Stuart Blumin puts it, the idea of the middle class in the United States has been 'pervasive and elusive; indeed . . . elusive precisely because it is pervasive'. In the early to mid-nineteenth century there was not necessarily a clearly defined or organised middle-class consciousness, but there were sets of behaviours and 'broadly homogeneous' social positions that could adopt this label, and in this book I take that to mean educated, professional White men and their families.[34] Being middle class was itself 'a permanent condition of liminality' between working class and old money – a status itself in flux depending on the market economy.[35] As the financial crashes of 1819 and 1837 demonstrated, socio-economic position was precarious; people moved into and out of social categories and the market economy moulded the literary careers and personal lives of writers. The authors in this book attempted – with varying degrees of success – to make a living through writing, but nearly all entered other professional roles that may be labelled as middle class. For example, Brown started his professional life as a lawyer, while Bird practised medicine before his prolific writing career in the 1830s and in 1841 returned to the University of Philadelphia's medical school to lecture. Melville came from a family whose social status rapidly declined as he was growing up; the family was downwardly mobile due to his father accumulating excessive debts. The White male author therefore becomes a representative figure for the most enfranchised and most vocal group in the nation, yet also a group aware and anxious of the slipperiness of social position.

Either in their proximity to middle-class characters or in being middle class themselves, the liminal White figure threatens liminality, dispossession and disenfranchisement as contagious or inevitable. For example, in Melville's 'Bartleby the Scrivener', the ghostly Bartleby's protestations against work and conversation challenge the lawyer-narrator's values of White citizenship, namely industry and sociality, key civic values expected of White men to survive and thrive in their careers. Confronted by a worker who chooses to disengage from both the professional sphere and – through starvation – the physical world itself, the narrator becomes increasingly exasperated and perturbed. The horror is not that Bartleby 'prefers not to' in itself, but that the utterances come from someone previously industrious and continually perplexingly polite. Bartleby is a contagion; he represents the frightening possibility that a professional White man, like the narrator, could himself abstain from these civic expectations. The only way to process these anxieties is to transform Bartleby into a less-than-White figure for the narrator to contain and control through the language of paternalism and objectification: Bartleby becomes a dependent, a charity case, a piece of furniture, a text. Throughout this book authors remove Whiteness from characters both to mark out those who refuse expected civic values, and to articulate anxieties about losing a claim on citizenship.

## TALKING WHITE IN THE EARLY UNITED STATES

In the early United States, civic identity was tied inextricably to both a metaphorical voice and manifestations of the physical voice. The voice is both 'the very texture of the social' and 'the intimate kernel of subjectivity'; it relays individual and social identity and allows us to interact with each other on a one-to-one basis and in larger communal arenas.[36] Post-revolutionary America was conceived as a logocracy with political power drawn from the power of words, and the 'grain of the voice' valued in national documents.[37] In his survey of democratic states in *A Defence of the Constitutions* (1787), John Adams repeatedly referred to 'the voice' of the people to connect citizens across the nation. When he wrote that 'the voice of the people is the voice of God', Adams saw an inherent power in the public metaphoric voice, a divine right in the will of the people to construct their own governance.[38] To naturalise was to publicly declare an oath of allegiance to America; to vote was to put to work your metaphorical voice for representatives to enact discursive democracy. However, 'the voice of the people' that Adams praised excluded large swathes of the national population: recent immigrants, White women, and in nearly all states, Black people, not to mention Indigenous peoples deemed to be outside of America. Even White men were silenced by political viewpoint: through the Sedition Act of 1798, the Federalists attempted to forge a unified national voice by shutting down dissenting voices; the purpose was to control who could speak and what could be said.

In this period, politicians and public figures were praised for their eloquent and powerful speeches. The political stump speech engaged with the public through storytelling to become the model means of democratic communication. The American most likely and able to master print and speech was 'implicitly, even explicitly, white, male, literate, and propertied', who by casting themselves as the disembodied abstracted citizen, claimed authority to shape the public sphere.[39] Throughout the early US, then, the voice retained its importance for civic identity. Outside of politics, discussion, deliberation, oration and rhetoric were necessary for interacting with and contributing to both local communities and the nation. From the late 1820s, lyceums acted as forums for 'culture-making rhetorical practice[s]' through debates and discussions, educational lectures and public recitations of magazine and newspaper articles – all content that would then be (re)printed and (re)circulated in newspapers and magazines.[40] The correct use of the English language was a marker of position in society, and cultural commentators and magazine writers voiced their concerns about improper usage in spelling, vocabulary or pronunciation. Speech policing takes shape in the figure of Dawkins in *Sheppard Lee*, a Philadelphia dandy who castigates his country cousins for their overfamiliar language. He educates them, saying, 'the first lesson I will give you is never to call me "Ikey" again, for that's vulgar; but always "Mr. Dawkins," or just plain "cousin;" . . . As for your brother, you must always call him "brother;" occasionally you may say "Wilkins," and it will sound aristocratic, as being a family name.'[41] Thinking and talking about language itself infuses literature of the period.

However, the voice also manifests itself in resistance to the nation-building work of lyceums and congressional speeches. Caleb Smith identifies two public exclamations – the oracle and the curse – in early US print culture. Both are persuasive, performative speech acts, yet they are uttered by two groups on opposite sides of the legal divide. The oracle, spoken by those in power, carries significant representational authority, such as a judge's sentencing. The judge speaks eloquently and reasonably to 'give voice to the spirit of the sovereign people', recalling Adams's claim of a united *vox populi*. In contrast, the curse – a pessimistic or damning prophecy – assumes the same power as the oracle, but is spoken by protesters, campaigners, convicts and blasphemers, representing those disqualified or alienated from citizenship. Their voices cut through the sentimental culture of the mid-nineteenth century, becoming a 'monstrous other' that reminds Americans of the failure of national ideals; Smith cites Nat Turner as a prime example of a curser who gives testimony condemning the nation and its institution of slavery.[42] At the same time, recent scholarship on nineteenth-century voices has also shown that those who opposed the exclusionary and discriminatory work of legal, political and cultural institutions also used eloquence as a form of protest. Disenfranchised and marginalised groups such as free and fugitive African Americans employed rhetoric and oratory to call for abolition and civil rights. For example, the lecture tours of Frederick Douglass and the theatrical readings of Mary Webb resonated Black cosmopolitanism and humanity through speaking in an 'Anglicized manner' and maintaining 'the performance of respectability'.[43]

The texts in this book were written at a time when Black and Indigenous groups were increasingly staking a claim on the public oral and print sphere, through either eloquent performance or searing protest. In contrast, unexpected and unusual speech in nineteenth-century fiction often acts as an aperture for the emergence of disenfranchised voices that, to quote Nancy Ruttenburg, are 'unanticipated, inarticulate, uncontainable, [and] heedless of the forms', and undermine the ideals set out in spoken and written discourses inhabited by middle-class and elite White men.[44] The fictional spaces I examine, in which the spiritual and physical worlds collapse into one another, offer up inexplicable voices: talking corpses, speaking spirits, enchanted bodies. 'Inexplicable' has two functions. First, it signals the supernatural nature of the voices heard at the intersection of life and death. It appears repeatedly as a descriptor in *Wieland* as the family attempt to grapple with disembodied and potentially demonic voices that disorder the senses and challenge the rational. Second, and most potently, 'inexplicable' indicates that White men speaking in such a way that challenges, negates or refuses tenets of White citizenship is unnatural, irrational and out of place. In *Dead Women Talking* (2013), Brian Norman brings together the literary dead body with the socially dead or disenfranchised by reading the speaking female corpse as a powerful dissenter against social oppression, a figure who enacts an uncanny haunting, imploring characters and readers to bring about change.[45] When who should speak and how they should speak carries political significance, what is at stake when citizens utter inexplicable voices? I pursue a different path from Norman by considering dead, dying and otherworldly White and often male characters who are not protesting the oppression of disenfranchised groups but, as stated earlier, are associated with Black or Indigenous people to articulate their own liminal position and the instability and uncertainty of Whiteness.

Taking on voices of colour has already received attention in scholarship on nineteenth-century mourning and spiritualism. Dana Luciano examines the Native American lament as an oral form ventriloquised by White Americans. The work of Cooper, for example, employs the unusual Indigenous mourning voice to position Native Americans as prehistoric, pre-national and therefore outside the nation. At the same time, taking on the spectral voice legitimises 'white indulgence in the Romantic time of lament', as White middle-class Americans experienced grief in capacious temporalities outside the linear.[46] Similarly, in her discussion of Indian Guides at mid-century séances, Molly McGarry argues that Native possession – marked through lament and war cries – was a form of 'cultural appropriation'. Mediums claimed a special access to pre-European spirituality, without necessarily pursuing reform for living Native Americans.[47] The non-White voice was exoticised, yet the political significance of those voices was held at a wary distance. On ventriloquised lament, Luciano states, 'taking on the Indian voice was a risky form of play because it also registered as a taking-*in*, something felt through the body', a claim that can also be made of cross-racial spirit possession.[48] Speaking as a Native American offered the utopian possibility of a shared cross-racial consciousness, but it also opened the White citizen and by extension the White civic body to contamination and contagion, and thus the fear of becoming less than White.

Growing in popularity in the mid-century, spiritualism and its cousin mesmerism questioned the boundaries of the self and self-possession, as mediums and mesmerists believed individuals could be controlled by the spirits of loved ones, strangers and historical figures, or by the manipulation of magnetic fluid in the body. The authors in this book do not depict cross-racial consciousness and, rather than the merging of racial identities, I attend to how these liminal encounters challenge White autonomy. Speaking without volition, or under the manipulation of another, either as yourself or as someone else, threatens the idealised unified and self-possessed White citizen, anxieties of which I discuss in my chapters on Poe and Melville. When I turn to Poe in Chapter 4, I argue that the horror of a blackened and disintegrating yet conscious and speaking mesmerised body is amplified for the White reader when we consider that Valdemar is an articulate intellectual manipulated and exploited by another educated professional. The blackness in Poe's tale is not Valdemar standing in for enslaved populations, but rather the possibility that White men could be treated as if they were no longer White. Gothic and speculative genres that feature mesmerised, enchanted, revenant, disembodied and spectral White voices function as safe fictional venues that imagine White marginality and contagion through exaggeration, and contain these anxieties within the printed pages of inexplicable events.

READING FOR WHITENESS

In this book, I argue for texts as fictive spaces of possibility where White loss can be imagined and allayed. New Americanism has long sought to connect this socio-racial context with the nation's literary production, but scholars have often criticised its focus on recovering 'residual ideology' and repressed 'potentially traumatic material' – the exclusion and disenfranchisement of African Americans, Native Americans, White women, immigrants and the working class – at the expense of formal recognition.[49] This is perhaps unfair on New Americanism – as Sam Otter points out, formal concerns have always been important to these historicist readings, particularly in elevating the position of White women and writers of colour.[50] But a movement towards (New) Formalism in the past fifteen years has encouraged scholars to push against the drive to become 'belated, secondhand historians' and instead view fiction as a realm of possibility.[51] Nineteenth-century Americanist scholarship of the last decade has sought to bring aesthetics 'in[to] fruitful conjunction with the historicist and political questions that have earned their central position' in literary scholarship and to 'reinstate close reading' as the 'basic materials that form the subject matter of even the most historical of investigations'.[52] Slowing down critique to focus on word choice, figurative language, structure, genre and tone recognises the text as a literary object itself instead of simply a historical one.

In this vein, Cindy Weinstein's recent work exemplifies the approach I take with close reading in this book. Focusing on American literature's relationship with – and representation of – time, her close reading concentrates on 'exact words, often adverbs, and the tenses of verbs' contextualised in a specific historical setting.[53] Weinstein's work does not exist in a historical vacuum, but like my own readings, close reading from this fusion of New Americanist and Formalist perspectives recognises that context can appear in these small units of meaning, and this close attention illuminates our readings of the text and our understanding of the early United States. Whiteness is on the surface of these texts; it is ingrained in descriptions of character gesture, voice, behaviours, reactions, emotions – all aspects that fit into the ideology of Whiteness as a constructed social identity and phenomenology. We can read Whiteness in the descriptions of characters that employ Native allusion – for example, Nick Handyside in Brown's 'Somnambulism', which

I discuss in Chapter 1. The same language that describes Indigenous populations as insensible and savage indicates White characters on the margins of Whiteness. Rather than reading Nick as a symbol or stand-in for Native violence, I read him as a liminal White figure, whom Brown frames in references to indigeneity to emphasise his precarity as a cognitively impaired young White man unable to participate in civic life. The specific language of racial character in much early US fiction enables us to think about discourses of ability and capability: who is included within the boundaries of citizenship, and who sits on its limen.

The written voice is the surface of the text. The oral and written forms discussed in this book – the gothic novel, ghost stories, blackface, slave narratives, medical case reports and séances – all carry social meaning. Returning to the formalist critique of Mikhail Bakhtin tells us that fiction brings together several types of layered narrative, authorial and character voices into one 'heteroglossic' written space.[54] In *Sheppard Lee*, Sheppard's first-person linear memoir is disrupted by his marked dialogue and subtly shifting narrative voice, which change when Sheppard merges with his transformations, including an enslaved Black man. The blackface minstrelsy that Bird draws on as a creative resource relies on stereotyped African American speech to continually mark Black Americans as outside an intelligent White society and its intelligible speech. At points in the text the reader is not sure whether Sheppard is professing his own opinions or those of a stereotyped lazy and childish Black man, inviting us to consider the possibility of cross-racial consciousness or, as I argue in Chapter 3, White disavowal of civic values. Close examination of the dialogue, free indirect speech and narrative that make up these written forms enables my discussion of the voice as the expression of liminal Whiteness in the early United States.

Across my six chronological chapters, a group of early US authors respond to the developing ideology of White citizenship through unusual and unexpected voices on the boundary between life and death. Each chapter focuses on a specific vocal context. Chapter 1 discusses how Brown communicates liminal Whiteness through sensational ventriloquism, which marks marginalised White men as non-White noncitizens along the shifting frontier. Itinerant Frank Carwin in *Wieland* and cognitively disabled Nick Handyside in 'Somnambulism' transform into haunting less-than-White figures through their ventriloquism and mimicry. Written in a context of environmentalist race theory, Brown uses liminal White characters to mark the permeable boundaries of Whiteness. The unusual and shape-shifting racially marked voices disturb the senses of White middle-class families who serve as prime fictional examples of rational White citizens in the early republic. In doing so, Brown fractures an early national society that elevated educated White middle-class families as model enlightenment citizens.

In contrast to Brown's scepticism, Washington Irving embraces the irrational and the supernatural in his early national ghost stories. In his historical folk tales, Irving makes colonial male characters ghostly by connecting them to the 'vanishing Indian' disappearing across the early nation. Irving employs liminal White figures marked by spectral indigeneity to enshrine a colonial vision of hierarchical yet interdependent community and citizenship, itself vanishing in the early national period. *Bracebridge Hall*'s spectral men are relics of a past America, who protest the increasing professionalisation of White male citizens and the destruction of colonial communal structures. In his intertwined tales of colonial America and Georgian England, Irving is involved in a project of 'spectral nostalgia', reproducing scenes of supernatural storytelling as a means of rescuing and propagating these fading civic structures of relation and feeling.

As Irving's protagonists and stories seem to travel through time, Bird's Sheppard Lee travels through bodies. Written after the environmentalist theories of the early republic have passed, *Sheppard Lee* experiments boldly with complete cross-racial transformation. Chapter 3 reads *Sheppard Lee* as textual blackface through two interwoven forms: blackface minstrelsy and the slave narrative. Sheppard's liminal journey into and out of an enslaved African American corpse mirrors the paradoxical demarcation and transgression of racial boundaries set up in early blackface minstrelsy. However, rather than offering a radical cross-racial consciousness, Sheppard's minstrel-inspired inhabitation of Blackness and his ventriloquisation of the burgeoning slave narrative genre mocks the White civic value of industry, while seeking to contain palpable threats of violent and fluid social and racial mobility in Jacksonian America.

How the supernatural can both enunciate and exorcise anxieties of White male citizenship extends to Chapter 4, on Poe. His work repeatedly engages with the destruction of White civic and individual bodies and in his fantastical horror tales, Poe employs scientific and medical experiments as narrative devices to voice White male civic fragility. Written in a context of 1830s and 40s medical graverobbing and dissection – a practice that often targeted unprotected African American bodies – Poe's medical narratives realise the frightening possibility that White men could also be controlled and manipulated in the name of medical progress. In subjecting his protagonists to near-death or fatal experiences, Poe asks what it means for citizens to lose their autonomy and instead become the property of others. In speaking of and protesting suffering, the voices of conscious cadavers seek to clutch to an autonomous citizenship, represented by – yet under threat from – the professional White male doctor.

In contrast to Poe's conversant cadavers, in my fifth chapter I examine a movement towards silence and wordlessness to express liminal Whiteness in Melville's late fiction. In *Pierre*, the otherworldly Isabel Banford voices her social and familial exclusion through shrieks and a spirit-possessed guitar. Cadaverous Bartleby in 'Bartleby the Scrivener' is a ghostly figure whose verbal refusals and withdrawals from conversation disavow the ideal of the social professional male. In response to these unusual utterances, Pierre and the narrator of 'Bartleby' turn Isabel and Bartleby into dependent figures that define their own roles in White social institutions as providers and protectors. Melville explores how one can move beyond language to testify experience, both in his characters' strange voices and in his own wrestling with language and writing itself in his later fiction.

Returning to the origin of critical Whiteness studies, early African American literature, the final chapter examines how tenets of Whiteness are performative and arbitrary in Webb's *The Garies and their Friends*. Assembling a cast of respectable free African American families and cunning and dishonest White men in antebellum Philadelphia, Webb reinforces Whiteness as a set of values not intrinsic to those coded as White, showing that the privileges Whiteness affords are not extended to Black Americans who embody those tenets. Influenced by the cross-racial oratory of his wife, Mary E. Webb, Webb conveys the permeability of the colour line through episodes of passing and White racial transformation in scenes of death and dying, and he articulates White male anxieties that they could lose the privileges of Whiteness themselves. In the final section, I consider prescriptive Whiteness itself as deadly through deathbed speeches in *The Garies* and across early African American fiction, in which White men express the failure of White mastery and the destructive power of White segregationist supremacy.

As I discuss in the coda, these texts articulate and often seek to contain anxieties of White loss and precarity, ideas that re-emerge in the contemporary moment. Repeatedly the fear of being treated as a minority, whether in the nineteenth or twenty-first century, finds form in the language of White exclusion, subjugation and death. The liminal White voice manifests itself in fiction as an inexplicable, forceful and haunting presence that disrupts normative communities, disturbs self-knowledge and challenges prescriptions of racial belonging in the United States.

## NOTES

1. Morrison, *Playing in the Dark*, pp. 46, 52.
2. Bergland, *The National Uncanny*, p. 13.
3. Castronovo, *Necro Citizenship*, pp. 3, 70.
4. Ibid. p. 8.
5. Melville, *Pierre: Or The Ambiguities*, p. 68.
6. Castronovo, *Necro Citizenship*, p. 22.
7. DuBois, 'The Souls of White Folk', in *Darkwater*, pp. 17–29 (p. 17).
8. See Baldwin, 'On Being White . . . and Other Lies', in *The Cross of Redemption*, ed. Kenan, pp. 135–8; Lorde, 'Age, Race, Class, and Sex: Women Redefining Difference', in *Sister Outsider*, pp. 114–25; hooks, 'Representing Whiteness in the Black Imagination', in *Black Looks*, pp. 165–78.

9. Yancy, *Look, a White!*, p. 6.
10. Examples include Lee Bebout on the US–Mexico border; Aileen Moreton-Robinson on Whiteness's dependence on claiming Indigenous land; Matt Wray on the development of 'white trash' to denigrate and exclude rural poor White people; Karen Brodkin, Noel Ignatiev and Matthew Frye Jacobson on Jewish, Irish and Eastern European exclusion and later assimilation into Whiteness; and Ruth Frankenberg on the importance of Whiteness to White women. Bebout, *Whiteness on the Border*; Moreton-Robinson, *White Possessive*; Wray, *Not Quite White*; Brodkin, *How Jews Became White Folks*; Ignatiev, *How the Irish Became White*; Jacobson, *Whiteness of a Different Color*; Frankenberg, *White Women, Race Matters*.
11. Levine-Rasky, *Whiteness Fractured*, p. 18.
12. Ahmed, 'A Phenomenology of Whiteness', p. 154.
13. This self-ownership enabled European Americans to take ownership of African Americans as human property and colonise land belonging to Native American tribes. See Harris, 'Whiteness as Property', pp. 1721, 1718; Moreton-Robinson, *White Possessive*, p. 52.
14. Ahmed, 'A Phenomenology of Whiteness', p. 159.
15. Jacobson, *Whiteness of a Different Color*, p. 40; Wray, *Not Quite White*.
16. Ahmed, 'A Phenomenology of Whiteness', p. 160.
17. Van Gennep, *The Rites of Passage*, p. 11.
18. Turner, *The Forest of Symbols*, p. 93; Turner, *Process, Performance and Pilgrimage*, p. 18.
19. Roach, *Cities of the Dead*, pp. 18–19, 181.
20. Turner, *The Ritual Process*, p. 95.
21. Viljoen, 'A Poetics of Liminality and Hybridity', in Viljoen and van der Merwe (eds), *Beyond the Threshold*, pp. 1–26 (p. 23).
22. Turner, *The Forest of Symbols*, p. 99.
23. Introduction to Soto (ed.), *A Place That Is Not a Place*, pp. 7–16 (p. 15).
24. Coviello, *Intimacy in America*, p. 12.
25. Ramsay, *A Dissertation of the Manners of Acquiring the Character and Privileges of a Citizen of the United States*, pp. 4, 3.
26. 'Naturalization' (26 March 1790), in Peters (ed.), *The Public Statutes at Large of The United States of America*, pp. 103–4 (p. 104); Kettner, *The Development of American Citizenship*, pp. 241–2.
27. 'Naturalization' (18 June 1798), in Peters (ed.), *The Public Statutes*, pp. 566–9.
28. Hyde, *Civic Longing*, p. 10.
29. Ricci, *Good Citizenship in America*, p. 97.
30. Young Welke, *Law and the Borders of Belonging in the Long Nineteenth Century United States*, p. 2.
31. An 1860 pamphlet of the reprinted decision included an introduction and appendix lauding the decision and, influenced by scientific racism, using anthropological 'evidence' of racial inferiority to support the denial of African American citizenship. *The Dred Scott Decision*, p. 17.
32. Coviello, *Intimacy in America*, p. 11.
33. Nelson, *National Manhood*; Roediger, *The Wages of Whiteness*.

34. Blumin, *The Emergence of the Middle Class*, pp. 2, 249.
35. Halttunen, *Confidence Men and Painted Women*, p. 29.
36. Dolar, 'The Linguistics of the Voice', in Sterne (ed.) *The Sound Studies Reader*, pp. 539–54 (p. 540).
37. Looby, *Voicing America*, p. 3.
38. Adams, *A Defence of the Constitutions of Government of the United States of America*, p. 127.
39. Warner, 'The Mass Public and the Mass Subject', in Calhoun (ed.), *Habermas and the Public Sphere*, pp. 377–401 (p. 382).
40. Ray, *The Lyceum and Public Culture in the Nineteenth-Century United States*, p. 2.
41. Bird, *Sheppard Lee*, p. 148.
42. Smith, *The Oracle and the Curse*, pp. 11, 4, 34.
43. Wright, *Lecturing the Atlantic*, p. 67; Black, 'Abolitionism's Resonant Bodies', p. 623.
44. Ruttenburg, *Democratic Personality*, p. 6.
45. Norman, *Dead Women Talking*.
46. Luciano, *Arranging Grief*, p. 82.
47. McGarry, *Ghosts of Futures Past*, p. 67.
48. Luciano, *Arranging Grief*, p. 79.
49. Preface to Pease (ed.), *Revisionary Interventions into the Americanist Canon*, pp. 1–37 (pp. 10, 12).
50. Otter, 'An Aesthetics in All Things', p. 117.
51. Dillon, 'Atlantic Practices', p. 208.
52. Introduction to Looby and Weinstein (eds), *American Literature's Aesthetic Dimensions*, pp. 1–36 (p. 1); Levinson, 'What Is New Formalism?', p. 560.
53. Weinstein, *Time, Tense, and American Literature*, p. 12.
54. Mikhail Bakhtin lists these overlapping literary voices at work in the novel: narration, *skaz* (oral narration), semiliterary written narration (such as the epistle), extra-artistic discourse (for example scientific description), and character speech. Bakhtin, 'Discourse in the Novel', in *The Dialogic Imagination*, ed. Holquist, pp. 259–422 (p. 262).

# I

# 'A SHRIEK SO TERRIBLE!': CHARLES BROCKDEN BROWN'S SENSATIONAL VENTRILOQUISTS

In *Memoirs of Carwin the Biloquist* (1803), Charles Brockden Brown's prequel to *Wieland*, the eponymous narrator recalls how he first learnt to ventriloquise by imitating a Mohawk in the western Pennsylvanian wilderness.

> I uttered the words which chanced to occur to me, and repeated in the shrill tones of a Mohock savage . . . 'Cow! cow! come home! home!' . . . These notes were of course reverberated from the rocks which on either side towered aloft, but the echo was confused and indistinct.[1]

The cries produce a response of 'the same words, with equal distinctness and deliberation, and in the same tone' from a dusky spot 'some hundred feet' behind Frank Carwin. The speaker is 'concealed from . . . view', located at a position 'inaccessible to man or beast'. Realising it is his own vocal power producing the responses, Carwin moves into 'new positions', penetrating the landscape with his inventive cries (pp. 230–1). In this episode, the savage 'shrill tones' reverberate through the air to create what Stephen Connor terms a 'vocalic body', an imagined Mohawk physically reinhabiting the frontier region where the young Carwin lives.[2] The echoes multiply this body to enact a spatial disturbance as the landscape fills with several Native voices in the shadows, behind rocks and above cliffs. At this moment, the Mohawk acts as a vocalic guise, one of many identities Carwin takes on using his voice. Carwin is a liminal figure, an Anglo-American who in this instance could be mistaken for a Native American.

Why are early national men shrieking in the wilderness? Taking this aural episode as a starting point, this chapter focuses on the significance of indigenised disembodied cries in Brown's *Wieland: Or, the Transformation, An American Tale* (1798) and 'Somnambulism: A Fragment' (*c.* 1799). The two texts feature families plagued by mysterious incorporeal voices and their attempts to locate and interpret the sources. In *Wieland*, Clara and her family – brother Theodore, sister-in-law Catharine and brother-in-law Henry Pleyel – are disturbed by a series of inexplicable cries, all performed by Frank Carwin, a man of swarthy appearance – his skin of an off-white 'sallow hue' – and itinerant lifestyle (p. 49). In 'Somnambulism', two travellers, Constantia Davis and her father, navigate a nocturnal journey haunted by the shadowy figure of Nick Handyside, an 'idiot' who shrieks in the darkness. Brown transforms these men into liminal White frontier figures in order to mark them as outside the family-as-nation microcosm. With their shape-shifting vocal powers, they unsettle the communities they encounter by throwing into doubt the reliability of the physical senses. In doing so, Carwin and Nick reveal the fractures of an early national society that elevated educated White middle-class families as model enlightenment citizens.

What citizenship looks like and how it interacts with the slippery nature of Whiteness and racial identity is an undercurrent running through Brown's depiction of early national society. As Katy Chiles has recently argued, race in the early national period was 'transformable'. Whiteness could be transitioned into and out of because race was 'potentially mutable' and 'continuously subject to change'.[3] New theories of natural history in the late eighteenth century, from writers such as Benjamin Rush, Samuel Stanhope Smith and Thomas Jefferson, hypothesised that the environment caused variations in race. These environmental theories exalted Whiteness by espousing that African Americans could erase their physical blackness over time and that Native Americans could be civilised and integrated into Anglo-American society.[4] In Brown's work there are a number of characters who transgress or blur the boundaries of Anglo-American Whiteness. For instance, in *Ormond* (1800), Ormond disguises himself in 'the complexion and habiliments . . . of a negro and a chimney-sweep'; racial masquerade enables Ormond to gain access to private spaces as an invisible American.[5] Similarly, in *Edgar Huntly* (1799), the eponymous protagonist performs 'racial cross-dressing', transforming into a violent savage by closely resembling Native Americans in his bloody, ragged appearance and animalistic movements.[6] Anglo-Americans taking on Native and African American physical markers, such as Brown's characters, could blur and transgress the distinctions between White and non-White.

As I discussed in the Introduction, Whiteness in the early national period was not monolithic, and groups of White men sat on or outside its borders: recent European immigrants, the rural poor, the institutionalised, the itinerant, the disabled. Those excluded from the commons became less than White and existed at a further remove, sidelined with groups like Native Americans, whom public thinkers and natural scientists viewed as unfit for citizenship due to their insensibility. On *Edgar Huntly*, Christopher Stampone argues that the wandering and wild Clithero does not symbolise Native Americans, nor 'falling into Indian-like savagery', but that he is 'always already savage' due to his Irish nationality, a group maligned as predatory and uncivilised.[7] It is this approach I take with *Wieland* and 'Somnambulism'. Native allusions in Brown's work serve to amplify deviation from Anglo-American middling Whiteness and mark out these men as liminally White. In *Wieland*, Carwin is a disowned son and itinerant wanderer moving across class lines, who invades a White middle-class family estate. In 'Somnambulism', Nick is a cognitively disabled young man unable to take part in society and community. Although Anglo-American men, Brown closely associates the pair's vocal dexterity with Native American speech, accentuating their position as less than White.

Foreign threat, democratic citizen, marginalised Native presence: scholars want to classify Carwin as symbolic of *something*.[8] At times he appears as Spanish, Native, a peasant, a devil, a thug, a woman – either in dress or speech – which supports these multiple alternative readings. I follow Ed White's claim that Brown does not 'identify the subaltern in an essentialist fashion', to argue for a reading of Carwin that focuses on his liminality and mutability.[9] Through mimicry, Carwin could be anyone: male/female, human/supernatural, Native/American/alien. His strange vocal abilities allow him to cross these national and ontological categories. His alignment with Native Americans emphasises his position as a liminal White man on the edges of the family-as-nation microcosm. It is this unknown quality that leads to the disruption of the senses in the Wieland family, who are alternately intrigued and terrified by Carwin's disembodied performances of family members, criminal thugs, and God.

Written between *Wieland* and *Edgar Huntly* but not published until 1805, 'Somnambulism' is chiefly viewed as a precursor of *Edgar Huntly*, with monstrous 'idiot' Nick Handyside an early formation of savage Native American behaviour in the 1799 novel.[10] However, I believe the text holds much significance for examining the discourses surrounding ability, race and citizenship in the early national period. Reading 'Somnambulism' in its own right, I contend that Nick is a liminal less-than-White figure, rather than a symbol of Native violence. Brown frames him in references to Indigenous behaviour and speech, emphasising his marginality as a cognitively impaired young White man unable to participate in civic life. Sustained attention to the fragment enriches our understanding of how Brown and early national literature attended to the place of young Americans within a nexus of gender, class, race and ability that determined their position on the margins of society. Nick's position on the peripheries of White society illuminates a concern in early national literature that the rights Whiteness accrued could be lost because of an inability to demonstrate civic qualities. Through Nick, Brown asks to whom citizenship is to be extended at a time when the concept was shifting, unsettled and still contested.

In these texts Brown pairs speaking, and its counterpart, listening, to bring to the fore and question ideals of rational White citizenship. After tracking how Nick and Carwin are indigenised through early national discussions of ventriloquial speech, in the second half of the chapter I argue that Carwin and Nick's liminal voices disrupt the hearing of the White familial communities in each text and therefore ideals of rational citizenship in the early national period. In this context, strange vocal talents such as ventriloquism and mimicry were part of a rational entertainment industry employed in early national communities to test and refine citizens' senses. In public spaces such as Philadelphia pleasure gardens, the public encountered a host of spectacles, from 'magic lanterns, perspective boxes, and solar microscopes to speaking figures, automata, and cosmoramas'. These were designed to enchant, intrigue and hone the senses of city-dwellers; they were seen as an aide for negotiating an environment of 'forgers, counterfeiters, conspirators, imposters, and demagogues'.[11] In *Wieland* and 'Somnambulism', this is a test the Wielands and Davises fail. When confronted by these seemingly inexplicable voices, the White families display an over-reliance on the senses and sensory experience alone, which leads to misrecognition and sensational gothic imaginations. In *Wieland* the family misinterpret Carwin's voice to be a supernatural event; in 'Somnambulism', the Davises mistakenly imagine Nick's savage cries as part of a gothic frontier fantasy. I argue there is a significant shift from the senses to the sensational, and from observation and empiricism to imagination, in the figures of Clara and Constantia. In examining the heroines' reactions to Carwin and Nick's voices, this chapter positions Clara and Constantia as poor readers of the gothic, blinded by unclassifiable and sensational scenarios from the dangerous men in the domestic space: obsessive and violent Althorpe and fanatical murderer Theodore. In *Wieland* and 'Somnambulism', Brown employs the liminal White figure to critique the fragile ideals of an exclusive White citizenship based on government of the senses.

### Rational Citizenship and Liminal Whiteness in the Early National Period

During the 1790s, it was Whiteness that began to unite existing and new citizens. As discussed in my Introduction, the Naturalization Acts reinscribed the nation as composed of White citizens only, the only group of American inhabitants viewed as capable of demonstrating the values of autonomy, industry, rationality, respectability and sociality. Cognitive competency underpinned these discussions of civic ability. Outlining this cultural ideology of citizenship, Justine S. Murison claims that 'the status of citizenship fused morality, memory, and residency . . . citizenship became a psychological question . . . as much as political definition of rights and requirements', termed 'moral citizenship'.[12] I would extend Murison's psychological definition of character as a combination of morality and memory to include the regulation of the senses, a racialised concept in the 1790s. Empiricism as formulated by Scottish philosopher Thomas Reid – the belief that truth is established through correctly using the five senses – was at the heart of American enlightenment concepts of white citizen building. The ideal citizen, in this respect, has a sound relationship between body and mind, governing their senses in order to make correct judgements and actions, the 'good character' demanded by the Naturalization Acts.

In an early diary entry, Brown specifically connects the senses with communal citizenship:

> Man possesses five senses or inlets to his mind. Of these the sight is the most useful, extensive and delicate in its formation . . . The importance of sight to men, and the exquisite organization of that matter in which it is centered, demand and have a separate theory . . . Man may be considered as one and alone; or he may be considered as a member of a community, and connected with others.[13]

Sensory experience connects a man to the external world and to others around him, bringing together individuals in local and national communities. Bonds of community and relation are predicated on individuals agreeing on what they have observed. One half of sense – soundwaves vibrating the ear drum, light reflecting off an object and entering the eye – is a corporeal event; the other half of sense – identifying correctly where the noise has been produced, who or what is the object in the light – is an act of judgement in response to external stimuli. Reid notes this second meaning of sense in his 1786 *Essays on the Intellectual Powers of Man*: 'In common language, sense always implies judgment. A man of sense is a man of judgment. Good sense is good judgment.' He claims, 'All knowledge and all science, must be built upon principles that are self-evident; and of such principles, every man who has common sense is a competent judge.' At a national level, the 'self-evident' truths of the Declaration consist of statements that all men can agree to be true. The influence of Scottish Enlightenment philosophy is patent: all men are connected by shared physical senses and by shared common sense – knowledge of how the physical world operates and what is correct.[14]

Although Reid's principles 'put all men upon a level', including the philosopher, the savage and the layman, in the early national US they narrowed to the exclusive realm of the middle class, the elite, the educated and the White.[15] The Wieland and Davis family initially serve as prime examples of 'the sensible "artificers" of middling and elite status: sedentary whites' – citizens who correctly regulate their senses and use reason to make sound judgements.[16]

In *Wieland,* the temple at Mettingen – previously a religious sanctuary constructed by Wieland Sr – is transformed by Theodore into an intellectual meeting place, where he and Pleyel debate philosophy, national politics and metaphysics, 'bandying quotations and syllogisms' (p. 28). Pleyel is held up as a man of critical thought – 'the champion of intellectual liberty' who 'rejected all guidance but that of his reason' – and as I turn to later, Clara is lauded for her level head (p. 23). As Sophia Rosenfeld writes, the philosophy of common sense created 'new forms of exclusion, just as much as interclass solidarity or identity'. Elevated as a 'prized American value' necessary for the good character of the natural born or new citizen, it excluded the uneducated, the mentally handicapped, Native Americans and African Americans.[17] Viewed as incapable of possessing common sense, all these groups existed on a sliding scale of states below full social, legal and political citizenship. Early national political theorists grouped together all those deemed incapable of being responsible citizens, contrasting 'idiots, lunatics, women of all races, people of indigenous nations, and African Americans with those considered worthy of full citizenship'.[18] A supposed lack of sense connected all these groups excluded from the vote and political participation. Without good sense, one could not participate in quotidian or political deliberation – both needed to assert one's position as a worthy citizen and member of the community.

Insensibility and irrationality appear in many early national texts, such as Susanna Rowson's *Charlotte Temple* (1789) and Sarah Wood's *Dorval; or The Speculator* (1800).[19] In these novels, temporary or sudden female lunacy shows the damage of unscrupulous seduction plots on unfortunate heroines. In such cases, insensibility stems from having too much sensibility to begin with – being too aware of and receptive to external stimuli. Nick in 'Somnambulism' stands apart from this group because his is a permanent debility. As an 'idiot' he lacks the mental understanding to take part in civic discussions, both at a quotidian and political level: his actions are 'entirely bereft of reason' (p. 15).[20] He is not over-sensitive, but, like the Native American, lacks sense and therefore reason. The Native American fully represented the lack of good sense as a debility, disqualifying participation in a rational society. Stanhope Smith noted a cognitive dullness in Indigenous populations, identifying a 'vacant eye' and 'look of idiotism' in their faces.[21] Rush, in a lecture to the American Philosophical Society in 1774, commented on the abilities of Indigenous men 'to bear the most exquisite pain without complaining', which contributed 'to give a tone to the nervous system'. He noted too that cold baths and the use of grease and clay to paint the body served to 'lessen the sensibility of the extremities of the nerves', making them impervious to the damaging effects of extreme heat or cold.[22] From this deadening of the senses came their cruelty, indifference and inability to participate in shared discussions necessary to civic life.

Turning to 'Somnambulism' explicates this intersection of race, citizenship and ability in the figure of Nick. The Davises encounter him after visiting Richard Althorpe, the tale's narrator and a nervous, romantic young man with an unrequited love for Constantia. Althorpe protests their departure, claiming the nocturnal journey is 'attended with uncommon danger', but he is 'unable to explain' to them or himself why (p. 8). Undeterred, the Davises set off, and Althorpe falls asleep in a chair, dreaming that he is on the roadside shooting a potential assailant. He awakens in the morning to the news that disaster has struck. While the Davises traverse rural Norwood, 'a region, rude, sterile, and lonely, bestrewn with rock, and embarrassed with bushes', a farmer tells them about Nick Handyside, a local simpleton who enjoys lurking in the darkness and scaring travellers with his shrieks (p. 15). The Davises' curiosity and speculation increases to a heightened state of excitement, until they hear Nick's cries, at which point Constantia is attacked by an unseen assailant and dies of her wounds. With the aid of Brown's introductory note on a sleepwalking murder, the reader is to infer that Althorpe's violent dream was reality and that he is the attacker.

In the short story, Brown employs Native allusions to demarcate Nick outside the exclusive realm of good sense and therefore good citizenship and Whiteness itself. Nick shares with the Native American physical, behavioural and vocal characteristics. However, to read Nick as simply a prototype Native figure (replaced by Lenni Lenape in *Edgar Huntly*) glosses over the text's racialised discourse of ability, in which familiar markers of indigeneity amplify his debility. Like the Native American who is often represented as a 'vanishing Indian' on the edges of society, Nick is an 'invisible American', elided in society and physically unseen during the text, yet framed through tropes of animalism and monstrosity.[23] Simultaneously, Nick is ghostly yet strongly physically demarcated. Althorpe describes him as a grotesque simpleton, a deformed half-man, half-beast figure.

> Near the spot where they are now, lived a Mr. Handyside, whose only son was an idiot. He also merited the name of monster, if a projecting breast, a mis-shapen head, features horrid and distorted, and a voice that resembled nothing that was ever before heard, could entitle him to that appellation. This being, besides the natural deformity of his frame, wore looks and practiced gesticulations that were, in an inconceivable degree, uncouth and hideous. (p. 14)

These are cruel words but this early American lexicon of disability – idiocy, monstrosity and deformity – conveys Nick's mental and physical debility and societal attitudes towards him. Rather than a singular label of 'disabled', impairment manifests in texts through descriptions of idiocy, monstrosity and deformity, and through discourses of inability versus ability and capacity versus incapacity.[24] Attending to these lexical choices avoids presentism and helps us to think about Nick's 'idiocy' in relation to the concept of citizenship, which is predicated on the ability to display civic values, namely rationality. Brown's description typifies late eighteenth-century American thought on the 'idiot' as a brutish figure whose body as well as mind was deformed. For example, a 1771 Boston newspaper article considered that the idiot, 'approaching so near the bestial kind, . . .'twould be difficult, if not impossible, to distinguish him from the beast, were he not covered with a human body'. Furthermore, the author jocularly asks that when this man dies, 'Will his spirit go down to the earth with the beast, or upwards with the man?'[25] The 'idiot' inhabited a position of earthly and spiritual limbo, in between human and animal.

Brown's descriptions of Nick as a monstrous 'idiot' are racialised. His 'natural deformity', as if an inherited physical trait, evokes early national race science accounts that repeatedly compared the 'savage' body to Euro-American bodily norms. Rush commented that Native men and women often had a much slower pulse 'than in persons who are in the constant exercise of the habits of civilized life', whilst Stanhope Smith observed that Indigenous populations had muscles 'generally smaller and more lax . . . than among a civilized people' with 'less beautifully turned' limbs.[26] Animal hybridity frames both the idiot and the Native American, reflecting how race scientists like Rush and Stanhope Smith applied theories of animal adaptation in new climates to its human population.[27] Hidden by the gloom, Nick is a shape-shifting figure, slipping between man and animal and interchangeable with 'a sheep or a cow . . . or hog' ('Somnambulism', p. 14). Brown's observational tone fixes Nick as a strange creature possessing peculiar talents and skills particular to the wilderness landscape: he is 'fleet as a deer' and 'patient, to an incredible degree, of watchfulness, and cold, and hunger' (p. 15). Like Rush's observations of Indigenous insensibility to the elements, Nick too displays an insensibility that physically marks his lack of good sense and reason.

This racialised lack of sense and reason is most powerfully conveyed through Nick's voice. Nick's disembodied cries produce imagined physical forms yet are ephemeral and intangible. Brown renders his thrown voice distinctly other-worldly: Althorpe describes it as resembling 'nothing that was ever before heard' (p. 14). The strange savage shrieks once again associate Nick with a Native presence. Nick's cries carry through the country landscape.

> Unable to extricate himself, and, at length, tormented with hunger, he manifested his distress by the most doleful shrieks. These were uttered with most vehemence, and heard at greatest distance, by night. . . . [He] improved the flexibility of his voice, till his cries, always loud and rueful, were capable of being diversified without end. Instances had been

known in which the stoutest heart was appalled by them; and some, particularly in the case of women, in which they had been productive of consequences truly deplorable. (p. 15)

Shrieking in the darkness, Nick's cries produce a savage 'vocalic body'. His amorphous shape-shifting voice projects 'inexpressibly wild and melancholy' howls that remind Althorpe of 'a troop of hungry wolves', another animalistic trope for Native Americans (p. 15). His shrieks inspire not just a fear of someone unusual and otherworldly, but primarily a fear of savage attack by a Native American, the unspeakable danger of the country road. Nick preys on the 'timidity of women' and his cries often appall and frighten female travellers (p. 14). Althorpe's obsessive thoughts over Constantia at the beginning of the text, combined with his dream of rescuing her from an unknown assailant, means that in his mind 'consequences truly deplorable' has a clear subtext of female sexual violation at the hands of the Native American. As Nick is a roaming 'monster', the reader is led to assume that he would perpetrate any attack. This remarkable yet othered vocal ability serves to underline Nick's insensibility and sever him from the White civic community. A *'dysarticulate'* man – James Berger's term for those blocked from language – Nick is disarticulated or forcibly dislocated from the early national community.[28] He is deficient and defective and so appears as a Native American, a non-White and non-American subject excluded from the polity. Brown's Native coding of an impaired White man reinforces citizenship as exclusively for the sensible.

Returning to Frank Carwin, the ventriloquist's disembodied shouts render him another encroaching irrational indigenised figure on the frontier. The Mohawk cry not only fashions Carwin as a Native subject but the manner in which he produces sounds emulates a vocal practice firmly associated with non-White and non-Christian groups. Writing on ventriloquism, Leigh Eric Schmidt suggests that M. de la Chapelle's *La Ventriloque* (1773), which Brown refers to in *Wieland*, 'offered a naturalistic lens . . . to provide a way of making sense of indigenous conjurers encountered through colonial contact'. In colonial America, the ventriloquial voice was the sign of witchcraft, either real or fraudulently performed to torment believers. Ventriloquism began to transform into a form of popular entertainment at the end of the eighteenth century – as I discuss shortly – but it still connoted the pagan, and was therefore implicitly non-Christian and non-White.[29] In Rush's lecture 'On Speech' (1792), he in fact portrays Native speech as a ventriloquial act: 'The Indians in this country, use their tongues and lips as little as possible in conversation. Even at public treaties, they grunt their assent to what is proposed to them, through their throats. All their languages partake largely of guttural sounds.'[30] Similarly to Rush, Thomas Reid viewed 'savage' speech as 'an exercise, not of the voice and lungs only, but of all the muscles of the body'.[31] Carwin uses the generic 'organs' to describe the source of his vocal power encompassing his throat and abdomen, suggesting a guttural source and matching the Latin etymology of 'ventriloquism' as speaking from the stomach (pp. 186, 232, 233). His ventriloquism is an act of physicality, 'every muscle tense' in his face when Clara sees him throwing his voice (p. 136). It is this peculiar production that Carwin uses not just to imitate a Mohawk, but in all his vocal guises in the text: Catharine Wieland, the 'sweet and delectable' sounding Clara, 'hoarse and manlike' whispering thugs, and an omnipotent deity (pp. 123, 56).

Sounding Indigenous – in language or vocal production – placed one on the borders of Whiteness. In Volume I of Hugh Henry Brackenridge's *Modern Chivalry* (1792), Captain Farrago meets an 'Indian treaty-man' who sources faux Native Americans amongst recent immigrants. Generally approaching 'Welch [sic], or Low Dutch, or Irish' men to pretend to be Indigenous, the treaty-man explains these groups are so apt because 'some unknown gibberish is necessary, to pass for an Indian language'. The ease with which their non-Anglophone speech could be mistaken for Indigenous tongues by White listeners compounds their marginal status in White society. The treaty man continues that failing one of those Europeans, he could obtain an American 'ingenious fellow . . . who can imitate a language by sounds of his own, in his mouth and throat', once again rendering Indigenous speech as beyond White vocal practices.[32] In *Wieland* and *Memoirs*, Carwin is that ingenious American man. Rather than marking out an immigrant nationality, his out-of-bounds indigenised voice articulates his unclassifiable liminal position along the edges of the family unit and the nation as a wandering American. For Brown, the ontological uncertainty and multiplicity of the ventriloquial voice represents those who are mutable in society, cross boundaries and are disconnected from the White family-as-nation, nation-as-family view of America.

Carwin takes on multiple guises before he throws his voice. He is a frontier figure, appearing at the isolated Mettingen estate on the banks of the Schuylkill a few miles outside Philadelphia. The Wieland family's grounds are set within a wild and chiaroscuro natural landscape, the shore of the river 'chequered by patches of dark verdure and shapeless masses of white marble, and crowned by copses of cedar' (p. 44). Mysterious traveller Carwin enters the enclosed lives of the family in the appearance of a rustic figure that Clara has only seen in the past 'on the road or field' (pp. 46–7). His clothing, coarse and weathered, suggests he is a wanderer or peasant. We can read this as the first of Carwin's physical guises, as he 'put on the garb and assumed the manners of a clown' to conceal his identity and turns itinerant to avoid detection by Ludloe, his villainous guardian in Europe (p. 183). In this guise he is afforded a form of invisibility; as an impoverished figure he fades into the background of a number of politically unimportant yet economically necessary domestic workers and poor labourers. Disguised as such, he is able to access different locations in the city and the surrounding countryside without attention; he is both outside the borders of the Wieland community and out of bounds, entering and leaving as he pleases, including sleeping on the 'smooth turf' on the estate during the summer (p. 186).[33] As such, from her distanced perspective Clara dismisses him as not part of the educated company she keeps at Mettingen. However, if Carwin chooses plain dress in order to have largely unimpeded movement and to avoid attention, this is negated by the remarkableness of his face:

> His cheeks were pallid and lank, his eyes sunken, his forehead overshadowed by coarse straggling hairs, his teeth large and irregular, though sound and brilliantly white, and his chin discoloured by a tetter. His skin was of coarse grain and sallow hue. Every feature was wide of beauty, and the outline of his face reminded you of an inverted cone. (p. 49)

Compared to the Wieland family, who are noticeably bodiless in Brown's descriptions, Carwin's grotesque visage is closely detailed by Clara. Carwin's distorted physique is emphasised first in person and then again when she sketches his face, a 'rare and prodigious' form that she cannot remove from her mind, which accentuates his uncategorisable strangeness and his distinct position outside the family (p. 50). Simultaneously, Carwin is socially invisible yet strongly physically demarcated as a strange less-than-White figure.

María DeGuzmán reads the above description of Carwin as one of 'racial ambiguity' due to his off-white physical appearance.[34] This, combined with his residency in Spain, she argues, represents a Spanish threat to the new nation. This is another of Carwin's physical guises; Clara identifies Carwin's 'garb, aspect, and deportment' as 'wholly Spanish' (p. 62). He is tainted and darkened through his '*transformation* into a Spaniard', not least due to his conversion to Catholicism (p. 63). Recent European immigrants, in particular Catholics and Jews, hold a liminal position in Brown's fiction, as both insiders who have many of the freedoms of White Americans, and outsiders who have distinct threatening political and religious beliefs. For example, in *Arthur Mervyn* (1800), Achsa Fielding, an English Sephardic Jew, is both part of Philadelphian society and economy and an exotic darkened figure (as 'tawney as a moor') who attracts Arthur.[35] Multifaceted American identity shifts and transforms along geographic and racial lines in the early national period.

When Carwin enters Mettingen his Mohawk cry re-emerges as a further series of known and unknown voices that intrude on the White domestic space and wreak havoc on the Wieland family. Drawing on the Mohawk cry, Hsuan Hsu identifies Carwin's voice as an Indigenous spatial disturbance to colonial possession of the land, that 'destabilize[s] the Jeffersonian grid by importing colonial voices back into the inmost cells of the colonizing nation'.[36] Carwin's is a liminal intermediary voice that brings together the expansionist aims of the early republic – it is a colonising force that enters and takes over the Mettingen estate – and the voices of those removed from the land in this expansionist project – the Mohawk cry. In my reading, the Native presence, like the Spanish one, is not what Carwin represents, but a destabilising allusion. Spaniard, Native, peasant: Carwin's signifiers of multiple identities indicate an unknowable and unclassifiable national subject divorced from the structures of family or community. His perceived foreignness is not a threat, but the combination of all his identities is because they destabilise readings of character, obscuring who Carwin is. If someone looks Spanish or looks like a peasant, but is not, then trusting the senses is thrown into doubt. Amorphous, without a locatable source, and taking up space where it is not, the ventriloquial voice more profoundly confuses sensory understanding.

## SENSATIONAL VENTRILOQUISM AND THE EARLY NATIONAL GOTHIC IMAGINATION

Brown chooses to populate each text with liminal less-than-White ventriloquial voices in order to test his republican characters and readers. In this context, we can see ventriloquism and unusual vocal powers to be a 'form of rational entertainment' testing the judgement of Enlightenment citizens' senses.[37] Although the majority of these spectacles (magic lanterns, cosmoramas, automatons) prized accurate vision in order to distinguish truth from falsehood, accurate hearing was valued in the same way and ventriloquism was, 'perversely enough, pressed into service for the refinement of the ear'.[38] In the accounts of ventriloquism appearing in British and American magazines in the late eighteenth century, including *The Weekly Magazine* edited by Brown, the ventriloquist attempts to trick or mislead the listening audience. Sixteenth-century French ventriloquist Petrus Brabantius, for example, 'put divers cheats on several persons' and mimicked the voice of one man's deceased father, tricking him into giving Brabantius six thousand francs.[39] Others, such as German nobleman Baron de Mengen, performed as dinner-table entertainment, leading the audience to speculate how the voices were produced. A similar episode occurs in *Memoirs of Carwin*, as an outdoor audience hears a disembodied voice singing Ariel's song from *The Tempest* and wonders where the singer is positioned (p. 241).[40] In these ventriloquial episodes, hearing is continually tested, with most listeners failing to correctly identify the human source of the voice. The test carries outside of the text too, so that readers of these magazine pieces can ask themselves if they would be able to work out the ventriloquial trick – could their ears detect the location and source of the voices, or would they too be hoodwinked?

This is a question that can be asked of fiction readers as well. Fiction provided a readership – presumed by social commentators to be largely female – with moral education and lessons in fortitude, virtue and rationality. In the face of innumerable essays on the danger of novel reading for naïve young women caught up in the narrator's intimate voice and unable to differentiate between fiction and reality, early American novels asserted their veracity to emphasise their moral value. Successful texts such as *Charlotte Temple*, William Hill Brown's *The Power of Sympathy* (1794) and Hannah Webster Foster's *The Coquette* (1797) all employ subtitles with these claims – *A Tale of Truth, A Novel; Founded on Fact* and *Founded in Truth*, respectively. In *Wieland*, Brown makes plain the moral usefulness of the text to illustrate 'some important branches of the moral constitution of man' based on factual accounts of ventriloquism and legal cases of homicide (p. 3). As part of this educational purpose, Brown performs his own ventriloquism, writing in the first-person voice of a young woman (Clara) or man (Althorpe) and creating dialogue and narrative that is designed to perplex, frighten and entertain. Writing, in particular fiction, that involves sensational and mysterious events equally tests the reader and challenges them to decipher clues and reach correct conclusions. In particular in *Wieland*, Clara, Pleyel and Theodore all act as representatives of the poor fiction reader; they misread situations and people, fundamentally misinterpreting Carwin's voices.[41]

Returning to Reid's work on the senses, ventriloquism is 'only such an imperfect imitation as may deceive those who are inattentive, or under a panic'. Pressing the point that a good citizen would carefully use their senses in the face of this perplexing act, he maintained that 'an attentive ear would be able to distinguish the copy from the original'.[42] At the beginning of each text the two women serve as prime examples of 'good' citizens precisely because they cast off the irrationality or poor sense ascribed to their sex. The ideal of republican womanhood, as Linda Kerber and more recently Lucia McMahon outline, granted women rationalism while delimiting them to the private sphere. The archetypal republican woman was 'competent and confident . . . rational, benevolent, independent, self-reliant'. She attained an acceptable level of education that would prevent her from becoming a sexualised, silly coquette and at the same time retain her femininity in order to become a suitable wife and mother for the civically engaged male citizen.[43] In literature of the 1790s the republican daughter functioned as a figure of virtue, often guiding her family through the tumultuous and uncertain new national landscape. The republican daughter navigated the American city, protecting and securing her family's finances and using her rationality to avoid rogues, tricksters and sexual predators. For example, in *Ormond*, Constantia Dudley is 'the consummate embodiment' of the constant, rational and courageous republican daughter who overcomes the mysterious Ormond and his sexual advances.[44] She would not be fooled by automaton and magic lantern shows on display in town.

In 'Somnambulism', the prototype Constantia initially uses her senses to perceive and judge what she and her father encounter on the road. She criticises Althorpe's overactive imagination, telling her father: 'I am not so much a girl as to be scared merely because it is dark.' Althorpe himself is 'ashamed' of the effeminate 'weakness' of his superstitious mind too; he is the irrational one with a 'mind . . . too powerfully excited' and 'ideas . . . full of confusion and inaccuracy' to which he inexplicably clings (p. 10). Constantia begins as eminently rational, employing her sight to ascertain who is there. Mr Davis, a victim of poor sight and ageing eyes, believes he sees a shady figure, but 'the young lady's better eyes enabled her to detect his mistake. It was the trunk of a cherry tree that he had observed' (p. 13). She warns her father against jumping to conclusions, assuring him there is no danger on the road. Later, Mr Davis believes that he has seen a light ahead, signifying a house where they can rest and get advice for the journey. Constantia again corrects him: 'the light which you saw is gone: a sufficient proof that it was nothing but a meteor' (p. 14). Language of observation and deduction permeates the first half of the text as Constantia uses her common sense to dismiss inaccurate assumptions.

In *Wieland*, Pleyel praises Clara for her temperament in comparison to the overtly feminine figure of his sister Catharine – 'her strength of mind is inferior to yours' – who is defined in the novel by her gender, existing as little more than Theodore's wife and mother to his children (p. 39). Clara's reputation as a rational woman precedes her. Carwin desires to test whether she is 'a woman capable of recollection in danger, of warding off groundless panics, of discerning the true mode of proceeding, and profiting by her best resources' to make her a 'prodigy' (p. 185). Clara is not swayed by testimony or 'tales of apparition and enchantments', which she sees as 'ignorance and folly', and she seeks to discriminate truth from fantasy on what she can observe (p. 42). When Carwin seeks to induce panic, superstition and fear through his strange cries, he tests these values of citizenry. However, despite her rational reputation, Clara is not a fully engaged republican woman. She admits that the family shut themselves off from the world and republican society: 'We gradually withdrew ourselves from the society of others, and found every moment irksome that was not devoted to each other' (p. 19). Through the Wieland family, Brown suggests that citizens must do more than display their education and reason; they must act and engage in the world. Those who shut themselves off politically or socially also shut out dissenting or sceptical voices that would rectify their increasingly irrational assumptions.

Nick and Carwin's ventriloquism and mimicry, which blur the boundary between the physical and spiritual, tests the hearing and judgement of the Wielands and Davises. Carwin deliberately uses his voice to create disorder in the community; he confesses to producing 'a mysterious dread' through a number of vocalic guises in order to destroy the reputation of Clara, mislead Theodore and Pleyel, and satisfy his own curiosity (*Wieland*, p. 192). However, as Eric Wolfe argues, the danger of Carwin's ventriloquism is not his deliberate misrepresentation through a number of vocalic guises, but the *'misrecognition'* of Clara, Pleyel and Theodore.[45] In the Wieland microcosm,

Brown presents a national community so disturbed that the very foundation of its identity – empirical reasoning, rooted in the senses – is shown to be fallible in the presence of an unclassifiable chameleon such as Carwin. These disturbed states of fear, confusion, doubt and awe when listening to onto-logically inexplicable voices lead the protagonists to return to their bodies, accepting and trusting their senses and dismissing extra-corporeal evidence. When confronted with what cannot be explained easily or at all, the Wielands assume truth in the senses alone, which are fallible through manipulation or delusion. In the early ventriloquial episodes, the family use the senses to justify their conclusions on who is delivering the voices, using prolific legal language to establish truth. They must weigh up the testimony of family mem-bers against the testimony of their senses. The first time the inexplicable voice is heard, Theodore returns from visiting the temple, claiming to have heard Catharine's voice beckoning him to the house. While Catharine, Clara and Pleyel seek to dissuade him, he states, 'your assurances . . . are solemn and unanimous; and yet I must deny credit to your assertions, or disbelieve the testimony of my senses, which informed me, when I was half way up the hill, that Catharine was at the bottom' (p. 30). Per Reid, man's faith in his senses 'remains as firm as if it were grounded on demonstration'.[46] For Theodore, his belief in his hearing takes precedence, even though he has no supporting visual evidence of Catharine speaking in front of him.

This acceptance of the senses as truth in the face of competing testimony is most apparent in the incident between Pleyel and Clara. Pleyel judges Clara to be 'the most abandoned and detestable of human creatures' after supposedly hearing an illicit meeting between her and Carwin. Pleyel, usually 'skeptical in a transcendant degree' fully accepts the aural 'evidence' presented. He exclaims, 'That my eyes, that my ears, should bear witness to thy fall!' (pp. 109, 103, 95, 95–6). His empiricism creates the legal framework with which he puts Clara on trial. Clara's lament that 'he has judged me without hearing' is ironic because Pleyel has judged her on his hearing almost exclusively, relying on the testimony of his ears over her version of events. Relaying how he heard the lovers' meet-ing, Pleyel recalls: 'My sight was of no use to me. Beneath so thick an umbrage, the darkness was intense. Hearing was the only avenue to information, which the circumstances allowed to be open' (pp. 97, 125). In these few sentences, Pleyel's senses are restricted to hearing alone; his sight would have remedied his 'inexplicable and momentary phrenzy' to show that the figures he heard were Carwin and Clara's servant Judith, part of Carwin's plot to set up Pleyel and toy with his and Clara's emotions (p. 110). In a text composed of long passages of descriptive monologue and dialogue, 'saying makes it so'; other characters speak the plot into existence, retelling events that Clara has missed.[47] Carwin's ventriloquism dictates the plot; through his mimicry he creates an entire alter ego for Clara, painting her as a scandalous woman embroiled in an affair with the traveller, a guise that Pleyel fully accepts. At the same time, hearing makes it so: characters construct their truths through what they have heard; Pleyel brings to life Clara's alter ego through retelling the conversation he has heard.

The idea that sensory experience alone creates truth is most apparent in the transformations of Clara and Theodore. The novel reaches a climax when Theodore murders Catharine, their children and servant girl Louisa Conway, claiming to hear the voice of God ordering him. The inexplicable disembodied nature of the voices, spoken where no man is present, leads Theodore, mis-guided by his empiricist learning and theism, to believe that these voices have a supernatural origin. After Carwin reveals himself as the ventriloquial source of the earlier voices, Clara struggles to decide whether Theodore is delusional or has been deceived by a demonic Carwin. From Carwin's entry, there is a clear shift from the senses to the sensational in Clara. By this I mean that Clara moves from using her senses to reach common-sense judgements, to her senses feeding a sensation-driven, gothicised imagination. Upon hearing shrieks that she believes to be from an assailant entering her house, Clara recalls:

> O! may my ears lose their sensibility, ere they be again assailed by a shriek so terrible! Not merely my understanding was subdued by the sound; it acted on my nerves like an edge of steel. It appeared to cut asunder the fibres of my brain, and rack every joint with agony . . . Shuddering, I dashed myself against the wall. (p. 78)

The voice disorders Clara's mind. Unable rationally to process the sounds, all she is capable of is a physical response that signifies a return to the body and a reliance on the senses alone. Reflecting on this incident a few nights later, Clara struggles to rationally process the speaker, imagining 'an invisible hand and of preternatural strength'. The incorporeal voice in the text overwhelms and disorders her mind – led by her hearing alone, she constructs the improbable 'vocalic body' of a phantom-man with 'all places . . . alike accessible' in this threatened home invasion (p. 78). For Clara, as the vocal intrusions increase, her other sense of deduction – sight – is increasingly unreliable. Instead of following Rush's advice that the senses should be used in tandem to ward off deception and mistakes, when Clara uses her sight it is distorted and further lends to her sensational imagination.[48] In a heightened state of trepidation, Clara experiences visual and aural hallucinations where 'slight movements and casual sounds were transformed into beckoning shadows and calling shapes' (p. 176). When she sees Carwin practise his ventriloquism, the monstrosity of his shrieking 'vehement expression' is accompanied by 'the eyes emitt[ing] sparks, which, no doubt, if I had been unattended by a light, would have illu-minated like the coruscations of a meteor'. The sight of a figure whom she deduces to be Carwin, giving off sparks, convinces her that he 'exceeded the standard of humanity' (p. 136). Even when Carwin confesses his ventriloquial ability, a human if strange bodily quirk, Clara prefers her sensory, subjective explanation that his voices are a supernatural occurrence: 'Was there not reason to doubt the accuracy of my perceptions?' (p. 203).

Unable to distinguish between imagination and reality and failing to recall all events, Clara becomes an increasingly unreliable narrator. Her fainting spells again signify a return to the body, a physical response overwhelming her processing of events, and throughout her narrative she relies on her uncle's recollections to fill in the gaps. Narrative voice is disrupted throughout the text, as Clara's narration is replaced with a transcription of Theodore's court testimony, which narrates the events of his murders, and Carwin's confessional, a speech that crosses chapter breaks, therefore temporarily removing Clara as the narrator. With such an unstable narrative voice, Brown places further responsibility on the reader to navigate these seemingly inexplicable events and reach their own conclusion.

When Clara 'transform[s] from rational and human into creature of nameless and fearful attributes' it is due to her heightened sensational imagination (p. 165). Carwin's inexplicable voices and his appearances stoke Clara's desire for imaginative reverie. Throughout her narrative, she admits finding pleasure in the unknown and dangerous. Against a life of domestic duties and conversation, the mysteries and danger of Carwin's vocal power, whether human or spiritual, offer Clara the opportunity to indulge her imagination. Originally presented as a rational, empirical citizen, Clara in fact takes pleasure from experiences that plunge her into states of melancholy or fear, often meditating on strange and violent events. Clara is not only a gothic heroine but also a reader of the gothic. There is a catharsis and pleasure in experiencing terrors from which the reader is somewhat distanced. We can see that the trauma of Wieland Sr's inexplicable death by spontaneous combustion leads to Clara's repeated attraction to and musings on danger. We are not told of Clara reading novels, but news of the recent French–Indian war – perhaps an oral report, perhaps a printed newspaper – is a source of excitement before Carwin's arrival, 'agitating our minds with curiosity' (p. 24).

This thrill intensifies upon Clara encountering Carwin. His strange and exotic form, racially ambiguous, throws Clara into a 'fit of musing' and she suddenly finds herself experiencing an outpouring of sensibility, which she can't explain: 'Why was my mind absorbed in thoughts ominous and dreary? Why did my bosom heave with sighs, and my eyes overflow with tears?' Clara can't decide whether Carwin is 'an object to be dreaded or adored', in part because of his liminal appearance; he can look darkened and grotesque yet has features that 'betoken a mind of the highest order' (pp. 49, 50, 65, 49). The combination of attraction and repulsion Clara feels from encountering Carwin and the compulsion she has to reimagine and revisualise his face in her drawings emphasises that he reawakens her sensory and sensational imagination. Clara is firmly rooted in her body, and her imagination anticipates sensory experiences: having a physical relationship with Carwin or Pleyel, escaping violence from assailants known and unknown, thinking about her father's inexplicable violent death, imagining the sensations of war. She admits of her imagination, 'I was tormented by phantoms of my own creation,' which leads to flights of fancy, shapes transformed into creatures and seeing flashes from Carwin's eyes, believing it as proof that he is 'leagued with hell' (pp. 76, 200). The scene in which Clara sees Carwin's ventriloquial act – a face emitting sparks in a horrifying contorted expression – has parallels with sensational phantasmagoria, in which audiences were subjected to grotesque moving images, terrifying sounds and atmospheric light shows. The phantasmagoria is a staged gothic fiction; both are forms of entertainment designed to deliberately scare and entertain an audience, and Clara is a willing participant.

This shift from the five senses, and more specifically hearing, to the sensational takes place in 'Somnambulism'. While Constantia begins as eminently rational and the archetypal republican daughter, she is swayed by her imagination and seduced by the idea of frontier romance, presented in the form of Nick. His ventriloquism and mimicry, which blur the boundary between the material and the invisible and between human and animal, test the hearing and judgement of the Davises. The father and daughter accept and trust their senses yet do not follow through with the good sense required of republican citizens, instead falling into sensation, adventure and romance. This shift from critical, rational hearing to sensation and the sensational takes place because the liminal figure's savage voice is the catalyst for Constantia's imagination. Narrating Constantia's journey, Althorpe imagines that his own fears may have 'infected her' or that she has 'imagined evils that my incautious temper might draw upon me'. They share a sensational imagination, prompted by thinking about the frontier. When Constantia and Mr Davis are first assailed by the mysterious figure on the roadside, he becomes a 'topic of abundant speculation' (p. 12). After meeting with the farmer and hearing about the wandering savage Nick, they consider him to be 'so singular a specimen of the forms which human nature is found to assume' that he deserves 'a variety of remarks' (p. 16).

Upon being told of Nick's wild exploits and in anticipation of hearing the shrieks, the Davises indulge in a moment of frontier fantasy.

> They pictured to themselves many combinations of circumstance in which Handyside might be the agent, and in which the most momentous effects might flow from his agency, without its being possible for others to conjecture the true nature of the agent. The propensities of this being might contribute to realize, on an American road, many of those imaginary tokens and perils which abound in the wildest romance.

He would be an admirable machine, in a plan whose purpose was to generate or foster, in a given subject, the frenzy of quixotism. – No theater was better adapted than Norwood to such an exhibition. . . . Yet the choice of Handyside, varied with the force and skill of which he was known to be capable, would fill these shades with outcries as ferocious as those which are to be heard in Siamese or Abyssinian forests. The tale of his recent elopement had been told by the man with whom they had just parted, in a rustic but picturesque style. (p. 16)

Here, the combination of Nick's cries and the frontier location renders him simultaneously exoticised and abhorred, as Norwood temporarily transforms into Siam or Abyssinia, nations not only harbouring ferocious animals but populated by indigenous peoples who had resisted European colonisation. The Davises' imagination is at work as they picture a number of scenarios in which Nick may appear. Their speculation creates a romanticised savage vocalic body in Nick, who serves as 'an admirable machine' to shock and frighten travellers. Here, 'machine' resonates with early national ideals of citizenship; Rush expected citizens to become 'republican machines' who 'perform their parts properly' to improve society, a role from which Nick is excluded.[49] The Davises and Nick play parts in this 'wild romance', with Constantia casting Nick in the 'Indian' role. Using the language of theatrical performance, Nick is a figure of entertainment. As a cognitively impaired liminal figure, he becomes the less-than-White bogeyman who can be vanquished. Constantia is particularly swayed by this frontier romance, declaring 'she should be highly pleased by hearing his outcries, and console[s] herself with the belief, that he would not allow them to pass the limits which he had prescribed to his wanderings, without greeting them with a strain or two' (p. 16). The senses lead to the sensational; Constantia finds pleasing terror in the idea of the frontier monster she can repel.

The picturesque savage figure is a product of White literary imagination. Constantia's frontier fantasy of a wild savage haunting her at a safe distance illuminates readings of *Edgar Huntly*, which was written shortly after, as a piece of diverting Anglo-American gothic imagination. In the frontispiece to the novel, Brown writes that he wants 'to exhibit a series of adventures, growing out of the condition of our country'. Instead of the 'puerile superstition and exploded manners; Gothic castles and chimeras' found in European gothic, he instead claims, 'The incidents of Indian hostility, and the perils of the western wilderness, are far more suitable; and, for a native of America to overlook these, would admit of no apology.'[50] Brown aims to create a distinctly American form of the gothic in the dangers of the American landscape, namely Native Americans and the frontier wilderness. In *Edgar Huntly*, Edgar must navigate the natural world, survive the elements and battle a host of Lenni

Lenape whom Brown presents as ghostly, unreal figures. Native Americans serve as an obstacle to be overcome in the gothic narrative, providing a pleasing terror to the reader familiar with the genre, especially as in *Edgar Huntly*, where the sources of terror are more familiar to an American audience than the castles and Catholicism found in Ann Radcliffe or Monk Lewis. Constantia serves as a representative of both Brown and his readership. Through her imagination she creates in Nick a savage vocalic body tied to the frontier, writing in her mind a 'wild romance'. She becomes a playwright, populating the set of the Norwood frontier with Nick as a savage antagonist and herself as the republican heroine who can protect her family from the perils of the road. At the same time, despite her claims of rationality and empiricism, upon hearing about Nick's cries Constantia transforms into one of Brown's gothic readers, eager to hear the shrieks, which she transposes into a musical 'strain or two', attesting to its pleasing terror ('Somnambulism', p. 16).

As the savage shrieks mislead the Davises, leading to sensational imagination, the liminal figure serves as a gothic narrative technique to increase and decrease tension. In 'Somnambulism', this tension escalates with each appearance of the shadowy figure, only to decrease each time Constantia dismisses her father's fears. The farmer's condensed history of Nick heightens anticipation of his appearance and the assumption that he will commit the violence. Brown simultaneously offers clues and diversions towards the source of the violence, requiring the text to be re-read after it ends and creating a test by which the reader can prove their claim to rationality. Brown's introductory note regarding a sleepwalking homicide is the most obvious clue, guiding the reader to infer that Althorpe's violent dream was reality and that he was Constantia's attacker. An intelligent gothic reader would not be distracted by Nick, and would recognise Althorpe's dream of shooting an assailant as a confession of his somnambulistic murder.

Just as the ventriloquial figure Nick throws his voice, Brown throws his narrative, misdirecting and diverting the reader from the source of violence in the text – the White, middle-class Althorpe. If we position Constantia as a poor gothic reader or listener, enjoying the pleasing terror of Nick's sensational ventriloquism, her imagination of a frontier romance blinds her to the danger in the woods, Althorpe himself, her sleepwalking attacker. Michael Cody offers a Freudian reading of Althorpe to argue that it is sleepwalking that reveals his savagery, contending that 'when his id is separated by sleep from the control of his ego, he becomes a far more dangerous unknown than Handyside'.[51] It is true that the only act of violence Althorpe admits to is in his sleep, dreaming that when fighting off an assailant he 'did not employ the usual preliminaries which honour prescribes, but, stimulated by rage, attacked him with a pistol, and terminated his career by a mortal wound' ('Somnambulism', p. 11). This dream mirrors the nature of Constantia's attack, acting as a veiled confession that Althorpe has committed the murder. However, Althorpe's savagery is also made clear when he is awake, at the end of the fragment when he narrates Constantia's death.

> The dying lady was removed to the house. The ball had lodged in her brain, and to extract it was impossible. Why should I dwell on the remaining incidents of this tale? She languished till the next morning, and then expired – (p. 18)

Althorpe's chilling detachment, unusual for a man who has earlier professed his love for the victim, comes through in his matter-of-fact tone. He displays an insensitivity different from Nick's; this is cruelty and indifference underneath a façade of gentility. The true terror of the text is revealed not to be the haunting, savage simpleton, but the middling gentleman capable of an act of obsessive, violent rage. Throughout his fiction, Brown undermines the ideology of the respectable and rational White man as the model citizen: Theodore Wieland murders his family in an act of delusional rage; Edgar carries out racist violence against the Lenni Lenape; Ormond violates domestic spaces and threatens republican daughters. 'Somnambulism' is not only a cautionary tale against the perils of insensibility, like the sleepwalking homicide, but a warning to early national citizens not to be swept up in frontier romance and fears of the racialised Other, while oblivious to the potential danger of the republican White male.

In Brown's works, the liminal White figure blurs racial boundaries to reflect the slippery and indistinct nature of White citizenship in the early national period. In doing so, the liminal figure, on the physical and symbolic margins of society, both critiques and challenges the expectations of White citizens. Nick and Carwin's ventriloquial cries transgress the boundaries of race, gender, class and species, and blur the demarcation between the material and the immaterial. In particular, Carwin's multiple physical and vocalic guises, as later seen in Robert Montgomery Bird's *Sheppard Lee* (1836), offer an alternative vision of identity that is dislocated from genealogy, property, geography and race. These liminal manifestations of Whiteness are resistant to the increasing essentialising of identity and formalising of Whiteness as the early national and antebellum period progresses. As I discuss in Chapter 3, Sheppard's racial transformation offers the opportunity to escape the confines of White middle-class civic responsibilities, while presenting the frightening possibility of rapid and violent racial movement.

In *Wieland* and 'Somnambulism', Native allusion signifies Carwin and Nick's exclusion from a community of enlightened citizens. The liminal figure, in its marginal mischief, exposes the fragility of this ideal of White citizenship where the senses will inevitably lead to 'good sense'; citizens require reason and suspicion as well as empirical sense on the unfamiliar frontier. Brown calls for intelligent readers of men who can distinguish between Nick and Althorpe and between

Carwin and Theodore. Brown's American gothic reflects the social concerns of a young nation through recognisable Native allusions and asks for intelligent citizens and readers to show good sense in the face of seemingly inexplicable and turbulent events. In my next chapter I turn to Washington Irving, whose 1820s ghost stories again employ Native-inflected White male figures in frontier spaces. He does so, I argue, to create nostalgia for colonial communities that embrace the irrational and supernatural storytelling, a contrast to Brown's resounding scepticism.

## Notes

1. Brockden Brown, *Wieland; Or the Transformation, and Memoirs of Carwin the Biloquist*, ed. Elliott, p. 230. Further citations of this edition are given in parentheses in the main text.
2. Connor, *Dumbstruck*, p. 35.
3. Chiles, *Transformable Race*, p. 2.
4. For example, the physician Benjamin Rush argued that endemic leprosy had led to Africans developing black skin. The remarkable case of Henry Moss in 1796, a free Black man from Maryland whose skin began turning white, suggested to Rush that physical blackness could be gradually erased or remedied. Brown printed a report on Moss in *The Weekly Magazine* in February 1798 and reprinted Rush's account in *The Monthly Magazine* in April 1800. These discussions of malleable race extended to perceptions of Native Americans. Unlike African Americans, however, this group were expected to assimilate by changing their behaviour, not physical appearance. Thomas Jefferson contended that through educational and agricultural programmes, Native Americans would move from savagery to civilisation. D.W., 'Account of a Singular Change of Colour in a Negro', *The Weekly Magazine*; Rush, 'Reasons for Ascribing the Colour of Negroes to Leprosy', *The Monthly Magazine*; Dain, *A Hideous Monster of the Mind*, pp. 24–5, 28–9.
5. Brockden Brown, *Ormond, Or the Secret Witness*, ed. Chapman, p. 154.
6. Gardner, 'Edgar Huntly's Savage Awakening', p. 446.
7. Stampone, 'A "Spirit of Mistaken Benevolence"', pp. 420, 423.
8. Shirley Samuels views Carwin as a threatening alien from revolutionary France against which America must be 'inoculated', whereas Jane Tompkins sees him as an internal threat, a 'child of the revolution' who wreaks violence on a young nation, and argues that Brown calls for 'the restoration of civic authority in a post-Revolutionary age'. Writing on *Memoirs*, Paul Downes interprets Carwin as 'an insistently *democratic* subject'. Hsuan Hsu takes the view that Carwin represents a colonised subject re-entering the White domestic space. Samuels, '"Wieland": Alien and Infidel', p. 54; Jane Tompkins, *Sensational Designs*, pp. 52, 61; Downes, 'Constitutional Secrets', p. 110; Hsu, 'Democratic Expansionism in "Memoirs of Carwin"'.
9. White, 'Carwin the Peasant Rebel', in Barnard, Kamrath and Shapiro (eds), *Revising Charles Brockden Brown*, pp. 41–59 (p. 52).
10. Brockden Brown, 'Somnambulism: A Fragment', in Crow (ed.), *American Gothic: An Anthology, 1787–1916*, p. 14. Further citations of this edition are given in

parentheses in the main text. Philip Barnard and Stephen Shapiro posit the short story is 'possibly written as draft "fragment" in the process of planning *Sky-Walk* or *Edgar Huntly*', while Jeffrey Weinstock traces the development of the frontier from Norwood in 'Somnambulism' to Norwalk in *Edgar Huntly*. Brockden Brown, *Edgar Huntly, or, Memoirs of a Sleep-Walker*, ed. Barnard and Shapiro, p. 244; Weinstock, *Charles Brockden Brown*, pp. 34–6.

11. Bellion, *Citizen Spectator*, pp. 5, 15.
12. Murison, 'The Tyranny of Sleep', p. 244.
13. Dunlap, *The Life of Charles Brockden Brown*, vol. 1, p. 20.
14. Reid, 'Of Judgment', in *Essays on the Intellectual Powers of Man*, vol. 2, pp. 168–372 (pp. 196, 199). Gary Wills meticulously traces the influence of Reid on Jefferson's framing of the Declaration in *Inventing America*, pp. 61–94.
15. Reid, 'Of Judgment', p. 177.
16. Knott, *Sensibility and the American Revolution*, p. 102.
17. Rosenfeld, *Common Sense*, pp. 15, 154.
18. Nielsen, *A Disability History of the United States*, p. 50.
19. Charlotte Temple goes insane and dies shortly after lover Montraville abandons her. In *Dorval*, the eponymous bigamist seduces and imprisons Elizabeth Dunbar. After she escapes she is incarcerated in a Philadelphia asylum, mad with guilt. Karen A. Weyler connects female madness in these novels with early national discourses on female sexuality in *Intricate Relations*, pp. 75–104.
20. Taking an empirical world-view, Samuel Johnson defined 'idiot' in his dictionary as someone in 'want of understanding' and therefore outside of rational society. Halliwell, *Images of Idiocy*, p. 7.
21. Stanhope Smith, *An Essay on the Causes of the Variety of Complexion and Figure*, p. 199.
22. Rush, 'An Inquiry into the Natural History of Medicine Among the Indians of North-America', in *Medical Inquiries and Observations*, vol. 1, pp. 1–68 (pp. 12–13).
23. Bergland, *The National Uncanny*, p. 3; Stern, *Plight of Feeling*, p. 2.
24. As Sari Altschuler and Cristobel Silva recently explain: 'The idea of *disability* – that is, a set of stigmatized physical and cognitive impairments around which certain exclusionary practices are organized – was . . . at work in early America, but *disability* was not yet the singular word used to describe it.' Altschuler and Silva, 'Early American Disability Studies', p. 2.
25. 'To the Curious and Observing', *Boston Evening Post*, 29 July 1771, quoted in Clemente, 'A Reassessment of Common Law Protections for "Idiots"', p. 2778.
26. Rush, 'An Inquiry into the Natural History of Medicine Among the Indians of North-America', p. 15; Stanhope Smith, *An Essay*, p. 156.
27. For example, Stanhope Smith looked to species variations and adaptations in different climates to argue that the Native's complexion and 'savage' behaviours came from the inhospitable North American environment. Stanhope Smith, *An Essay*, pp. 77–79.
28. Berger, *The Disarticulate*, p. 2.
29. Schmidt, *Hearing Things*, pp. 151, 138–43.

30. Rush, 'Of Speech', in *Benjamin Rush's Lectures on the Mind*, ed. Carlson, Noel and Wollock, pp. 196–214 (pp. 204–5).

31. Reid, *An Inquiry into the Human Mind*, p. 96.

32. Brackenridge, *Modern Chivalry*, ed. Newlin, p. 55.

33. In *Wieland*, Judith serves as a prime example of the ignored servant: she continually resides in the domestic space and is privy to intimate information, yet Clara regularly overlooks her subjectivity. For example, on first meeting Carwin, Clara quotes the stranger yet demotes Judith's words into indirect speech. See Pethers, 'The Secret Witness', in Lawson (ed.), *Class and the Making of American Literature*, pp. 40–55 (p. 42).

34. DeGuzmán, *Spain's Long Shadow*, p. 25.

35. Stephen Shapiro views Achsa's Jewish identity as a cover for her '(Caribbean) mixed-race' and connects her to the circum-Atlantic slave trade that Brown weaves through the novel. He contends that Achsa's marriage to Arthur at the novel's conclusion puts forth an argument for interracial marriage, which supports Brockden Brown's abolitionist writings published in the early 1800s. Shapiro, *The Culture and Commerce of the Early American Novel*, p. 287; Brockden Brown, *Arthur Mervyn, or, Memoirs of the Year 1793*, ed. Barnard and Shapiro, p. 320.

36. The 'Jeffersonian grid' – a stable and structured sense of social and geographic place in the early national period – originates with Wieland Sr's landgrab at the beginning of the novel, with the Wieland microcosm representing a nation seeking democratic expansion across the continent, appropriating Indigenous land for White domestic estates. Hsu, 'Democratic Expansionism in "Memoirs of Carwin"', p. 144.

37. Schmidt, *Hearing Things*, p. 136.

38. Ibid. p. 137.

39. 'An Instance of Ventriloquism', *The Weekly Magazine of Original Essays*, 2.22 (1798), p. 277. This anecdote originally appeared as 'Singular Anecdote Relative to Ventriloquism', *Weekly Magazine, Or Edinburgh Amusements*, 1.25 (1774), pp. 275–7.

40. In one account, the Baron produced a small wooden doll, who was so 'impertinent' in her ventriloquised speech that the Baron stuffed her in his pocket to quiet her, much to the worry of an Irish officer who 'was so firmly persuaded that the baron's doll was a real living animal' that he attempted to rescue her from the confines of the pocket. 'Singular Anecdote Relative to Ventriloquism', p. 277.

41. The novel's opening foreshadows the family's critical misreading in Wieland Sr's misinterpretation of the Bible, a part of his Christian fundamentalism that leads to his emigration to America. Brown writes, 'His constructions of the text were hasty, and formed on a narrow scale. Everything was viewed in a disconnected position.' Brockden Brown, *Wieland*, p. 8.

42. Reid, 'Of the Powers We Have by Means of Our External Senses', in *Essays on the Intellectual Powers of Man*, vol. 1, pp. 81–360 (p. 356).

43. Kerber, *Women of the Republic*, p. 206; McMahon, *Mere Equals*, p. 9.

44. Tavor Bannet, 'The Constantias of the 1790s', pp. 451–2.

45. Wolfe, 'Ventriloquizing Nation', p. 436.

46. Reid, 'Of the Powers We Have by Means of Our External Senses', p. 326.

47. Seltzer, 'Saying Makes It So'.
48. Rush, 'Of the Subserviency of the Senses to Each Other, and on the Knowledge Derived from Them', in *Benjamin Rush's Lectures on the Mind*, ed. Carlson, Noel and Wollock, pp. 351–61.
49. Rush, 'Of the Mode of Education Proper in a Republic', in *Essays, Literary, Moral and Philosophical*, pp. 6–20 (p. 14).
50. Brockden Brown, *Edgar Huntly*, pp. 3–4.
51. Cody, *Charles Brockden Brown and the Literary Magazine*, p. 143.

# 2

## 'THIS IS A STORY-TELLING AGE': SPECTRAL NOSTALGIA IN *BRACEBRIDGE HALL*

In his historical tales, Washington Irving makes colonial male characters ghostly by connecting them to the pre-modern 'vanishing Indian' disappearing across the nation in the early national period. Like Charles Brockden Brown, Irving uses Native-coded speech and appearance to mark White men as liminal and outside the structures of early national society. Whereas Brown uses liminal Whiteness to significantly challenge and test ideals of exclusionary rational White citizenship, Irving's liminal White men speak against changes in early national conceptions of civic economic masculinity. This chapter argues that Irving employs liminal White figures temporarily marked by spectral indigeneity to enshrine a colonial vision of hierarchical yet interdependent community and citizenship, itself vanishing in the early national period. I propose that Irving is involved in a project of 'spectral nostalgia', using ghostly White male figures to critique an early national citizenship predicated on individual success and mobility, which is driven by progress but racked by instability, intangibility and disconnection. In his collection of tales and sketches, he employs scenes of supernatural storytelling to transmit this nostalgia for colonial masculinity, citizenship and community.

In this chapter I examine the prevalence of spectral figures and supernatural storytelling in *Bracebridge Hall* (1822), Irving's episodic novel of sketches of rural Yorkshire life and international ghostly tales. The supernaturally inflected Hudson Valley in *The Sketch Book* (1819–20) and *Bracebridge Hall* is itself a liminal space between fantasy and reality, inhabited with otherworldly Native figures, mischievous Indigenous spirits and the ghosts of Dutch explorers and settlers. A natural space seemingly removed from the modern world, it acts as a fitting location for Antony Vander Heyden, who blurs the boundaries between citizen and noncitizen, the propertied gentleman and roaming Native figure in 'Dolph Heyliger'. *Bracebridge Hall*'s lone American piece, 'Dolph Heyliger' is a ghost story by fictional historian Diedrich Knickerbocker, set in the colonial Hudson Valley. In it, the dead are repeatedly invoked and intrude upon the imaginations of communities across decades, from 1720s New York, the setting of the short story, to 1820s Yorkshire, where the story is recited. Geoffrey Crayon, Irving's travelling narrator and observer of British life, tells the story one evening to entertain his hosts at the Bracebridge estate. The ghost of the piece is Killian Vander Spiegel, a Dutch settler who in the 1640s buries significant wealth in Dolph's native Manhattan. After meeting the ghost, Dolph embarks on a dreamlike journey up the Hudson River to the outskirts of Albany. Lost in the wilderness, he encounters Vander Heyden, who appears as an uncanny reminder of the Dutch ghost and who slips in and out of Native appearance and spaces. Antony is a spectral figure made ghostly through an association with vanishing Indians and Dutch settler ghosts. In the wilderness, he tells stories of these Dutch ghosts and vocally protests the changing world around him.

Irving conceives of liminality as a transformational period between removal from and return to society. Liminal figure Antony transitions from propertied White settler to racially ambiguous outsider and back to colonial landowner, as Irving roots prosperous White citizenship within a supernatural and Indigenous-inflected frontier. Antony is part of a multiracial group and appears as Native American. He vocally protests an increasingly professionalised, cerebral form of masculine citizenship detached from community and the land. In tying propertied fathers to propertyless, socially excluded and otherworldly non-White counterparts, *Bracebridge Hall* positions its White patriarchs as vanishing figures themselves, out of place in Georgian England and the early United States. Through 'spectral nostalgia', Irving enshrines faded structures of communal citizenship that indigeneity marks.

In these spectral figures such as Antony, the past seems to re-enter the present. *Bracebridge Hall* comprises scenes of supernatural storytelling, and tales of ghosts appear alongside sketches of rural English life. Thinking about haunting as a 'collision of temporalities or spaces', as María del Pilar Blanco does, we can apply this ghostly frame to many of the texts within Irving's collections, in which the past and present seem to blur.[1] We can read a figure like Antony performing the same purpose as ghosts in that he appears to be from another time and when he talks he invokes nostalgia for White colonial masculinity. His presence enacts a collision of temporalities within the text because he embodies a form of White male citizenship that Irving conceives to be from the past. Spectrality, or the appearance of ghostly figures, enacts a collapse of the linear progression of time, as the present seems to become the past. By bringing these ghostly figures into the present, the supernatural is a key apparatus of Irving's project of spectral nostalgia.

Irving's work has often been called 'nostalgic' for its use of idealised rural English landscapes and sleepy New York villages.[2] However, what is missing is an examination of the apparatus of this nostalgia and what spectral figures and supernatural storytelling adds to Irving's projection of an idealised past. Nostalgia is not just a descriptor for the effect of Irving's fiction on the reader but also refers to a literary technique in which time appears to be amorphous and the past re-enters the present. Originally conceived of as a disease of homesickness (the etymology of nostalgia meaning 'home-longing'), during the eighteenth century nostalgia transformed in cultural understanding into a practice of accessing a past that no longer existed. Nostalgia became a creative act that reimagined the past through selectively omitting or adding, diminishing or exaggerating aspects of either a recent or distant period. In *The Sketch Book* and *Bracebridge Hall*, Crayon continually enters an environment of nostalgia during his journeys. In these two collections, the past and the present collide as Crayon meets a number of men 'out of time': men like the Squire and Romani gypsies of Bracebridge Hall, who seem to be from an idealised past outside of living memory but are alive in Georgian England. Both the ghost story and nostalgia look backwards to previous eras, but also forwards. As work by Svetlana Boym, Alastair Bonnett and Jennifer Ladino has shown, nostalgia has a radical or 'critical edge' in which the past is used to critique the present and put forward an alternative future.[3] It is radical in offering attachments to the past and denying progression, futurity and change. In Irving's 'spectral nostalgia', the liminal Antony gives voice to a form of White male colonial citizenship attached to the natural environment, land ownership and communal structures. By associating Antony with a primitive Native shadow, Irving presents Dutch American communities as artefacts of colonial America but hopes to reinstate their values of stability and kinship within a contemporary United States.

Irving's interest in propertied patriarchal figures on both sides of the Atlantic and their association with propertyless and otherworldly non-White counterparts serves to emphasise that the citizenship these men represent is a fading relic and out of place in conceptions of citizenship in 1820s America. The Jeffersonian ideal of detaching property from citizenship in an attempt to dismantle hierarchical structures (although only for White men) developed into the male citizen's value being signified by his ability to earn and control capital.[4] Economic shifts towards finance capitalism, the stock market and entrepreneurialism in the early national period significantly changed social relations.[5] What Walter Sondey describes as 'corporatism' in Irving's works, an attachment to community and institutions, was overshadowed by self-interest, self-reliance and the pursuit of social mobility.[6] By the 1820s, with the expansion of the franchise to all White men in most

American states, the paternalist citizenship embodied by figures like Antony is outdated, and yet Irving resurrects and propagates it in his supernatural tales. As new demographics found their metaphorical and physical voice, Irving instead casts in favourable light colonial structures of hierarchical and paternalistic societies. I argue that he brings together past and present to offer a vision of financial and social stability in an increasingly fragmented and unstable economic landscape. In 'Dolph Heyliger', Irving overlays nineteenth-century economic and social developments onto colonial characters and settings. In his association with supernaturally inflected and socially excluded Native Americans, Antony offers a 'masculinity unscathed by the forces of commerce and market' and stands apart from the progression towards an increasingly individualised society, disconnected from community and property, that would have been familiar to Irving's readers.[7]

From a discussion of colonial White masculinity in *Bracebridge Hall*, I turn to Irving's wider project of colonial nostalgia in his work. Crayon's English sketches complement the Knickerbocker stories to show idealised communities negotiating an increasingly industrialised and progressive society on both sides of the Atlantic. Furthermore, beyond individual pieces, the apparatus of a hybrid assemblage of sketches and tales contributes to Irving's nostalgic vision. In Irving's work, it is not just the liminal White figure that is important to his nostalgia project, but the act of supernatural storytelling itself. In the final part of this chapter I argue that Irving's supernatural storytelling apparatus, which uses multiple narrators, is crucial in his spectral nostalgia project, because his vision of community and citizenship depends on a continued genealogy of oral cultures. Storytelling and the passing on of stories through generations propagates an alternative mode of history, one which values communal experiences, folklore and myth. Supernatural storytelling is a vehicle that carries Irving's nostalgia for interdependent yet hierarchical stable communities.

## An 'Indian mode of life': Indigeneity and Nostalgia in 'Dolph Heyliger'

Irving's storytelling is inspired by a unique natural landscape tied to Native Americans and the supernatural. His portrayals of Native populations in *The Sketch Book* show that they are already spectral figures on the edges of American society, vanishing from the landscape due to a campaign of White expansionist violence. In particular, his 'Traits of Indian Character' and 'Philip of Pokanoket' in *The Sketch Book* – whilst attempting to elicit sympathy towards Native tribes – present them as noble yet insubstantial half-formed figures. In 'Traits' they are 'mere wrecks and remnants of once powerful tribes, who have lingered in the vicinity of the settlements and sunk into precarious and vagabond existence'.[8] Not only will they soon be gone 'like a vapor from the face of the earth', but they will be forgotten from history and 'the places that now know them will know them no more forever'. In the biographical sketch of King Philip, Pequod,

Narragansett and Wampanoag warriors 'stalk like gigantic shadows in the dim twilight of tradition' instead of the pages of history books. In fact, if memories or 'tradition' are to sustain their presence, it will only be as an ornamental supernatural presence in the 'romantic dreams of the poet', who depicts Native figures as fabled forest creatures.[9] Fading Indigenous tribes become a mythical part of the landscape, a reliquary for lost histories and a source of artistic inspiration.

The limited amount of scholarship on non-White figures in Irving has primarily focused on how his depiction of Native culture marks *The Sketch Book* as a work of identifiably 'American' literature. Laura Murray is right to argue that Irving uses the Native figures above to discuss the position of America as a young country. Irving creates an 'aesthetic of dispossession' by placing the Indian essays within a collection of romanticised English sketches. The closing speech from an unnamed warrior in 'Traits' is an example of Native oratory and culture that has been 'subsumed' by White writers in order to cultivate 'their [own] sense of vulnerability with respect to Britain'.[10] Native figures serve Irving's construction of White Americans as passive peoples, since they too have been victims under English colonial rule, an analogy that masks their own involvement as colonisers of Indian land.[11] As I discuss shortly, Irving frames his White characters in indigeneity to mark out a specific type of colonial American masculinity, writing a subset of 'vanishing Indian' Americans alongside 'vanishing Indians' in the early nation.[12]

The subsumation of Native culture Murray identifies in the Indian essays extends to Irving's fiction. Native figures, although absent from the upstate New York community, are the bedrock of the ghost story in 'Rip Van Winkle' (1819). Their myths of the landscape are part of Knickerbocker's explanation for Rip's disappearance and reappearance: the Native Americans are the original storytellers in the Hudson Valley. For the Indigenous population, the mountains were 'the abode of spirits' and terrorised by a Manitou that 'took a mischievous pleasure in wreaking all kind of evils and vexations upon the red men', often masquerading as a wild animal leading them through the forests until they come upon 'the brink of a beetling precipice or raging torrent'. In what Michelle Sizemore calls an act of 'half-erasure', Irving builds a Native fantastical into his tales; he locates Indigenous culture as a space of enchantment, but incorporates this storytelling into a new Euro-American culture where Rip, Knickerbocker and Irving are the narrators.[13]

As in Brown's frontier works, 'Dolph Heyliger' imprints the Native American upon the wild landscape. Dolph, a young doctor's assistant in Manhattan, encounters Killian Vander Spiegel, a Flemish ghost who mysteriously and silently haunts a local house. This encounter prompts Dolph's adventure along the Hudson River to upstate New York. During a storm, Dolph is thrown overboard onto the banks of the Hudson, and when seeking a path through the forest he finds a 'savage and trackless' landscape, almost totally impenetrable due to 'wild vines and briers, which completely matted themselves together, and opposed a barrier to all ingress'.[14] Furthermore, this landscape lacks the markers of Euro-American colonisation or civilisation to which Dolph is accustomed in Manhattan, with 'no signs of cultivation, nor any smoke curling amongst the trees, to indicate human residence' (p. 331). The wilderness and its Indigenous inhabitants represent not only a pre-modern but a pre-human life. This wild, unknown and dangerous landscape, framed in indigeneity, is an ideal environment for Dutch Americans to implant their own ghostly figures.

Antony is one of the spectral Dutch American figures inhabiting this new American environment. Dolph is within a liminal space between fantasy and reality, full of uncanny reminders of an earlier dream in which he travels up the Hudson and returns with bags of gold. Fragments of the dream reappear in the daytime as he somnambulistically embarks on the same journey; he is a passive body 'under supernatural influence' and 'unconsciously carried along' the pier to a sloop heading to Albany. Things seem to happen to Dolph without much reason or causality as Irving moves him from house to town to ship. Encountering the sloop's captain, Dolph is 'surprised and aroused' to find him 'short and swarthy, with crisped black hair; blind of one eye, and lame of one leg – the very commander that he had seen in his dream!' Upon meeting Antony, Dolph is struck by the older man, who reminds him of Killian, although not in physical appearance: 'it was hard to define where the vague resemblance lay – but a resemblance there certainly was'. Throughout his encounter with Antony, Dolph is 'repeatedly perplexed' by the reappearance of the phantom in the form of Antony, again claiming this 'vague resemblance' in spirit 'that could not be fixed upon any precise feature of lineament, but which pervaded the general air of his countenance and figure' (pp. 326, 333, 337). Antony appears as a Dutch–Native spectral presence, in a hybrid liminality that unites Native culture, Dutch colonial communities and the supernatural in Irving's fiction. Irving places Antony within a spectral and 'primitive' Native American society inhabiting the Catskill Mountains in order to emphasise that he is a relic of a colonial society, another vanishing American. At first Dolph thinks only Native Americans comprise the hunting party he stumbles upon; on closer inspection, he discovers Antony is White, a 'hale and hearty' older man whose 'face was bronzed almost to the colour of an Indian's . . . He wore a hunting-frock, with Indian leggings, and moccasons, and a tomahawk in the broad wampum belt round his waist' (p. 333). Antony is a racially liminal figure whose ambiguous appearance signals his integration with the Native group.

Irving associates non-scripted and oral communication with Native American communities. In his 'Traits' essay, Irving ventriloquises Native speech by quoting at length an unknown Indigenous chief. Native oratory is forceful yet eloquent. It is an oral form of which early national writers take ownership, setting it in print to capture a vanishing pre-modern society, as seen in 'Traits'. Native oral culture underlies Antony's ghost stories; the White settler supplants these Native voices with his own. Settling around a campfire for the evening, Antony 'sing[s] a stave or two of a Dutch drinking song' before his Dutch American 'myrmidons' or companions 'join in the chorus'. Like Brown in *Memoirs of Carwin the Biloquist*, Irving describes the liminal voice filling up the frontier space 'until the woods echoed again' (*Bracebridge Hall*, p. 336). However, as opposed to Carwin's racially ambiguous ventriloquism in *Memoirs*, in 'Dolph Heyliger' Antony replaces Indigenous speech and oral culture with his own and colonises the Catskill woods with more European settler vocalic bodies. After the singing, Antony begins to tell 'legendary tales . . . about the river, and the settlements on its borders'. Explicitly developing Native mythology found in the 'Rip Van Winkle' postscript, Antony says Indigenous incantations brought about 'the misadventure which befell the renowned Hendrick Hudson, when he sailed so gallantly up this river in quest of a north-west passage, and, as he thought, run his ship aground' (pp. 337–8). His interweaving of Native mythology and Dutch ghostly past encapsulates Irving's own interpretation of the Hudson Valley.

Irving writes, 'the sturdy bush-beater sat in the twisted root of a tree, that served him for a kind of arm-chair, dealing forth these wild stories, with the fire gleaming on his strongly marked visage' (p. 337). This storytelling scene draws on both European and Native influences to create a domestic scene along the frontier, in which the wild and untraversable natural space transforms into homely furniture. The settler reconfiguration of the natural space further supplants Native Americans by mirroring Antony's possession and transformation of an Indigenous legend into a Dutch ghost story. As a patriarchal and proper-tied White man, Antony can easily appropriate the culture and storytelling of propertyless non-White figures to indulge in fantasies of frontier masculinity and the wild lifestyle of the Native American. At the same time, this liminal storytelling space acts as a fitting setting for him to protest changes in society that would see his form of colonial citizenship vanish.

Antony becomes the indigenous focal point of the text. The African American and Native characters in the 'Dolph Heyliger' story collection all exist as margin-alised and silenced figures, there to centre the value of the White Dutch American character. In 'The Storm Ship', Antony's house in Albany is full of 'pet negro[es]' who joyfully surround him on his return and eagerly wait to hear his stories of adventure in the wilderness, and the Indigenous hunting party are reduced to a pack of dogs, 'sleeping like hounds in the sunshine' around his house (pp. 350, 335). Whilst Irving reduces these two groups to a 'spectralized supporting role', according to Sladja Blazan, Dutch settlers fill the landscape with their own ghosts and spectral figures.[15] Blazan argues that Irving populates his texts with Dutch–Native ghosts to construct a legacy for Dutch Americans, like the Native

American figures have, and write their claim of ownership onto the land. These ghostly Euro-Americans use the supernatural to 'elevate' themselves into 'the role of mediator and spokesperson for disempowered inhabitants of early America'.[16] Making the Dutch American into a form of Native ghost does not just legitimise Dutch American involvement in European colonisation but also expresses anxiety about a vanishing form of colonial male citizenship. Instead of speaking for the dispossessed Native Americans or exculpating their own colonialism, I argue that Antony speaks of his own threatened type of White colonial citizenship. Irving's portrayal of liminal Dutch Americans as another colonised group does not just represent adolescent national identity in relation to English rule, as Murray and Blazan discuss, but also values a structure of communal citizenship vanishing from the newly independent nation.

Irving distinguishes between Dutch Americans and English Americans by depicting differences in the structure and behaviours of their communities. They are two distinct ethno-regional groups that Irving maps onto northeastern America. As Donald Ringe notes, in Knickerbocker's faux histories Dutch American New Yorkers exist in opposition to the Yankee New Englander, who practises a roaming self-interest and represents an intangible economy based on a speculative stock market. In response, Irving offers Dutch American villages as places of 'permanence and social stability'.[17] Ringe focuses on Dutch American communities in *A History of New York* (1809) and *The Sketch Book*, but his argument can be mapped onto Irving's portrayal of 1720s New York in 'Dolph Heyliger'. Irving presents a European colonised group in 'Dolph Heyliger'. The Dutch population in Manhattan 'groaned under the tyranny' of English powers and is both metaphorically and physically silenced, as Lord Cornbury 'carried his cruelties towards the Dutch inhabitants so far as to allow no Dominie, or schoolmaster, to officiate in their language, without his special license' (p. 304). Against this dominance, Albany is completely untouched by 'the restless people of New England', as the English have yet to reach that far north. Knickerbocker idealises Albany 'in all its glory', in particular suggesting that it is a steady, stable and slow environment: 'Every thing was quiet and orderly; every thing was conducted calmly and leisurely; no hurry, no bustle, no struggling and scrambling for existence' (pp. 349–50).

The liminal White voice and references to Native appearance and speech within 'Dolph Heyliger' invoke nostalgia for a White male citizenship that Irving attaches to vanishing Dutch American communities. Furthering Ringe's arguments on competing regional values of change versus stasis, however, I add that Irving uses liminal White figures and their connection to Native culture to offer an alternative, older view of time that challenges a modern idea of development and progress, in particular with regard to shifting ideas of urban economic male citizenship. A 'culture of capitalism' significantly affected communal structures and interpersonal relations in the early national period, when the ideal male citizen had a strong Protestant work ethic, was self-disciplined and self-possessed. However, instead of investing these traits in a 'moral economy' of communal exchange that existed in colonial towns, he directed these virtues into finance capitalism and entrepreneurialism in the growing early national city.[18] The certainty and stability of paternalism shifted to the risk and independent success of individual endeavour. In a 'culture of capitalism', social interactions are framed in terms of value and accumulation of capital. These new self-made men in the early national period used their voices, in acts of public speaking and writing, to further their social and economic position.

Irving overlays these early nineteenth-century developments onto his early eighteenth-century tale. Dolph's journey from Manhattan to Albany and its surrounding wilderness is a movement backwards in time, towards a period untouched by English colonisers and the Yankee economic masculinity they represent. Antony enacts a 'natural' way of life on his hunting trips with his Native guides, taking time out of his life in Albany to indulge in the adventure of an 'Indian mode of life'. He owns a large swathe of inherited wild land and derives his wealth from the environment, but he seeks a closer connection with the earth away from the sleepy town and patriarchal domesticity in Albany. This involves taking hunting parties into the forests, sleeping outdoors, fishing, hunting and 'living the Lord knows how' with his 'several Indian hangers on'. As a 'man of property' and because of his commanding wealth, he can appropriate Native culture and 'indulge his humours without control' or refusal (pp. 334–5).

As Philip Deloria writes, 'playing Indian' – the appropriation of Indigenous dress and behaviours – allows White Americans to 'encounter the authentic amidst the anxiety of urban industrial and postindustrial life'.[19] In being mistaken for a Native American, Antony steps outside the social structures of White colonial America, but only temporarily. His appearance and temporary mode of living signifies the propertyless Native excluded from legal, social and economic citizenship, but Antony can and does return to Albany to enjoy his wealth and patriarchal power. Antony embodies an early form of White protest from the colonial period onwards that Deloria identifies, in which settler communities employ Native traits to make their own claims on American selfhood. These moments in the forest when Irving associates Antony with a Native presence show that Antony's form of White masculinity – a physical and robust outdoors 'authentic' existence – is out of step with ideas of the successful urban citizen in the increasingly professionalised and market-driven America of the 1820s. In the forest, Antony bemoans the increasing professionalisation and education of young men at the expense of 'manly accomplishments' (p. 348). On finding out that Dolph is a doctor's apprentice, Antony is appalled that his natural and masculine 'talents and accomplishments' have been 'cramped and buried under a doctor's wig'. Holding a 'mortal grudge' against the medical profession, he decries that a young man such as Dolph, 'who could shoot, fish, run, jump, ride, and wrestle, should be obliged, to roll pills and administer juleps for a living – twas monstrous!' (pp. 348–9). He instructs Dolph to disregard his apprenticeship and rely on his natural skills, and he takes a paternal role over the young adventurer, offering to house him until he can make his own way in life away from the regiment, toil and tedium of the physician. Antony's free indirect speech, mediated through Knickerbocker's narration, protests the progression away from a 'natural' masculinity attached to household systems, moral economy and the land. He fulfils his purpose as a figure of spectral nostalgia by critiquing contemporary society, a critique that he develops through his tale of Killian Vander Spiegel.

Irving revisits the division between Dutch Americans and English Americans when Antony relays the story of Killian. After the 1664 English purchase of New Amsterdam, Killian

> fell into a melancholy apprehending that his wealth would be taken from him and that he would come to beggary. He turned all his property into cash, and used to hide it away. He was for a year or two concealed in various places, fancying himself sought after by the English, to strip him of his wealth; and finally was found dead in his bed one morning, without any one being able to discover where he had concealed the greater part of his money. (p. 354)

Killian is a figure of male economic anxiety, concerned with the vulnerability of any intangible wealth and hoping to find security in hard cash. His paranoia paints the English – genealogical forerunners of the speculating Yankee – as avaricious villains who roam from house to house stealing Dutch wealth. By taking over the narration, Antony employs the story of Killian's lost wealth from fifty years earlier to support his own protest against changes in a colonial male citizenship attached to landed property, a dependency on the natural environment and 'manly pursuits'. And by extension, Irving employs a supernatural tale from the previous century, brought forward to the 1820s through a chain of oral and written narratives, to challenge citizenship in the early national period and its dependence on economic masculinity.

Killian's story fits into Irving's modes of economic masculinity that David Anthony describes at work in *The Sketch Book* and *Tales of a Traveller*. In these collections Anthony sees two options for White American economic masculinity: the instability and flux of the financial market as seen in 'The Legend of Sleepy Hollow' (1820) and 'The Devil and Tom Walker' (1824), and the fantasy of tangible treasure in 'The Golden Dreams of Wolfert Webber' (1824). Anthony argues that Irving retreats to the fantasy of finding gold in the face of fluctuating and insecure financial situations, in particular the loss of the Irving family business in 1817 and the financial panic of 1819.[20] Considering *Bracebridge Hall* in light of Anthony's thesis offers a third formation of economic masculinity: a success story predicated on inheritance. Dolph is a wish-fulfilment figure; through both finding gold and marrying into fortune, he succeeds and demonstrates a citizenship attached to property and rooted in community. Dolph's 'up-from' narrative from adolescent apprentice to wealthy community leader offers security because the means by which he becomes wealthy are rooted in the traditional made fantastical. In other words, Dolph's treasure-finding is a mediated form of inheritance. Whilst Dolph's trajectory embodies the 'phenomenon of social mobility in America', it is not, as William Hedges claims, devoid of 'aristocratic exclusivities'.[21] In taking Dolph to Albany and narrating his ancestor's lost wealth, which is waiting to be recovered, Antony becomes a surrogate father. After hearing Killian's story from Antony, Dolph asks himself: 'Why the plague could not the old goblin have told me . . . without sending me all the way to Albany to hear a story that was to send me all the way back again?' (pp. 354–5). By having Antony speak for Killian instead of the ghost speaking for himself, Irving brings to the fore a paternal relationship between the older and younger man, as Dolph inherits the story of Killian and subsequently secures the ghost's treasure. Dolph realises that both he and Antony are descendants of Killian and thinks to himself that if he can marry Antony's daughter, 'both branches of the family will be again united, and the property go on in the proper channel' (p. 355). Unifying estranged branches of the family tree through a new marriage confirms the fortune as a stable rather than unbelievable mediated inheritance. Finding the gold reclaims his ghostly ancestor's inheritance and continues a traditional genealogical line. In marrying Marie Vander Heyden, Dolph regenerates Antony's successful patriarchal citizenship, making 'good use of his wealth' and becoming 'a distinguished citizen, and a valuable member of the community' (p. 362). The fantastical coincidence of paternal inheritance enables Dolph's self-making. In the tale's conclusion, Irving offers a balm for early national anxieties about unstable economies and the societal pressures for young men to display independent economic male citizenship.

## A 'NEW STOCK OF STORIES': STORYTELLING AND COLONIAL COMMUNITY AT BRACEBRIDGE HALL

Irving employs inherited storytelling throughout *Bracebridge Hall* to propagate the conceit of a good and valuable citizen, who supports and leads his community and looks after those less fortunate than himself. The voice is integral to forging and developing this enshrined colonial vision of citizenship and Irving closely explores the conceit of oral storytelling in the collection's English sketches. As Sizemore contends of *The Sketch Book*, by just reading the American pieces on their own 'critics have circumvented the chaotic heterogeneity of the Atlantic world conflated in the collection'.[22] Described by Irving as a 'connected series of tales and essays', *Bracebridge Hall* again jumps across space and time, crossing the

Atlantic between colonial America, Georgian England, pre-Revolutionary France and early modern Spain through the narratives of Crayon's travelogue, the stories of Squire Bracebridge's guests and Knickerbocker's historical manuscripts.[23] It is necessary to read this tale *in situ* to understand Irving's wider project of nostalgia, which involves Crayon's English travel narratives and Knickerbocker's faux New York history, as well as the storytelling apparatus of which they are a part. For Crayon, travel around England is a process of nostalgia because it unites different periods from his own past. By encountering the landscapes and scenes that he read about 'in every stage of his existence' he is overcome with the 'recollected ideas of infancy, youth, and manhood; of the nursery, the school, and the study', which 'come swarming at once' in a 'delightful train of remembrance' (p. 8). Travelling to England is not just a trip back in time to encounter Old World customs and traditions, but is also a way Crayon can access his own past, experienced as a selective editing of his own life through a transatlantic lens.

Irving's English scenes feature nostalgic communities. Irving is aware that the English community he presents in *The Sketch Book* and *Bracebridge Hall* is a fading relic of previous generations. The *Blackwood's Edinburgh Magazine* reviewer of *Bracebridge Hall* agreed, criticising that characters were 'not drawn from life, but from musty volumes'.[24] Reintroducing the aristocratic Bracebridge family in 'The Hall', Crayon calls the Squire 'a lingering specimen of the old English country gentleman'. Irving's sketches of the Squire are similar to his essay on James IV (1473–1513) in *The Sketch Book*. Both men are paternalistic figures who socialise with the 'lower orders' and rule for their best interests (*Bracebridge Hall*, p. 13). In 'A Royal Poet', James promoted 'every thing that could diffuse comfort, competency and innocent enjoyment through the humblest ranks of society' and 'mingled occasionally among the common people in disguise; visited their firesides; entered into their cares, their pursuits, and their amusements'.[25] In the same vein Crayon praises the Squire's attentiveness to his tenants – 'inquiring into their concerns, and assisting them in times of difficulty and hardship' – which makes him 'one of the most popular, and of course one of the happiest, of landlords' (*Bracebridge Hall*, p. 192). However, he admits that the example set by the Squire is but a 'Utopian dream', not upheld by many landed gentry in England. Crayon criticises self-exiling wealthy families for fleeing in the face of financial crisis, and urges them to retire to their estates and exercise 'noble simplicity', 'good sense' and a frugality that their poor neighbours already observe (pp. 195–6). Irving recognises that the Squire is a man 'out of time' and that his memories of communal traditions and customs belong to an Elizabethan age, 'stored with the accounts given by Stow, in his *Survey of London*', a city history completed in 1598 (p. 204).

In opposition to the Squire, Irving sets up his neighbour Mr Faddy as a model of wealthy citizenship embodying a self-interested society. Establishing a country pile after accumulating 'a large fortune by dint of steam-engines and spinning-jennies', Mr Faddy prioritises finance – he has 'a face full of business' – instead of fostering inter-rank relationships. After hearing about the upcoming May Day celebrations, his capitalist dogma colours his criticism: instead of 'fiddling, dancing, and carousing', the rural poor should be 'staying at home to work for their families'. Imposing his 'territorial rights' over his estate, he blocks public right of way and threatens prosecution for trespass. Mr Faddy is a Yankee in English guise, transforming the landscape and 'bent upon improving and reforming' the village under his plans for urbanisation (pp. 202, 203, 269).

Irving's creation of English parallels for his American types extends to his portrayal of the 'gypsies' living on the estate. Irving's representation of the Roma at Bracebridge Hall was partially influenced by Walter Scott's historical romances, such as *Guy Mannering* (1815) and its 1817 stage production, in which 'gypsy' witch Meg Merrillies appears as an exotic supernatural figure.[26] The British press understood 'Scottish gypsies' to have originated from India and positioned them as Asiatic figures who had 'retained almost unaltered their distinct oriental character, customs, and language' after centuries in Britain.[27] At the same time, the 'vanishing Indian' inflects Irving's depiction of this less-than-White group. Crayon mythologises the Roma presence by describing them as spectral figures 'haunting the purlieus of the Hall'. Despite creating mischief and invading local poultry-yards to steal food, they serve as figures of nostalgia for the Squire, who sees 'the race as belonging to the good old times' of feudal patriarchalism (*Bracebridge Hall*, p. 207). For the Squire, they are exotic relics of a lost rural idyll he seeks to regain through paternal ownership of the land and control of its residents. Crayon too shares this attraction, but for slightly different reasons. He is drawn to their sexualised exoticism, 'their clear olive complexions, their romantic black eyes, their raven locks, their lithe, slender figures' and their connection to popular myth and superstition as they speak 'in low silver tones, dealing forth magnificent promises, of honours and estates, of world's worth, and ladies' love'. The Roma are simultaneously a link to the past as a wandering and primitive community outside the civic bounds of 'county gaols and country magistrates', who roam the landscape as 'free denizens of nature', as well as a bridge to the future, offering to tell visitors' fortunes (for a fee) with supposed supernatural powers (pp. 209–10).

Crayon's description of wildness and spectrality renders the Roma Eurasian cousins of Native Americans ghosting the Hudson Valley. Crayon muses:

> They seem to be like the Indians of America, either above or below the ordinary cares and anxieties of mankind. Heedless of power, of honours, of wealth; and indifferent to the fluctuations of the times, the rise or fall of grain, or stock, or empires, they seem to laugh at the toiling, fretting world around them. (pp. 209–10)

The Roma and Native Americans are both out of step with worldly developments, whether financial, political or technological. As a result, they stand against the movement of time itself, the 'toiling, fretting world' that continually strives for progress and success. Irving presents a nightmarish picture of this toiling world when the Squire relates a visit to industrialised Dudley, where '[t]he pale and ghastly people, toiling among vile exhalations, looked more like demons than human beings; the clanking wheels and engines, seen through the murky atmosphere, looked like instruments of torture in this pandemonium' (pp. 203–4).[28] For the Squire and Crayon, the Roma offer an alternative means of survival away from this hellish world of industrial capitalism, and like the Native Americans in 'Dolph Heyliger' they offer both a vision of a pre-modern way of life, dependent on the land, and a static point in time. Seemingly ungoverned by and disinterested in politics, laws or a financial economy, they appear not to have changed over generations. In this increasingly industrial and urban nation he visits, Crayon's only way to understand the Roma is to transform them into Indigenous, mythical figures that serve his nostalgia.

Crayon, and by extension Irving, is invested in the utopian ideal of interdependent communities practised at Bracebridge Hall. The attraction to English rural life creates a vision of communal existence that Irving sees disappearing in America and remaining only in the underrepresented and forgotten Dutch American towns. As Elisa Tamarkin writes, this attachment to England or 'anglophilia' in antebellum writing presents 'an aesthetics of return to colonial structures of feeling'.[29] In other words, independent Americans wanted the relationships found in English towns that were predicated on interdependency and communal customs as well as hierarchy, a structure from which they had previously rebelled. Tamarkin writes about US literature and culture after Irving, but this statement holds true for his fiction as well. By the 1820s, attitudes in America had softened from openly criticising British culture and communities in the Paper War 'battle of words' (1815–19), and writers sought to find commonalities with their transatlantic kind, despite a 'proclamation of an end of ties to Britain'.[30] The English sketches in partnership with the Knickerbocker stories create nostalgia for an alternative vision of community relations to which Americans such as Irving could opt in. When Crayon comments in *The Sketch Book*, 'We may thus place England before us as a perpetual volume of reference,' he justifies his attachment to the country. Just as if using an encyclopaedia or dictionary, he can dip in and out, using different aspects of the nation as good or bad examples of citizenship and community in order to 'avoid the errors and absurdities that have crept into the page' and draw out 'golden maxims of practical wisdom' to improve American character.[31] His anglophilia meditates on the fostering of communities and White male citizenship in relation to an increasingly progress- and success-driven individualist society on both sides of the Atlantic. At the opening of *Bracebridge Hall* Crayon claims not to be politically minded, and to be more interested in the 'ancient and genuine characteristics of my "fatherland"', but through his portrayal of the members of Bracebridge's rural community and their rituals he presents both a utopian paternalistic society and the reality of these communities increasingly faced by drives for profit, exploitation and separation (p. 13).

Irving's sketches perform nostalgia in that they present time as fluid. Past customs and traditions are alive at Bracebridge Hall, and men from the past seem to appear in the present on Crayon's travels around the country. Irving portrays Bracebridge Hall as simultaneously of the past and the current moment. Readers do not gain a strong impression of specifically what year events are taking place, due to the focus on cyclical communal events and traditions over political discussion.[32] Returning to Crayon's first visit to Bracebridge Hall in *The Sketch Book*, 'The Christmas Dinner' embodies this amorphous time as different members of the family are 'metamorphosed' into folk characters by wearing their ancestors' clothing.

> The irruption of this motley crew with beat of drum, according to ancient custom, was the consummation of uproar and merriment. Master Simon covered himself with glory by the stateliness with which, as Ancient Christmas, he walked a minuet with the peerless though giggling Dame Mince Pie. It was followed by a dance of all the characters, which from its medley of costumes seemed as though the old family portraits had skipped down from their frames to join in the sport. Different centuries were figuring at cross hands and right and left; the Dark Ages were cutting pirouettes and rigadoons; and the days of Queen Bess jigging merrily down the middle through a line of succeeding generations.[33]

The Elizabethan figures performing in Georgian England emphasise the Squire as a man out of time. In this masque, time is multiplicious as different periods dance in an interweaving choreography. Past and present co-exist as time is punctured, allowing for the illusion of time travel. At the same time, Crayon is aware that these 'fleeting customs were posting fast in oblivion' and time is moving forward, just as he acknowledges that the Squire is a relic of a fading society 'of long departed years'.[34]

The form of the sketch itself contributes to this project of spectral nostalgia, because it is inherently contradictory in how it presents time. It is deliberately fragmented, a quick account of a character, location or event that can exist within a series or as a standalone piece. This fragmentation suggests that time is moving quickly, that the writer only spent a very short period with the subject of the sketch, and is constantly moving just like a tourist making visual sketches on a trip. However, by only focusing on singular moments with no plot arc, the sketch simultaneously creates a space outside of time's progression. The sketch is transgressive as it challenges a linear idea of time by instead offering overlapping temporalities found in landscape depiction, character description and narrative digression, which suggests time may not be moving at all. For Amanpal Garcha, nineteenth-century sketches are an 'alternative fantasy of a break, or an exemption, from temporal change'.[35] They rebel against the flux and instability found in a newly industrial society that always needs to drive forward, by offering moments without any change or development. The sketch's stasis stands against the idea that the printed form is inextricably tied to modernity and progress, offering the reader a respite. The same can be said of Irving's sketches in *Bracebridge Hall*. Irving preserves a form of narrative that itself stops the progression of time by focusing on painterly descriptions of characters, places and events whilst overlaying them with the meanderings and musings of a fictional persona, who provides a sense of cohesion between pieces.

Irving's collections bring together stories and sketches, which formally 'embody radically different conceptions of temporality and coherence', with the sketch a plotless form whilst the story is dependent on plot. On *The Sketch Book*, Garcha claims that Irving navigates these substantially different forms by creating two separate narrators: Crayon, who observes English life, and Knickerbocker, who writes fantastical American history.[36] Crayon and Knickerbocker are increasingly interconnected in *Bracebridge Hall*. They are united by a project of nostalgic storytelling that Irving constructs through scenes of storytelling within the sketches and a narrative apparatus that connects sketches with stories. This creates a chain of narration that promotes Irving's spectral nostalgia for colonial community and citizenship. Each of the tales within *Bracebridge Hall* ('The Stout Gentleman', 'Annette Delarbre', 'The Student of Salamanca' and 'Dolph Heyliger') are narrated by guests at the hall, who regularly meet to entertain each other with stories of adventures, horror or humour.[37] Each story follows a short scene describing the narrator about to tell the tale. Irving carefully structures these sections to move from a scene of oral narration to Crayon's 'reprinted' ghost stories. Furthermore, although Irving claimed he did not mind which volume of the text was published first, the collection clearly structures its episodic English sketches in a loose plot and moves towards resolution in the second volume.[38] The position of the 'Dolph Heyliger' sequence within the larger text mirrors the plot progression of *Bracebridge Hall*. Placed immediately before Crayon's last sketch at the Hall, 'The Wedding', Dolph's marriage to Maria reflects the collection's ending, in which the Squire's ward Julia Templeton marries his son Guy Bracebridge.

In 'Dolph Heyliger' there is a chain of narration as different characters set up the story of Dolph, Killian and the haunted Storm Ship. This matryoshka-like narrative passes through and around several narrators and storytellers: Crayon, Knickerbocker, Pompey, John Josse Vandermoere, Antony, and Mynheer Selyne.

In 'The Historian', Crayon agrees to read a story aloud to his fellow guests, before reintroducing the reader to Knickerbocker and his project of reclaiming Dutch American history. Following this, within 'The Haunted House' – the manuscript that Crayon has reprinted – Knickerbocker reminisces on a childhood encounter with Pompey, a free African American man, who tells the young boy fearful stories of the possessed property, accompanied by 'such awful rollings of his white eyes'. Pompey does not expand on his stories; he is swiftly killed off and absorbed into the supernatural legacy of the haunted house, and Irving replaces him with the 'pleasant gossiping' Vandermoere, who promises more frightening stories than Pompey (pp. 302, 303). Once again, non-White characters are diminished or spoken over, with Vandermoere taking over the story just as Antony and Irving replace the Indigenous storytellers of Henry Hudson's disappearance. A non-White story is subsumed by White storytellers who move action forward as narrators and protagonists, but Black and Indigenous speakers remain frozen in the sketch-like frame narrative. Adding more concentric circles of narration, Irving evades Vandermoere's voice and substitutes it with Knickerbocker's retelling. Further in 'Dolph Heyliger' and 'The Storm Ship', the narrative passes from Knickerbocker to Antony telling a story about the haunted ship, taken from the work of early Dutch American poet Selyne. Knickerbocker republishes this story, but it is not clear whether these are Antony's words, that of the poet, or Knickerbocker himself.

Irving repeatedly mediates his narratives of a New York village to support a specific type of history he wishes to pursue, tied to a specific storytelling market. From *A History of New York* onwards, Irving creates a folk history that is predicated on oral narrative and the circulation of quasi-supernatural occurrences. Traditional histories such as the satirical object of *A History*, Samuel L. Mitchill's *Picture of New York* (1807), exclude these events and focus instead on detail and statistics. In the late eighteenth century, an Enlightenment school of historiography conceived history as a series of 'exemplary narratives' which aimed to 'discover "the constant and universal principles of human nature"'. According to Hannah Spahn, in the 1800s this view of history began to shift into a 'Romantic' historiography, one that prioritised the testimony and lived experiences of individuals and communities. Historiography divested its didactic futurity in order to connect with the experiences of the past, as Irving's faux history of New York employs mutable myth, folklore and fiction to create communal 'Romantic' history and recreate communal experiences.[39] In all of Knickerbocker's texts, Irving creates entire Dutch American families and communities as 'an alternative set of ancestors for nineteenth-century, republican New Yorkers'.[40] For this genealogy to continue, Knickerbocker's stories depend on multiple overlapping narrators and the perpetuation of oral storytelling. The embedded oral forms of narration that Irving seeks to replicate in *Bracebridge Hall* simultaneously reach farther and farther back in time to pre-colonial

American history in Antony's recounting Native myth, and at the same time reach forward, as each narrator or storyteller is succeeded by another, ending with Crayon but no doubt to be retold again by both Crayon's audience at the hall and Irving's readers.

For Irving, storytelling creates an anti-individualist society because it is dependent on a shared bond between the speaker and the listener and shared experiences of performance. When Crayon remarks in 'The Historian' that 'this is a story-telling age', he reflects on the popularity of the oral tale during the late eighteenth and early nineteenth centuries. Irving's letters attest to his own role as a storyteller (p. 297). Whilst composing *Bracebridge Hall* he wrote to Thomas Storrow that he had received a 'new stock of stories' whilst staying in Edgbaston and had relayed them to 'the most experienced little story mongers in all Birmingham', his nieces.[41] Storytelling unites people of different ranks and ages within communities on both sides of the Atlantic. Crayon is a liminal figure himself, a foreign outsider who resides with an English family; through storytelling he is incorporated within the Bracebridge community, acting as both listener and speaker. Storytelling is citizen-building as it asks listeners to consider alternative viewpoints, engage with complex emotional territory and broaden their own experiences. Within scenes of supernatural storytelling this is especially relevant. In 'St. Mark's Eve', Crayon remarks that he 'never knew the most gay or the most enlightened of audiences, that were not, if the conversation continued for any length of time, completely and solemnly interested' in ghost stories (p. 103). Sasha Handley comments that ghost stories in eighteenth-century England were 'embedded within working patterns and life-cycle structures' of town and village life, sustained through oral heritage and the growing circulation of printed pamphlets and periodicals.[42] In *Bracebridge Hall*, the ghost story acts the same way; it is woven into quotidian communal life and considered as a necessary part of civic life.

In particular, Crayon draws attention to the suspension of disbelief that ghost stories and supernatural tales encourage. Reminiscing on popular superstitions 'brings up with it a thousand delicious recollections of those happy days of childhood, when the imperfect knowledge I have since obtained had not yet dawned upon my mind, and when a fairy tale was true history to me'. He regrets that he no longer lives in an age 'when the fictions of poetry were believed' (p. 282). Unlike Brown, who seeks to dispel superstition and irrationality in *Wieland*, Crayon recognises the importance of taking pleasure in the 'pleasant errors' of superstitious thoughts and supernatural daydreams, which provide a reprieve from quotidian reality. In *Wieland*, the ventriloquial voice disrupts the text and the White citizen's belief in the authenticity of oral communication and the reliability of the senses. In contrast, Irving utilises oral narratives to recreate the experience of hearing a supernatural tale and create authenticity within his writing. In *Bracebridge Hall*, supernatural tales offer an escape from the 'cold realities of morning' – the constant drive of progress, work, politics and the instability of the financial market, which contribute to an increasingly fractured and individualist society (p. 282). To return to the world of the supernatural is to return to communal 'structures of feeling' predicated on shared acts of imagination and emotional exchange.[43]

Whilst this storytelling apparatus is most apparent in *Bracebridge Hall*, it provides a frame for reading the earlier 'Rip Van Winkle' – the passing on of stories rescues the displaced Rip and propagates a nostalgic community found in the Hudson Valley. In the short story, Rip is threatened with ostracism from the Catskill village to which he has returned after a twenty-year supernatural absence. Rip's worried cry, 'Does nobody here know Rip Van Winkle?' voices a social anxiety that he is a self that no longer has a place within a cohesive whole.[44] Within the post-Revolution town, Rip is a foreign body, accused of being a spy and a refugee: he is also a superfluous figure, whose position, as well as name, has been usurped by his now adult son, Rip Jr. He is another liminal figure who experiences a disconnection and exile from community, and must negotiate his place when returning to this transforming community.

Crucially, Irving employs scenes of storytelling to rescue Rip and put him back into the structures of the town, after the local sage Peter Vanderdonk verifies Rip's story of being spirited away. This corroboration exists in Vanderdonk's own fantastical tale, inherited from a historian ancestor, 'that the Kaatskill mountains had always been haunted by strange beings', including the ghost of Hendrick Hudson, whom Rip encounters before his disappearance.[45] After Vanderdonk's intervention, Knickerbocker's narrative jumps forward in time, briefly covering Rip's return to family and community, much in the same way that the narrative at the end of 'Dolph Heyliger' jumps to Dolph's marriage and his successful communal leadership years later. However, rather than the town completely changing in the face of the Revolution, Irving presents the town as a hybrid of change and stasis – the 'modern' and the 'premodern' together – rendering the village a space of nostalgia where past and present coexist.[46] The Catskill village is bustling, consumed with the election fever of 1796, but its Dutch American form of communal life stays, and it welcomes back Rip and allows him to continue the role he played before his disappearance. He seemingly slips back into village life, resuming 'his old walks and habits' and taking 'his place once more on the bench at the inn door', which remains a space for communion and gossip, despite its new name 'The Union Hotel' reflecting the nation's radical change.[47] The village remains a nostalgic space for Irving, a place where communal colonial values and structure remain, even after the Revolution.

Setting up his stories of pre-Revolution America amongst the circulating gossip and unfamiliar terminology and politics of a new nation, Rip becomes 'a chronicle of the old times "before the war"'. Concluding the tale, Irving focuses on Rip's role as a storyteller, as he narrates his supernatural disappearance and reappearance 'to every stranger that arrived at Mr. Doolittle's hotel'. 'Rip Van Winkle' comes full circle as Rip resumes his role as a supernatural storyteller and entertainer, passing on stories that become embedded in community so that 'not a man, woman, or child in the neighbourhood, but knew it by heart'.[48] The neighbourhood is therefore united by the shared experience of hearing Rip's story. These are stories to be passed on over and over, first through the universal experience of oral storytelling and then through the print media of Crayon's travelogue.

In his work, Irving makes Dutch Americans 'vanishing Indians' to challenge an economic mode of masculinity in the 1820s. He frames his propertied patriarchs in markers of indigeneity not to speak against the treatment of Native Americans but to protest shifts away from colonial structure of feeling and White masculinity rooted in the land. In selectively editing America's colonial past and populating colonial spaces with indigenous Dutch ghosts, he creates spectral nostalgia for colonial forms of citizenship and community. After Irving, the White indigenised voice finds its most potent speaker in James Fenimore Cooper's *The Leatherstocking Tales*. Throughout the series, Natty Bumppo/Hawkeye stresses his Whiteness and maintains a desire for racial purity, yet Cooper frames him in markedly Indigenous dress, behaviour and speech to distinguish him from Euro-American settlers. Hawkeye's liminality between settler and Native – while still asserting Whiteness – is most powerfully expressed in his deathbed scene in *The Prairie* (1827).

The novel ends with Hawkeye's death, surrounded by both Pawnee and White characters. Looking out west to less cultivated land, with 'the glorious tints of an American sunset' falling on his face, Hawkeye experiences an Indigenous death.[49] Teton elder La Balafré eulogises the trapper on the final page:

> 'A valiant, a just, and a wise warrior has gone on the path, which will lead him to the blessed grounds of his people . . . When the voice of the Wahcondah called him, he was ready to answer. Go, my children; remember the just chief of the Pale-faces, and clear your own tracks from briars.'[50]

Although asserting his Christianity throughout the series, the Indigenous characters comprehend his death through their spiritual framework. In a repeat of Chingachgook and Tamenund's speeches mourning Uncas in *The Last of the Mohicans* – written the year before but set forty-seven years earlier – Hawkeye becomes the vanishing Indian himself. He bemoans before he dies: 'I am without kith and kin in the wide world . . . when I am gone, there will be an end of my race.'[51] Hawkeye speaks in Native lament, co-opting the Indigenous speeches of the early US that spoke of the violence against them and mourned a vanishing world. Cooper employs Native genocide – the erasure of the Mohicans a year before – as a rhetorical frame for one White man's death, which both distinguishes him from the Mohicans and Uncas and elevates him. In this way, making Hawkeye Indigenous 'absorb[s] the Native Other's difference, coded as pain, the "not-I" into the "I"', as Eve Tuck and K. Wayne Yang claim of *The Last of the Mohicans*.[52] As the sympathetic centre of the text, his death becomes more important in this moment than the loss of whole Indigenous tribes. At the end of *The Prairie*, White readers are asked to mourn Hawkeye's heroic form of grounded White masculinity that has sought to protect the land and unite Indigenous and settler communities, rather than think too much about the ongoing violence against Native Americans in the early nation.

Like Rip van Winkle, Hawkeye does not disappear for good. As Cooper's series plays with time, criss-crossing from the 1740s to the 1800s over five novels, Hawkeye reappears in *The Pathfinder* (1840). Unlike Uncas, Hawkeye gets to come back to life in 1758, the fictional form resurrecting his noble, rugged masculinity through literary time travel for two more novels. The supernatural and the fictive reincorporate the liminal subject back into society and into print, a stroke of fortune that also occurs in Bird's body-hopping novel *Sheppard Lee*. As Irving and Cooper use Indigenous framing to praise a specific form of White masculinity, in my following chapter I argue that Bird's tale of White-to-Black racial transformation once again centres liminal White men, challenging constraining White civic values and expressing anxiety over Black social mobility in Jacksonian America.

## Notes

1. del Pilar Blanco, *Ghost-Watching American Modernity*, p. 1.
2. For example, works by Robert Hughes, Laura Murray, Michelle Sizemore and Walter Sondey all locate the Hudson Valley and Crayon's English travelogue as sites of nostalgia. See Hughes, 'Sleepy Hollow: Fearful Pleasures and the Nightmare of History', p. 7; Murray, 'The Aesthetic of Dispossession', p. 214; Sizemore, '"Changing by Enchantment"', p. 168; Sondey, 'From Nation of Virtue to Virtual Nation', in Pickering and Kehde (eds), *Narratives of Nostalgia, Gender and Nationalism*, pp. 52–73 (p. 54).
3. Ladino, *Reclaiming Nostalgia*, p. 15. See also Bonnett, *Left in the Past*, p. 2; Boym, *The Future of Nostalgia*, pp. xv, 5.
4. Jeffery Sklansky traces the development of economic citizenship in *The Soul's Economy*. In Chapter 3 I discuss further the civic value of work and industry in relation to *Sheppard Lee*.
5. Steven Watts argues that in the 1790s American economy shifted from a 'moral economy' of households that produced goods and services in communal exchange, to a market economy that 'spurred an ethos of entrepreneurialism and self-made success' centred on the individual. This he terms a 'culture of capitalism' and the bedrock of liberal America. Watts, *The Republic Reborn*, pp. 7–8.
6. Sondey, 'From Nation of Virtue to Virtual Nation', p. 52. 'Corporatism' has an unintended economic echo here with 'corporation'. However, whereas corporations

are 'invisible, intangible and artificial being[s]' greater than the sum of their founders and employees, corporatism is a world-view rooted in personal, social and economic interconnectivity. Chief Justice Marshall, *Bank of U.S. vs Deveaux* (1809), quoted in Smith, *Civic Ideals*, p. 194.

7. David Anthony writes specifically about *The Sketch Book* and *Tales of a Traveller*, but his discussions on forms of economic masculinity are pertinent to 'Dolph Heyliger' and *Bracebridge Hall* and I will return to them later in the chapter. Anthony, *Paper Money Men*, p. 56.

8. Irving, *The Sketch Book of Geoffrey Crayon, Gent.*, ed. Bradbury, p. 238.

9. Ibid. pp. 248, 246.

10. Murray, 'The Aesthetic of Dispossession', pp. 219, 207.

11. Ibid. p. 221.

12. Bergland, *The National Uncanny*, p. 3.

13. Irving, *The Sketch Book*, pp. 40–1; Sizemore, '"Changing by Enchantment"', p. 174.

14. Irving, *Bracebridge Hall, Tales of a Traveller, The Alhambra*, pp. 330–1. Further citations of this edition are given in parentheses in the main text.

15. Blazan, 'Silencing the Dead', p. 18.

16. Ibid. p. 14.

17. Ringe, 'New York and New England', p. 459.

18. Watts, *The Republic Reborn*, pp. 7–8.

19. Deloria, *Playing Indian*, p. 7.

20. Anthony, *Paper Money Men*, pp. 47–8, 7. Anthony builds upon a line of scholarship, most notably the work of Irving biographers William Hedges and Jeffrey Rubin-Dorsky, which argues Irving wrote *The Sketch Book* to soothe his personal psychological trauma. Rubin-Dorsky contends that Irving created the fictional Crayon persona as a buffer between himself and the world, through which he could negotiate the cultural position of American literature in the early national period and channel anxieties about economic failure into the realm of fantasy. Hedges, *Washington Irving*; Rubin-Dorsky, *Adrift in the Old World*.

21. Hedges, *Washington Irving*, pp. 187–8.

22. Sizemore, *American Enchantment*, p. 119.

23. Washington Irving to Ebenezer Irving, 29 January 1822, in *The Complete Works of Washington Irving*, eds Pochmann, Kleinfield and Rust, vol. 23: *Letters, Volume 1, 1802–1823*, eds Alderman, Kleinfeld and Banks, p. 661. This edition is hereafter cited as *Letters, Volume 1*.

24. 'Review: Bracebridge Hall', *Blackwood's Edinburgh Magazine*, 11 (June 1822), p. 689.

25. Irving, *The Sketch Book*, pp. 77–8.

26. Deborah Epstein Nord writes that Scott's 'gypsies' represent a lost national history and appear as dreamlike figures of 'primal phantasy'. A friend of Scott and an admirer of his historical romances, Irving too renders his Roma figures as representative of a displaced social and economic way of life. Epstein Nord, *Gypsies and the British Imagination, 1807–1930*, p. 40.

27. 'Notices Concerning the Scottish Gypsies', *Blackwood's*, 1 (April 1817), p. 43.

28. Having spent a significant portion of time living with his sister and brother-in-law Sarah and Henry van Wart in Birmingham whilst writing both *The Sketch Book* and *Bracebridge Hall*, Irving would have been familiar with the burgeoning industry around the city and in nearby Dudley. Whilst this chapter does not focus on Irving's depiction of English landscape, it is important to note that Irving deliberately locates Bracebridge Hall in rural Yorkshire and not in the West Midlands. Irving took the name Bracebridge from the family that built Aston Hall, a Jacobean mansion on the outskirts of Birmingham. His choice to avoid the obvious setting for the text and instead move to Yorkshire consciously contributes towards his project of nostalgia for communities less exposed to the demands and destruction of the industrial revolution.

29. Tamarkin, *Anglophilia*, p. xxviii.

30. Irving engages in this war of words in 1819 when he criticises English travelogues of America in *The Sketch Book*'s 'English Writers on America'. Clark, *The American Idea of England, 1776–1840*, p. 112; Eaton, *The Anglo-American Paper War*, p. 7.

31. Irving, *The Sketch Book*, p. 49.

32. There are a few mentions to very recent political events, such as in 'Little Britain' in *The Sketch Book*, when the speaker Mr Skryme refers to the 1819 Peterloo massacre as 'the bloody scenes in Manchester' and the 1820 conspiracy to assassinate Prime Minister Lord Liverpool and his cabinet as 'the great plot in Cato Street'. Irving, *The Sketch Book*, p. 210.

33. Ibid. p. 200.

34. Ibid.

35. Garcha, *From Sketch to Novel*, p. 18.

36. Ibid. p. 44.

37. Later British editions of *Bracebridge Hall* omit these four stories and their introductory pieces, which reconstructs the text purely as a travelogue focused on rural English life.

38. *Letters, Volume 1*, p. 661.

39. Spahn, *Thomas Jefferson, Time, and History*, p. 107.

40. Bradley, *Knickerbocker*, p. 5.

41. Irving to Thomas W. Storrow, 1 February 1822, in *Letters, Volume 1*, pp. 662–4 (p. 663).

42. Handley, *Visions of an Unseen World*, p. 209.

43. Tamarkin, *Anglophilia*, p. xxviii.

44. Irving, *The Sketch Book*, p. 38.

45. Ibid.

46. Pratt, *Archives of American Time*, p. 50.

47. Irving, *The Sketch Book*, p. 39.

48. Ibid.

49. Cooper, *The Prairie*, ed. Nevius, p. 385.

50. Ibid. p. 386.

51. Ibid. p. 383.

52. Tuck and Yang, 'Decolonization is Not a Metaphor', p. 16.

# 3

# 'WHAT HAD BECOME OF ME?': *SHEPPARD LEE'S* BLACKFACE TRANSFORMATION

At the end of Book 5 of Robert Montgomery Bird's *Sheppard Lee: Written by Himself* (1836), the shape-shifting narrator finds himself in peril, threatened with lynching by a group of angry pro-slavers and chased by a group of enslaved men in Virginia. His escape route takes an unusual and confronting form:

> There was but one resource left me, and that let the reader determine hereafter of how deplorable a character. I made a successful dodge, followed by a dash right through the screaming Africans, who perhaps hesitated to lay a rough hand on one of my colour, and, reaching the body of their companion, cried, half to myself and half to the insensible clay, 'It is better to be a slave than a dead man; and the scourge, whatever romantic persons may say to the contrary, is preferable, at any time, to the halter. If thou art dead, my sable brother, yield my spirit a refuge in thy useless body!'[1]

Throughout the novel, downwardly mobile Sheppard reanimates the bodies of six recently deceased men (a merchant, a dandy, a moneylender, a Quaker, a slave, an aristocrat), taking on their memories, voices and behaviours. Until this point in the text, death has provided a series of opportunities by enabling Sheppard to seek wealth and happiness. Coming across the insensible body of a young enslaved man, Tom, Sheppard chooses a life of bondage to escape extra-legal execution and the premature end of his body-hopping adventures. Just as

Tom's body acts as a physical resource to provide immediate safety, a life of enslavement soon becomes an emotional resource to offer comfort and enjoyment for Sheppard. Whilst asking his reader to 'determine hereafter of how deplorable a character' the enslaved figure and enslavement is, over the course of his several months in bondage Sheppard modifies his statement to posit that it may be better to be a slave than a *living* man.

In this chapter, I argue that Sheppard's liminal experience of supernatural racial transformation critiques White civic and economic value expectations. Like *Wieland*, Bird's shape-shifting text imagines the possibility of a radical fluidity of identity and social position across lines of race and class. However, whereas early national texts suggest that Whiteness can be erased through slippages into indigeneity, *Sheppard Lee* employs metempsychosis to suggest a White man can physically transform and live as a Black man. Sheppard enters the bodies of five other men, but it is when he occupies the happy yet rebellious enslaved Tom that he finds what Christopher Looby calls 'his nearest approach to inner contentment'.[2] This transition provides the most problematic yet fascinating invention of the novel: that a White citizen resides somewhere underneath the character of Tom, and that this White citizen could identify with and enjoy enslavement, which challenges expectations of industrious and autonomous Whiteness.

Since its republication in 2008, criticism of Bird's body-hopping novel has largely focused on its most daring episode, Sheppard's animation of an enslaved corpse. There are numerous interleaving generic influences on Bird's polyvocal imagination of racial metempsychosis: medical philosophy, race science, political discourse, abolition and anti-abolition print culture, the eighteenth-century it-narrative, the picaresque. Justine Murison discusses the impact of Bird's medical training on the connections between Sheppard's White and Black transformations. Studying antebellum theories of hypochondria, a racialised 'Southern' ailment, Murison compares Sheppard/Tom – human property who is happiest to 'go galloping on all fours' like a horse – to hypochondriac enslaver Arthur Megrim, Sheppard's last transformation, who believes he is 'now a chicken, now a loaded cannon, now a clock, now a hamper of crockery-ware' (pp. 336, 394). On Megrim's condition, Murison writes that 'Bird, in effect, sets up a fictional experiment in which he considers which is the worse slavery: a white man in a slave's body living under the rule of a kind master or the white man in the white body experiencing the luxurious disease of hypochondria.'[3] Yet, in this novel, slavery is not only preferable to death or madness but, for Sheppard, it is better to be a slave than a sane living White man. This preference is less surprising when we situate readings of the novel alongside a performance culture in which White men could enjoy temporary Blackness: blackface minstrelsy.

Less critical attention has been given to the influence of blackface on *Sheppard Lee*'s depiction of racial transformation, despite Bird's successful career as a playwright in the early 1830s. In this chapter I examine Sheppard's leap into Blackness through the lens of blackface minstrelsy. As Benjamin J. Doty notes, 'Blackface minstrelsy provides the representational foundation of Lee's portrayal of racial blackness.'[4] Spaces of performance are liminal zones of transformation and ambiguity, in which masquerade, make-up and costume blur and transgress class, race and gender stratification. The hybrid-voiced minstrel, a White man claiming to speak as Black, directly influences Bird's imagination of overlapping and merging racial selves. Growing in popularity in Northern cities in 1830s, the transgressive spectacle of racial cross-dressing directly influences Bird's fiction. He was surrounded by a culture of racial performance and social stereotype, which he filters into *Sheppard Lee* through exaggerated descriptions of the physical appearances and voices of different regions, classes, nationalities and races. On the antebellum stage, blackface transformations simultaneously fortified and demolished racial boundaries by emphasising yet engulfing the performer's own Whiteness. *Sheppard Lee* not only draws its conflicting racial stereotypes of lazy yet cunning and childish yet violent Black men from the raucous minstrel lyrics and performances, but both forms share the same racial politics, in which enslaved Blackness acts as an escape from the economic and civic pressures on White working men. Bird transplants into *Sheppard Lee* the minstrel's performance of a Blackness aware of its underlying Whiteness. The result is a novel that temporarily rejects White civic values by depicting racial transformation as a respite from the expectations of industry, autonomy, responsibility and property ownership. Like the early blackface minstrel, Bird employs the imagined Black body as a creative resource to critique Whiteness.

*Sheppard Lee* belongs to a nineteenth-century literary genre of textual blackface, in which White figures disguise themselves or masquerade as African Americans. Such figures include the eponymous Ormond in Charles Brockden Brown's 1800 novel, a group of fleeing White women in Leonara Sansay's *Zelica, the Creole* (1820) and Black Guinea in Herman Melville's *The Confidence-Man* (1857).[5] Whereas *Ormond*, *Zelica* and *The Confidence-Man* focus on episodes of physical disguise performed out of necessity or as trickery, *Sheppard Lee* centres on a racially liminal first-person narrative voice, which internalises the 'interracial identification' that Eric Lott recognises at the heart of blackface minstrelsy's attraction.[6] The supernatural plot device of metempsychosis enables Bird to turn the performance of blackface minstrelsy into real and complete racial transformation. Entering a Black body and mind is a fascinating and transgressive spectacle daring readers to imagine and identify with a wholly alien existence. However, despite Sheppard's repeated claims of Tom's difference, he coexists with the slave figure through slippages in his first-person narrative. In the act of speaking as Tom, remembering and writing first-person experiences of slavery, the previously White spoken and written 'I' of the text temporarily turns Black, and White and

Black selves coexist. Creating a faux slave narrative in Book 6 of the novel, Bird disavows the sympathetic purpose of the genre and instead turns it on its head to frame White labour as the real slavery of the period.

For Bird, stereotypes of the Black man as seen on the stage are a creative resource to build an exciting and humorous anti-abolitionist narrative. Doty views blackface as influencing Bird's satire on antebellum theories of embodiment, which 'reveals a more complex, ambivalent interaction between literature and medicine'.[7] I contend that Bird's ridicule is much more sweeping. Bird's audacious experiment dares the reader to identify with an alien Black existence to satirise Jacksonian citizenship. To read *Sheppard Lee* as textual blackface enables us to bring to the fore that Sheppard's racial transformation is not just a leap into Blackness but also out of Whiteness. In the second half of this chapter I argue that through Sheppard's racial transformation, Bird challenges a broader set of White civic values, such as the work ethic, responsibility, control of financial capital, ownership of property and self-possession. In writing his own slave narrative, Sheppard finds enslaved Blackness to be an emotional resource, one that offers respite from the pressures of economic success and civic conformity, which Bird paints as the true oppression of antebellum society. In this textual blackface, Bird reveals a liminal self that dances along the margins of Whiteness to perform desires for Black identification as it voices anxieties over White citizenship.

As Doug Jones has argued, the politics of blackface minstrelsy contained two contradictory messages: a punching up against White respectability politics and the market economy oppressing White workers, and a punching down against an enslaved and free Black population. The representational elasticity of the Black male figure enabled minstrels to perform 'polyvalent and ostensibly contradictory enactments' of African American men as childish yet cunning, lazy yet athletic, powerful yet bound: desirable yet a target of ridicule.[8] Although a White man could become Black, blackface performers and audiences simultaneously mocked yet feared the possibility of a Black man becoming White through increased rights for African Americans and the subjugation of White workers. Bird employs these contradictory politics in *Sheppard Lee*. The novel uses the slave stereotype as both an escape valve from the pressures of White civic values and a barrier to contain the threat of Black suffrage. Ending his slave narrative with an unsuccessful violent rebellion and Tom's gruesome death, Bird seeks to limit Black social mobility and alleviate fears of White oppression. As in minstrelsy, *Sheppard Lee* depends on a racial hierarchy that can be transgressed to offer a White escape fantasy, yet is ultimately maintained to uphold White social, legal and political privileges.

## RACIAL STEREOTYPE ON BIRD'S STAGE

For readers unfamiliar with this relatively obscure text, I begin with a brief summary of the novel's unusual and episodic plot. *Sheppard Lee* opens as an account of an unsuccessful New Jersey landowner who squanders his wealth and loses his acreage due to his overseer's mismanagement and his own ineptitude. Seeking financial salvation, Sheppard resorts to searching for mystical treasure buried in the village woods, accidentally fatally stabbing himself with a trowel. Fortunately, his misadventures have a silver lining: he discovers the ability to will his now disembodied spirit into the bodies of the recently deceased. Thus his adventures begin, taking him from New Jersey to Pennsylvania and Virginia, in the guise of six different characters who exist as socio-economic types: John H. Higginson, a successful and gouty brewer; Isaac Dulmer Dawkins, a penniless dandy on the make for a wealthy wife; Abram Skinner, a miserly Jewish moneylender with scheming sons; Zachariah Longstraw, a Quaker whose charitable intentions repeatedly end in his downfall, finally kidnapped and transported into the South; Tom, a lazy and happy Virginia slave who participates in a violent rebellion sparked by an abolitionist pamphlet he alone can read; and Arthur Megrim, a dyspeptic aristocrat who thinks himself to be, by turns, furniture, animals and the Emperor of France.[9]

Sheppard's entire journey is a liminal process, starting with his death in New Jersey woodlands – the separation of his spirit from his corpse and of Sheppard from his community – and concluding when he returns to his body and reintegrates into his village as a reformed man eighteen months later. Throughout his body-hopping adventure, he travels between his own enduring self and the character of each new incarnation, literally embodying Victor Turner's liminal persona in his transition between the fixed condition of 'legal status, profession, office or calling, rank or degree'.[10] Each of Sheppard's embodiments represents a fixed socio-economic type or condition; profession (merchant), rank (aristocrat) or legal status (slave) easily demarcates each man. During each incarnation, Sheppard submerges within the new character to varying degrees by taking on the thoughts, behaviours and emotions of each man to the point where he does not remember any previous existence. For example, when becoming Skinner, Sheppard observes: 'In entering his body, I became, as I have mentioned repeatedly before, the subject of every peculiarity of being that marked the original possessor' (p. 212). Repeatedly, Sheppard describes the original owner of the body as his 'prototype', rendering himself a copy that acquires the identity of the previously living man. Therefore, Sheppard's own sense of self during the narrative's events can be imagined as a wave; in the troughs, he has no recollection of his life and only faintly resides within each character in order to record events; during the peaks, which occur at the beginning and end of each incarnation, he remembers who he is in order to move between bodies.

Bird's dependence on flattened social types stems from his career writing for the antebellum stage. Before and after his brief yet prolific career in fiction, Bird had a varied professional life. Shortly after training as a physician at Pennsylvania College, he turned to playwriting in 1827. Bird completed nine dramas between 1827 and 1834, of which three tragedies – *The Gladiator* (1831), *Oralloossa* (1832) and *The Broker of Bogota* (1834) – were performed, with celebrity actor Edwin Forrest in the lead roles. Bird creates stock dramatic and comedic roles along the lines of race, class, gender and nationality. In his tragedies, racially ambiguous characters such as the enslaved Spartacus in *The Gladiator* are heroic yet savage figures. Bird is clearly aware of the abolitionist connotations in *The Gladiator*, which was written and performed soon after Nat Turner's unsuccessful insurrection. He notes in his diaries, 'If *The Gladiator* were produced in a slave state, the managers, players, and perhaps myself in the bargain, would be rewarded with the Penitentiary!' for celebrating a rebellious slave. However, as a less-than-White figure of antiquity, which Peter Reed terms 'classical blackness', Spartacus is safely removed from contemporary racial issues.[11] There is a clear distinction between Spartacus, an ethnically ambiguous figure whose violence is distanced by location and time, and Turner, who embodies contemporary fears of African American violence and sexual violation. Forrest's tanned and muscular Spartacus is an exoticised rather than reviled figure on the stage; a violent slave, yet one who speaks with both eloquence and raw power. In his diaries on *The Gladiator*, Bird praises Forrest as 'undoubtedly the best man for Spartacus in Christendom', in particular because 'his voice & muscle hold out to the last'.[12] With swarthy appearance and powerful vocality, Forrest's 'classical blackness' in portraying characters such as Spartacus, Metamora and Othello invoked a sense of cross-racial identification from the audience – with the colour barrier removed or blurred, White theatregoers could imagine themselves in those positions, without having to extend their sympathies to contemporary free and enslaved African Americans.[13] A *New York Standard* review lauded Forrest for his authentic Spartacus – 'the actor is lost in the slave' – a statement that could only be comfortably made with the assumption that Spartacus was not representative of Turner.[14]

Racial ambiguity moves from the stage to the page in *Nick of the Woods or The Jibbenainosay* (1837), in which Bird presents a darkened Whiteness as opposed to the lightened 'classical blackness' of historical tragedies. In this novel, a pacifist Quaker living on the Kentucky frontier during the Revolution – the ironically named 'Bloody' Nathan Slaughter – transforms into Nick, a vengeful maniac who scalps Native Americans in the forests to avenge the murder of his family. Known as the Jibbenainosay ('Spirit-that-walks') amongst the Shawnee, Nathan/Nick is spoken of as 'a great tall fellow, with horns and a hairy head like a buffalo-bull' and 'a blood-thirsty creature'.[15] Nathan/Nick is a White man who becomes increasingly indigenised in his appearance and behaviours. He dresses in 'Indian garments' and speaks fluent Shawnee. Vanquishing the Shawnee chief who killed his family at the climax of the novel, Nathan/Nick's step is 'like that of a warrior leaping through the measures of the war-dance' and when he speaks 'his words were of battle and bloodshed'.[16]

Bird attributes Nathan's 'extreme metamorphosis' to a head injury sustained during the attack on his family, and the irony of the Quaker's name turns out to be nominative determinism. Writing a virulent Indian-hating novel, Bird celebrates this violence as part of a righteous campaign against the 'barbarities of the savages'. He frames Nathan's revenge in Indigenous markers to show how far he has fallen from Christian Whiteness due to the Native violence inflicted upon him – an erasure of Whiteness differing from Sheppard's complete race abandonment in switching bodies.[17] The novel was quickly adapted as a melodrama for the stage by Louisa Medina in 1838, and Joseph Proctor's costume change from Nathan to Nick/Jibbenainosay heightened the racial ambiguity of a White man who could so easily be mistaken for a Shawnee warrior. Adding the Jibbenainosay's 'large Indian blanket' and 'Indian headdress of feathers' to Nathan's 'deerskin hunting shirt' and 'skin leggings', Proctor could easily slip out of Whiteness and into this performed indigeneity to heighten sympathy for an anti-hero driven to sensational – and for the audience, enjoyable – violence.[18]

Against these (melo)dramatic portrayals of racially ambiguous figures intended to foster audience sympathy, Yankee comedies like Bird's unpublished *The City Looking Glass* (1828) reduce non-White figures to peripheral comic characters. These productions draw heavily on Jacobean and Restoration comedies to create clear social types marked by speech and appearance; for example, a stock city gentleman, servants, a West Country sailor and an Irish-Southern plantation overseer in *The City Looking Glass* – a range of distinct voices from different regions, nations and social groups that also populates *Sheppard Lee*. During Sheppard's incarnation as Dawkins the reader encounters a number of these voices: the thickly inflected Irish accent of his housekeeper, Nora Magee; the over-familiar and common speech of his country cousins Sam and Pattie; and his own aristocratically nasal tones. In distinguishing non-White characters as distinctly African American, unlike the ambiguity in tragedies, Yankee comedy actors used burnt cork and lard to transform themselves and spoke in exaggerated African American vernacular.[19] Rather than the cross-racial identification of tragedy's blurred colour line, these productions uphold racial boundaries yet tease the possibility of transgression. Both Samuel Woodworth's *The Forest Rose* (1825) and *The City Looking Glass* feature scenes of White men tricked into kissing or escorting veiled Black women, eliciting horrified amusement from an audience fearing miscegenation.[20]

A combination of stage comic Blackness and street performance, blackface minstrelsy developed as a raucous and transgressive entr'acte in the 1830s. Originating in Northern cities, White musicians created entertaining African American personas to popularise African American dance and song. Performers such as Thomas Dartmouth 'Daddy' Rice were hugely popular for their portrayals of extravagant Black characters like runaway Jumping Jim Crow and dandy Zip Coon. Rice began 'jumping Jim Crow' in Kentucky in 1830, performing a lively jig, mimicking local African American speech and painting his face black with burnt cork. Throughout the period 1832–6 he toured major cities with comic songs, dances and plays.[21] In a 'simultaneous drawing up and crossing of racial boundaries', minstrels overstated African American appearance and speech to mark racial differences, but their performances repeatedly recognised they were White men inhabiting Blackness.[22] In 'Jim Crow', Rice explicitly reveals this hybrid voice to his audience, introducing himself thus: 'My name is Daddy Rice, as you berry well do know,/ And none in de Nited States like me, can jump Jim Crow', before moving into Jim's autobiographical song.[23] Audiences recognised the minstrel as performance but still 'mined it for improbable forms of authenticity'.[24] Both the transformation of a White man into Black and the range of Black stereotypes performed carried political and social weight for a White audience.

With his zanier register of comic songs and slapstick against authority figures, Jim Crow dared audiences, in the words of W. T. Lhamon Jr, to 'identify with a white man's embodied desire for blackness'.[25] In Rice's verses, Jim Crow is a trickster figure, wheeling about multiple national locations, outwitting both White and Black characters and inhabiting both anti- and pro-slavery positions. He mocks the pretensions of Black freemen in the North and literally strikes out against the respectability politics to which both Black dandies and the White middle classes ascribed, 'beating a Jarsey niggar,/ In de street de oder day'.[26] At the same time, in the 1835 farces *Virginia Mummy* and *Bone Squash Diavolo*, enslavers are outwitted by cunning Black manservants or succumb to comic deaths.[27] More than simple caricature, the freewheeling minstrel simultaneously frightened White audiences with the possibility of African American violence or miscegenation, while attracting and fascinating them with his African athleticism and virility.

In finding autonomy and agency within a piece of human property, the minstrel ridicules the tenet that White citizens possess true freedom. An anti-establishment figure, Jim has more freedom than White citizens who are expected to adhere to social norms of having a job, providing for their family and contributing to the economic and political wellbeing of the nation. Although a working-class performance, middle-class audiences that saw Rice could find pleasure too in White performances of Blackness, a transgressive opportunity for cross-class as well as cross-racial escapism. Jim offers the possibility that a White man could aspire for this freedom in the guise of enslaved or fugitive Blackness. Most provocatively, in 'The Original Jim Crow' (1836), Rice ironically teases, 'I'm so glad dat I'm a niggar,/ An don't you wish you was too'. With both Rice and his audience aware that the minstrel's Blackness is an act, Jim jokes that White men 'would spend every dollar,/ If dey could only be/ Gentlemen ob colour' to access his life of leisure, such is its appeal.[28] Although complete racial transformation is impossible for the audience (unless they are Sheppard Lee), the minstrel inhabits a privileged position in his ability to temporarily slip into Blackness through exaggerated appearance and speech, and he offers his spectators a glance at a pleasurable and rebellious life of drink, dance and debauchery.

However, as Doug Jones has recently disputed, prevailing scholarship on blackface can rest too easily on the idea that minstrelsy had the potential for cross-racial solidarity. Jim Crow's japing did not lead to increased support for the abolition of slavery or political rights for free African Americans. Jim Crow dared audiences to desire Blackness, but not to live as Black men in New York or Philadelphia. They could desire the laziness and play that the freewheeling fugitive represented but not the lack of suffrage and persecution inherent to the lived experience of real free and enslaved African Americans, a condition they instead wished to purport to protect their own freedoms. Northern performers and audiences depended on ongoing chattel slavery to offer up bodies for White performers to mimic. Minstrelsy enabled White working-class male performers and audiences to confront the constraint and exploitation of White civic and economic values but assert the privileges of Whiteness over Black suffrage: they 'expropriated black performance culture and developed a distinct strand of proslavery thought with which to bring about their socio-economic betterment at the expense of African Americans'.[29] Invested in 'black performance and political material, not black men', minstrelsy utilised the Black male figure as a creative resource to give shape to desires to escape the constraints of Whiteness, yet articulate White physical and political freedoms by controlling and containing performed Blackness to subjugate real African Americans.[30] These contradictory political messages of the enslaved Black man shape Bird's portrayal of Blackness in the Virginia section of *Sheppard Lee*.

### 'I THOUGHT IT QUITE BEAUTIFUL': RACIAL TRANSFORMATION IN THE NOVEL

Rice's blackface and Bird's stage tragedies inhabited the same performance spaces in Northern cities. For example, in 1834 New York's Bowery Theatre advertised that Rice would perform as the 'Celebrated Jim Crow' in *Oh Hush!* for a few nights before Forrest returned to the stage as Colombian Baptista Febra in Bird's *The Broker of Bogota*.[31] The theatre's drive towards populist and nativist productions in the 1830s made the Bowery the perfect place to see both America's leading stage actor and the increasingly popular minstrel. The two productions may have attracted different audiences in terms of taste, and possibly class – one interested in comic farce, the other interested in Shakespearean tragedy – but they both marked the non-White body as a spectacular yet identifiable figure. Staging his plays in close proximity to minstrel acts, Bird poaches this White working-class form – and its own poached Black material – and translates 1830s minstrel culture into *Sheppard Lee*'s ventriloquisation of slave speech. In Virginia, Bird transcribes the speech of slaves with pronounced African American vernacular or 'Congo tang', echoing the dialect in which blackface minstrels sang and spoke (p. 311). In one episode, after looking at an abolitionist pamphlet, Tom's fellow slave Governor breaks into rhyming song, exclaiming:

> Oh! de possum up de gum-tree;
> 'Coony in de hollow:
> Two white men whip a nigga,
> How de nigga holla! (p. 348)

The influence of blackface songs on Bird is clear. The first two lines of Governor's verse adapt Rice's 'The Original Jim Crow' ('Dere's Possum up de gum tree/ An Racoony in de hollow') and George Washington Dixon's 'Zip Coon' ('O ole Zip Coon he is a larned skoler,/ Sings posum up a gum tree an coony in a holler').[32] Furthermore, Governor's burlesque of enslaved Blackness, miming receiving the lash from an invisible master – 'now ducking to the earth, now jumping into the air, as though some lusty overseer were plying him, whip in hand, with all his might' – mirrors the athleticism of blackface entertainers' lively jigs, the jumping of Jumping Jim Crow, to mock abolitionists' claims of violence and degradation (p. 347). This doubling back of racial performance – the Black slave enacting an exaggerated anti-abolitionist Blackness through a White authorial mouthpiece – continues when Sheppard transforms into Tom.

At the beginning of Sheppard's transformation into Tom, Bird creates his own form of blackface doubling through a literal mirror. Like the play of racial masquerade in minstrelsy, at first Sheppard is well aware that he is a White man inside a Black body. Upon waking as Tom, Sheppard examines his new body:

> my hand, which I had raised to scratch my head, came into contact with a mop of elastic wool, such as never grew upon the scalp of a white man. I started up in bed and looked at my hands and arms; they were of the hue of ebony – or, to speak more strictly, of smoked mahogany. I saw a frag-ment of looking-glass hanging on the wall within my reach. I snatched it down, and took a survey of my physiognomy. Miserable me! my *face* was as black as my arms – and, indeed, somewhat more so – presenting a sable globe, broken only by two red lips of immense magnitude, and a brace of eyes as white and as wide as plain China saucers, or peeled turnips. (pp. 331–2)

None of Sheppard's other transformations have their physical appearance mapped in such an exaggerated and attentive manner. As Doty identifies, this description of Tom is taken from the minstrel's costume. These demarcations of racial appearance fed performances of blackface; illustrations of Rice show him with almost pitch-black skin, bright white eyes, large red lips and tight curly hair.[33] Bird's description of 'smoked mahogany' is an analogue for the burnt cork used in blackface costume. In looking in the mirror, Sheppard, seeing his new body, reflects a mixture of curiosity and revulsion. First seeing his new appearance, Sheppard fears a life of brutality and cruelty and 'could think of nothing but cowhides and cat-o'-nine-tails, that were to welcome me to bondage'. Later, divorced from this fear of violence, the Black body remains captivating – Sheppard recalls 'having peeped at [my face] a dozen times or more, my ideas began to alter, and by-and-by, I thought it quite beautiful' (pp. 332, 342). Like the spectacle of Rice's grotesque blackening, Sheppard's transformation is terrifying yet fascinating for the antebellum reader, as Bird's narrative moves out of the familiar experiences of White Philadelphia into the alien condition of chattel slavery.

Thinking beyond physical demarcations, when Bird describes Tom's mental condition, a clear connection emerges between racial physiognomy and interiority. From Sheppard's first transformation into Higginson onwards, Bird sets up an inextricable link between the body and the mind, with Sheppard often meditating on this relationship. As Dawkins, Sheppard states,

> I do verily believe that much of the evil and good of man's nature arises from causes and influences purely physical; that valour and ambition are as often caused by a bad stomach as ill-humour by bad teeth . . . sages who labour to improve the moral nature of their species, will effect their purpose only when they have physically improved the stock. (pp. 140–1)

This way of thinking about the body is indicative of Bird's medical training and his brief practice as a physician. Against dualism, antebellum medical philosophy believed physical ailments influenced psychological conditions and that, in Murison's words, 'mind was never divorced from matter'.[34] In the above quotation, this connection between mind and matter has evident links to race science, as Sheppard's breeding lexicon, adhering to antebellum theories of racial hierarchies, espouses a proto-eugenic approach to improving human intelligence and morality.

In Sheppard's transformation into Tom, then, Tom's biological race directly influences his mental condition. Tom's lack of memory is a key example of this influence. As in his previous incarnations, Sheppard/Tom cannot remember any of his previous selves: 'I was no longer Sheppard Lee, Zachariah Longstraw, nor anybody else, except simply Tom, Thomas, or Tommy, the slave . . . I had ceased to remember all my previous states of existence.' However, Tom cannot even remember his own past, finding himself unable to account for his ability to read; he is demarcated from Sheppard's previous incarnations, who quickly regain their memories. Sheppard posits, 'Perhaps my mind was stupefied – sunk beneath the ordinary level of the human understanding, and therefore incapable of realizing the evils of my condition' (p. 341). This explanation evidently stems from an understanding of 'The Ethiopian Race' as ranking far below 'Caucasian' intellect, prominent in American race thinking from Jefferson to Bird's later Pennsylvania College colleague Samuel George Morton. In *Crania Americana* (1839), Morton's claim that Africans were 'flexible' and could 'yield to their destiny, and accommodate themselves with amazing facility to every change of circumstance' is manifest in Tom's presentism, as Sheppard claims: 'I could not have been an African had I troubled myself with thoughts of anything but the present' (*Sheppard Lee*, p. 341).[35]

Tom's 'evacuated interior', in the words of Samuel Otter, mirrors exaggerated blackface stage presences and scientific racial categorisation. In his consideration of the novel as a comedy of manners concerned with social position, Otter asserts that 'the logical body for Lee to enter would not have been a Virginian slave but a member of Philadelphia's African American aspiring class', which would reflect the strained race relations in 1830s Philadelphia.[36] For Otter, Bird's use of the slave stereotype evades these pressing social concerns and reduces racial politics to abolition alone. However, this slave transformation does enable Bird to speak about racial politics beyond emancipation by satirising the value expectations of White male citizenship, namely industry, property ownership and self-possession. Although Tom's condition is 'tolerable', reading it through the narrative voice of Sheppard suggests the frightening possibility that lost rights are preferable to the legal, social and economic privileges and responsibilities of citizenship.[37] Sheppard/Tom's first-person narrative challenges the White reader to conceive of what is at the limits of their imagination by offering the possibility that a White citizen could identify with and indulge in the alien condition of Black enslavement.

This argument hinges on reading the presence of Sheppard underneath Tom in the plantation episodes, which enables him to not only remember but also reflect on his experiences. Although Bird employs essentialist racial stereotypes to portray Tom as completely physically and mentally different from Sheppard's White self, as the section progresses Bird crosses these racial boundaries when Sheppard begins to identify with an enslaved experience. In his transformation into Tom, Sheppard is racially liminal when the oppositions of Black and White selves temporarily coexist. He is a liminal figure who partially internalises each of his transformations, taking on the thoughts and emotions of each man, so that the first-person narrative refers to both himself and each incarnation. In this sense, Sheppard's liminality is manifest through slippages between his present narrative and Tom's interior during the plot. Sheppard must be present within his incarnation as Tom in line with the novel's logic that it is Sheppard's autobiographical tale.

In Sheppard/Tom, Bird balances extreme racial difference with the convergence of Black and White selves. The possibility of minstrelsy's performed interracial identification as reality emerges when it becomes harder to separate the voices, memories and character of Sheppard and Tom, which overlap and intertwine on the plantation. In the limited occasions Sheppard transcribes Tom's speech, the omission of an African American vernacular accent – which all the other enslaved characters possess and Bird ventriloquises – alerts the reader to the White self within the Black slave. If the Ebonics of Governor's songs distance the reader, alerting them to the alienness of the Jim Crow figure, then Tom's dialogic silence draws the reader further in to the first-person narrative centre of the text. Furthermore, Sheppard does not explain why Tom is the only enslaved man who can decode 'the mysteries of the pamphlet', or how he acquired literacy, just that, 'I had a feeling in me as if I *could* read' (pp. 355, 350). This ability counters the otherwise childlike portrayal of Tom, a field hand who is happiest when galloping as a horse. Where does his literacy come from? In a textual blackface reading of the text, literacy is Bird's acknowledgement of Sheppard's White self present within Tom. Sheppard/Tom is a hybrid of an enslaved Black mind and a White self. This, in effect, is manifest in Sheppard's first-person narrative voice during his racial transmigration.

The separation between Black and White selves, free and unfree selves, is left linguistically ambiguous in Sheppard's transformation into Tom. The text details Sheppard's autobiographic adventures, of course, but throughout the narrative the linguistic distinction between Sheppard recalling past events and his transmigration at the current point in the text is not always made clear. There is a confusion of first-person written voice as these multiple selves intervene in Sheppard's narration of his story. For example, after changing from Higginson to Dawkins, Sheppard uses in short succession, 'I – that is John H. Higginson –', 'me – that is, I. D. Dawkins –', and 'my body – that is, Higginson's –' (pp. 109–10). Sheppard must separate the individuals each time, such is the potential confusion when writing about his transformation. However, throughout the text, the distinction between past and present selves is not always made explicit. In chapter 14 of Book 3, the heading states: 'A short chapter, containing an account of the Author's cousin, Samuel Wilkins, Jr.' (p. 151). The identity of the author here is confused; Sheppard is the author of his memoir, yet Samuel Wilkins is Dawkins's cousin. In the novel, the linguistic centre of first-person narrative – 'my' and 'I' – shifts continually, as Sheppard refers to both his own present self and his past transformations. The instability of the first-person 'my' and 'I' in the text linguistically represents Turner's theory of liminality as a transformative space in which the self changes. Liminality is found in the spaces of the text where the 'I' of each transformation overlaps or replaces the present 'I' of Sheppard's narrative voice, meaning that old and new selves coexist.

In writing Sheppard's experiences as an enslaved African American, Bird creates hybrid utterances that refer to Tom and Sheppard simultaneously. We can frame them through Mikhail Bakhtin's definition of hybrid constructions as a single utterance or text that 'contains mixed within it two utterances . . . two semantic and axiological belief systems'.[38] Just as blackface minstrelsy contains both White and Black selves when the White performer speaks as Black, in *Sheppard Lee*, the first-person narrative contains two polar experiences and axioms – Black enslavement and White freedom – in a supposedly singular narrative voice. Looking back on his time as Tom, Sheppard reflects that 'there was less done by, and less looked for from, my master's hands, than I have ever known to be the case with the White labourers of New Jersey' (p. 340). 'My' refers to Tom's enslavement, but the 'I' clearly refers to Sheppard's knowledge of White labourers in New Jersey. This doubling of the Black 'my' of the past and the White 'I' of the present suggests a fundamental merging of identities. Sheppard's clear and repeated assertions of Tom's differences are undermined by those moments when in one sentence he is linguistically represented as both Black and White. Another day, he recollects:

> I found myself, for the first time in my life, content, or very nearly so, with my condition, free from cares, far removed from disquiet, and, if not actually in love with my lot, so far from being dissatisfied, that I had not the least desire to exchange it for another. (p. 341)

The repeated 'my' and 'I' of this sentence could refer to both men: in this moment, are these feelings of contentment Tom's, or Sheppard's? I contend the latter. The past tense of 'found myself' indicates that Sheppard is not making a comparison in the present, when he writes his narrative, but at the time of which he is thinking. Sheppard asserts that Tom has no memory of his previous existence as Tom or anyone else, and so should have no comparison to make. Sheppard's former life and his four previous transformations, on the other hand, have left him dissatisfied and in search of exchangeable bodies. He is present within Tom, even if he is not aware of this at the time, and so 'my life' refers to his life as Sheppard, while 'my lot' and 'my condition' refer to Tom's enslavement.

Although Sheppard claims that as Tom he cannot remember his past White existences, from the previous statements, it is clear that he is continually present within Tom. Moreover, later Sheppard remembers his enslaved existence; even if the physical body of the slave has perished, the memories are sustained when Sheppard returns to his own body. By presenting the experience of enslavement in the first person, in this section of the novel Bird moves from theatrical blackface stereotypes to a fictional slave narrative. In his study of non-human narrative, Jonathan Lamb identifies a connection between the popular eighteenth-century it-narrative and slave narratives. Lamb argues that in each form, 'a silent acknowledgement is being made of the unusualness of the first-person narrator insofar as a statement of the obvious is required in order to affirm that it was that very person who wrote or told' the tale.[39] In other words, both forms employ titles that make it clear who is writing the narrative, asking the reader to believe that an anthropomorphic lapdog or a sentient hairpiece or human property wrote the tale. *Sheppard Lee*, in part an it-narrative describing the adventures of Sheppard's circulating spirit and in part a slave narrative, echoes this stylistic quality in its subtitle: *Written by Himself.*[40]

Antislavery societies, proliferating in the 1830s, emphasised the humanity of enslaved people to elevate them above the sentient property of it-narratives and as deserving of civic rights, and to encourage identification and action from sympathetic White readers. As Christopher Castiglia argues, 'White reformers took on blackness not on the surface of the skin, but as suffering interior, a civic depth.' Abolitionists such as William Lloyd Garrison claimed identifying with Black emotional pain in order to propose 'a way for whites and blacks to merge through the imagination, suggesting an affective "sameness" once the burden of marked bodies is removed'.[41] A text such as Richard Hildreth's pseudo-slave narrative *The Slave* (1836) – originally published as a truthful account, but later revealed to be a White-authored fiction – partially removes the colour line in order to emphasise the universal sympathetic bonds between Black and White interiority. Hildreth makes his slave persona Archy Moore fair-skinned in order for White readers to identify with Archy's emotional suffering and support Hildreth's abolitionist aims.[42] However, as Castiglia argues, abolitionists' universalising claim bolsters White privilege to be virtuous, empathetic citizens who can temporarily feel the pain of the enslaved but maintain their own legal and social autonomy.[43] In *Sheppard Lee*, Bird offers the potential for this interracial identification through a merged racial interiority, Sheppard/Tom. However, his use of the liminal 'I' turns White affective privilege on its head. Rather than asking the reader to sympathise with the potential Black citizen of abolitionist literature, he instead dares them to identify with the limited psychology of the stereotyped Black noncitizen of minstrel culture. In doing so, this identification with the figure of the happy and lazy enslaved man is part of Bird's comic aim to challenge contemporary ideals of identity formation as tied to the Jacksonian marketplace and its civic and economic value expectations.

## 'AN'T *I* SLAVE?' TO 'WHO AIN'T A SLAVE?'

Sheppard's racially liminal narrative voice challenges the White middle-class reader to not only identify with an enslaved experience but to entertain the possibility that Tom's existence is preferable to that of the other five White incarnations, who are figures defined or driven by the pursuit of wealth and social standing. The stereotype of Tom as a happy and lazy enslaved man sits amongst a group of characters who consist of one or two exaggerated personality traits, a collection of behaviours, thoughts and emotions delineated by their socio-economic position. In the misfortunes of Sheppard's White incarnations who are continually on the make, Bird satirises the idea of identity as tied to the pursuit of wealth. An ethos, or culture of capitalism, frames social interactions and individual identity in terms of value and accumulation of capital. Within a developing industrialised market economy, earning and controlling capital was central to identity formation and civic contribution. As Jeffrey Sklansky notes, Americans cemented 'bond[s] between selfhood – or, in the language of the early republic, independence or liberty or virtue – and property'.[44] Epitomising such a connection, Skinner the moneylender has a pathological fixation on finance. He asks himself: 'What am I worth? how much more can I make myself worth?'; Bird mocks his selfhood, which exists purely as a monetary not moral concept (*Sheppard Lee*, p. 200).

Bird's textual blackface dares the middle-class White reader to go against the axiom of citizenship tied to White social markers. In contrast to the formation of the White individual through owning property and the self, the enslaved Black body denotes an inability to achieve these ideals of independence and democratic participation. If personal selfhood and citizenship is figured in the language of property ownership, Sheppard is happier in the opposite situation, happier being property, without the worries of the citizen. In becoming Tom, Sheppard finds 'everything black about himself'.[45] In other words, he finds his own desires for laziness, contentment and play that the African American slave represents. At the beginning of the novel, Sheppard's own inherited enslaved manservant, Jim Jumble, is so happy with his position that when Sheppard offers to free him,

> he burst into a passion, swore he would *not* be free, and told me flatly I was his master, and I should take care of him: and the absurd fool ended by declaring, if I made him a free man he would have the law of me, 'he would, by ge-hosh!' (p. 20)

Jim's desire to stay in bondage is due to an understanding of 'the difference between living, on the one hand, a lazy life, without any care whatever, as my slave, and, on the other, labouring hard to obtain a precarious subsistence as a free man' (p. 20). At first fearing enslavement in Virginia, Sheppard soon realises the idyllic conditions of his plantation. Revising his original abolitionist stance, Sheppard ponders: 'It may be however, that there is nothing necessarily adverse to happiness in slavery itself, unaccompanied by other evils.' Tom's group do not recognise physical punishment as part of their reality. In response to *The Fate of the Slave*'s depiction of beaten and chained enslaved men, Governor exclaims, 'An't *I* slave?', which inverts the affecting abolitionist cry 'Am I not a man and a brother?' (pp. 342, 351). Sheppard recalls that as Tom, 'Of one thing, at least, I can be very certain. I never had so easy and idle a time of it in my whole life,' and he claims to be 'contented with my servile condition', again refusing the third person to distinguish Tom's condition from his own (pp. 342, 344).

Bird's enslaved figures enact a common argument in anti-abolitionist writings that maintained the White working man had a harder life than the enslaved one. For example, in J. P. Kennedy's plantation romance *Swallow Barn* (1832), slave-owner Meriwether espouses that the enslaved are 'required to do less work than any other labourers in society, they have as many privileges as are compatible with the nature of their occupations; they are subsisted in general as comfortably, nay, in *their* estimation of comforts, – more comfortably than the tillers of the soil of other nations', a statement that convinces the Northern narrator.[46] As David Roediger has outlined, White workers used the metaphor of slavery to speak of themselves as experiencing a form of oppression – 'wage slavery' or 'slavery of wages' – worse than the life of easy dependence they believed those enslaved in the South enjoyed.[47] For Bird, co-opting the language of slavery extends beyond manual and mechanical labour to frame all paid work and urban living. In his short story collection *Peter Pilgrim* (1838), the narrator of 'A Night on Terrapin Rocks' seeks to escape 'the slavery of a city life, not to speak of the more intolerable bondage of trade', and 'throw off my chains, and turn savage'.[48] Throughout *Sheppard Lee*, Sheppard is a slacker who has no desire for the exertion of paid work, instead seeking treasure, inheritance and marriage to secure prosperity. However, in Philadelphia he is plagued by the stresses and 'disquiet' of his transformations – Higginson's gout and nagging wife, Dawkins's debt collectors and failed marriage plot, Skinner's scheming sons chasing their inheritance – that cannot be separated from the market economy and its pressures (p. 341). When Ishmael exclaims in *Moby-Dick* (1851), 'Who ain't a slave?' he acknowledges that everyone has to subjugate themselves to play a part in the market economy.[49] In concert with making anti-abolitionist claims on plantation slavery as an inherently neutral institution, Bird expands figurative slavery for White citizens who are legally free, yet constrained by civic and economic conditions. The minstrelised Blackness of happy and dependent Jim, Governor and Tom acts as a fantasy for Sheppard and White readers to release themselves from these constraints.

Inhabiting a paradoxical position just like early minstrels, Sheppard's liminality demonstrates White desires for Blackness, a desire to exist outside the market-driven pressures on individuals, while at the same time presenting African Americans as a threat to White social and political freedoms. Using an enslaved Black figure to critique White value expectations yet elevate and protect Whiteness reflects discussions by White workers to consider themselves as oppressed, yet refuse interracial solidarity. While White workers used the language of slavery to emphasise their drudgery, they refused collaboration with real enslaved populations. Roediger writes, 'Chattel slavery provided white workers with a touchstone against which to weigh their fears and a yardstick to measure their reassurance.'[50] Enslaved Black labour was a point of contradistinction for White workers – the language of slavery articulated a belief that they suffered economically, yet were still racially superior and alone deserving of legal and political rights. The scenes in Philadelphia feature several characters obsessed with their social position, which they frame in the language of race. When Longstraw encourages striking needlewomen to go into domestic service, they respond, insulted, 'he wants to make niggur servants of us! *us*, that is freeborn American girls!' (p. 280). In a society where free citizen implied White citizen, Frances Trollope noted it was 'petty treason to the republic to call a free citizen a *servant*'.[51] Profession had clear racial connotations, which equated the performance of domestic and manual labour with being less than White, because it suggested dependency as opposed to self-ownership.

Bird further discusses this relationship between work and race in *Peter Pilgrim*'s 'My Friends in the Madhouse'. Visiting an asylum, the narrator meets John, a man committed for coming up with an extraordinary innovation to end slavery. To fix enslaver concerns that they would suffer financially under emancipation, the man invents 'patent niggers', mechanical men of 'wood, iron, leather and canvas' that would replace freed African Americans and who 'never get tired, or sick, or sulky – never die, or run away, or rise in insurrection'.[52] Still carrying the racial slur, these automatons embody the enslaved's loss of freedom and mark out plantation labour as below White workers. Yet Bird's imaginary solution doesn't address what would happen to the formerly enslaved. While seemingly allaying fears for the Southern aristocracy, the invention inflames White anxieties of freed African Americans replacing White workers and securing equal political rights, a racial upheaval that Bird threatens in *Sheppard Lee*'s slave revolt.

## BLACK KINGS AND WHITE SUBJECTS

Bird clearly ridicules yet fears the possibility that an enslaved man could have self-determination and political agency leading to political power. In one episode on the plantation, preening Tom appears as 'something of a coxcomb', wearing Master George's old coat, 'a ruffled shirt, and a white neckcloth, with a pair of leather gloves' whilst holding a 'peeled beechen wand' as a cane (p. 342). Here Bird returns to blackface types – in this guise he mirrors Zip Coon, the minstrel dandy that Rice and Dixon portrayed as foolish and proud.[53] Through Tom's pretensions, Bird mocks Black aspirations of social mobility that genteel clothing and mannerisms represent. While Sheppard ironically finds 'his fullest experience of political consciousness and revolutionary agency' through the revolt, when he writes his memoir he is quick to dismiss this political participation from a Black man.[54] Sheppard vigorously rejects the idea that as Tom he could be a president or king as 'sentimental notions' and 'stupid ambition' (p. 357). Sheppard/Tom becoming president is as unrealistic as Sheppard's transformation into a Black man, and yet both versions of Sheppard believe their situations possible. In minstrelsy, Jim Crow's freewheeling attitude extends into the nation's highest office. Rice's runaway slave suggests that as president he will 'drink mint julep, an swing upon de gates' of the White House, which dismisses effective Black political power.[55] In *Sheppard Lee* these comic aspirations turn tyrannical. The image of a Black president is troubling enough for many antebellum White readers, but the prospect of a Black king threatens the entire democratic foundation of the nation when the enslaved wish to become masters themselves. In their rebellion, which sees Bird drawing on the Turner revolt again, the enslaved men seek to 'exterminate all the white men in Virginia' and take their daughters and wives. The self-appointed king of the slaves, Governor, threatens: 'I lick any nigga I like! . . . I shall hab my choice ob de women: what you say *dat*? I shall hab Missa Isabella faw my wife!' (pp. 360–1).[56] Sheppard/Tom's aspirational realisation that he has the freedom to be a 'great personage' poses the threat of radical social fluidity and miscegenation (p. 357). Throughout the novel, social position is shown to be shifting and liminal in Sheppard's transformations and circulation through antebellum society. Tom's belief in the potential of Black political participation further threatens the idea of a racially stable and hierarchical society.

The fictive containment of Tom's social mobility and prospective Black governance allay Bird's personal anxieties over emancipation. Bird considers the threat of Black power and the loss of White freedom in his personal notes, concerned over rises in the Black demographic.[57] Although supportive of abolition in theory, calling slavery 'a moral cancer . . . eating its way into the vitals of this otherwise healthful country', in a letter to his brother Bird asks what should be done with a free Black population. Contending 'there should be no negroes in the country' after emancipation, he formulates a plan for a domestic colony. Firmly segregationist, Bird argues that freed African Americans should be transported past the Rocky Mountains and governed by a White head of state, putting up geographical borders to replace the existing political barriers to Black suffrage. When the population are able 'to take care of themselves' in a few generations, America should grant this colony independence and set a 'treaty of eternal amity'. Concluding the letter, Bird wonders if it 'would be easier or more effectual . . . to murder 'em all', revealing the extent to which he saw Black social mobility jeopardising the freedom, prosperity and even convenience of the White population.[58]

Threats of racial violence are in partnership with anxieties that White citizens could lose their social position and freedom at the hands of both White and Black Americans. Sheppard's movement into Tom is not the first time in the text that a White man is transformed into and treated as a less-than-White figure, more so than domestic workers' association with Black servants. Acts of physical blackening mark Longstraw's exclusion from the community for his paternalism. A group of youths he scolds pelt him with mud, and two wrestlers whose paid fight he interrupts tar-and-feather him (pp. 279, 283). Later, slave-catchers kidnap and transport him down to Virginia, mistaking him for 'a roaring lion of abolition', in an episode that mirrors anti-abolitionist violence against Garrison in October 1835. In taking the place of the missing slave, Longstraw is subsequently blackened and receives the same treatment as the runaway: bondage and execution. Furthermore, in a reversal of racial hierarchy, the enslaved men who will later rebel against their masters set up a lynching for the 'cussed bobolitionist', propelling Sheppard/Longstraw towards the body of Tom, where this chapter began (pp. 314, 325).

Bird returns to these fears of White subjugation in *The Adventures of Robin Day* (1839). Like *Sheppard Lee*, *Robin Day* follows a downwardly mobile young man who navigates turbulent social conditions, this time during the War of 1812. Robin's journey too is a liminal one, as he transitions between several social positions during his adolescence and young adulthood. Moving through Philadelphia, Southern plantations, the frontier, the Gulf Coast and Cuba, Robin repeatedly appears in several guises across profession, class and race. He transforms through a picaresque series of accidents and incidents, inhabiting different social statuses through masquerade and misrecognition, and like Sheppard, takes on several names: Sammy September, Robin Rusty, Robin Day, Sy Tough, Chowder Chow. Robin transitions between indentured child servant, young middle-class gentleman, rebellious schoolboy, accidental burglar, soldier (for both British and American armies) and pirate. The fear of White unmaking and degradation is palpable throughout the text. On the Philadelphian streets, 'almost a citizen' Robin, a fugitive for taking part in a violent school rebellion, is knocked about by free Black porters who shout at him, 'Git out of *my* way, will you?'[59] Angered by the arrogance of the true aristocracy of the town, Robin is equally astounded by the 'general submissiveness' of genteel White citizens who meekly acquiesce to the porters' yells, and aghast that if he retaliated he would be 'immediately taken up and carried before a magistrate; by whom I would be heavily fined for the liberty I had taken'.[60] Integrated society threatens to invert racial hierarchies, leading to White deference for Black tyrants, the feared outcome of emancipation that Bird outlines in *Sheppard Lee*.

Finally returning to his body after one last transformation, Sheppard finds his financial situation greatly improved. His brother-in-law has managed the estate, while his former corrupt overseer has died and left Sheppard a generous inheritance. Sheppard's eighteen-month journey, whether supernatural or hallucinatory, enables his disengagement from the real economic and civic demands of citizenship that his brother-in-law has taken up on his behalf. By his return, his dreams of contentment have been realised neither by the fantastical nor by the market economy, but by the traditional paths of inheritance and land management. In this neat conclusion, Sheppard does not grapple with the ramifications of the disastrous and bloody slave revolt, in which he remembers participating, nor does he revisit the broader politics of abolition and enfranchisement considering his cross-racial transformation. Instead, liminality is temporary; one moves forward into a new self just as the blackface performer easily washes off the burnt cork and returns to their free White self.

Victor Turner views the liminal process as one of reflection, during which the liminal persona gains insightful knowledge from their transformational experience. He writes:

> knowledge or gnosis obtained in the liminal period is felt to change the inmost nature of the neophyte, impressing him, as a seal impresses wax, with the characteristics of his new state. It is not a mere acquisition of knowledge, but a change in being.[61]

Sheppard does not retain specific characteristics of each of his transformations, but combined, the bodies and memories of the six transformations act as emotional resource, which he draws on at the end of the novel to enable his personal and civic development. Sheppard's change in being manifests in becoming less concerned with money and position than before his supernatural journey. He learns from all his negative experiences of the past eighteen months that 'there is nothing peculiarly wretched in my lot, and that I can be happy or not, just as I may choose to make myself' (p. 416). Sheppard's message at the end of the novel when he returns to his body – 'to make the best of the lot to which Heaven has assigned me, and to sigh no longer with envy at the supposed superior advantages of others' – is an appreciation of a stable identity, a fixed social position and body, which acts against and limits Tom's aspirations of legal freedom and political rights (p. 415). Sheppard's earlier enjoyment of slavery challenged the civic ideals of property, industry and autonomy, but these tenets return once his fortunate social station has been re-established. The 'moral' of Sheppard's tale – 'My estate is small, and it may be that it will never increase. I am, however, content with it; and content is the secret of all enjoyment' – reinforces the idea of static social positions, of contentment with what one has (pp. 418, 424). However, this ultimately seems unrealistic in the world of the text, in which Sheppard's own journey is set amongst the potential for actual rapid, fluid and, in the case of Tom's attempt, violent social movement.

Bird's exercise in textual blackface, in particular his racially liminal narrative voice, is an audacious attempt to inhabit an alien experience across the heavily demarcated racial divide. However, like the cross-racial escapism of Jim Crow,

Sheppard's transmigration is ultimately transitory, an experiment that entertains, terrifies, challenges and comforts the White antebellum reader before returning to the safe confines of social conformity. A novel that radically suggests a merged racial interiority returns to both its social and physiological borders. Bird's racial experiment depends on Blackness as an emotional and creative resource yet contains its unruly Blackness to secure White prosperity and self-possession. If a White man can turn Black, social position and civic expectations become topsy-turvy, an almost unimaginable inversion of the racial hierarchy, which ultimately prevents meaningful affiliation across the antebellum colour-line.

As I discuss further in my next chapter, Sheppard's possession of dead bodies for his personal gain sits in an antebellum context of growing medical and scientific experimentation on the human body. Near the conclusion of Sheppard's body-hopping travels, Sheppard/Tom is executed for his failed slave rebellion. Unable to escape Tom's body before death, Sheppard/Tom is hung and buried, before a group of doctors exhume and examine him. 'Desirous to show their skill in anatomy', the medical students source Tom's cadaver and two other enslaved corpses for practice (p. 371). Lacking legal possession of their own bodies in life, and with no protection after death, the enslaved men are prime targets for medical bodysnatching, a practice that targeted the nation's noncitizens: African Americans, Native Americans, the itinerant and the institutionalised. In front of a dozen 'respectable gentlemen', the doctors attempt galvanic reanimation, resuscitating the corpses and enabling Sheppard to escape into another body before the dissection (p. 372). Later, Sheppard finds that his original body has been stolen and embalmed by German doctor Feuerteufel for the 'especial benefit of science and the world'. When confronted by his own exploited corpse, Sheppard is horrified that *his* body could be treated with such little dignity. His 'sorrow and affliction' compel him to reclaim his body, his estate and by extension, his property-in-himself (p. 406). In a novel in which bodies are acquired and discarded in pursuit of wealth and social ascendancy, the body of medical and scientific experiment that educated White men control and manipulate serves as a stark reminder of Sheppard's loss of self and the vulnerability of White, as well as Black, unprotected bodies after death. In the following chapter I examine how Edgar Allan Poe imagines medical experiments on dying and dead White men to explore and exorcise these fears of fragile White self-possession and autonomy.

## NOTES

1. Bird, *Sheppard Lee*, pp. 326–7. Further citations of this edition are given in parentheses in the main text.
2. Looby, 'Introduction', in Bird, *Sheppard Lee*, pp. xv–xliii (p. xxxvii).
3. Murison, 'Hypochondria and Racial Interiority in Robert Montgomery Bird's *Sheppard Lee*', p. 11. For more on the influence of Bird's medical and scientific

study on *Sheppard Lee* see DeRewal, 'The Resurrection and the Knife'; Rebhorn, 'Ontological Drift'; Altschuler, 'From Empathy to Epistemology'.

4. Doty, 'Satire, Minstrelsy, and Embodiment in Sheppard Lee', p. 153.

5. Ormond covers himself in 'the complexion and habiliments . . . of a negro' to enter a home as a chimney sweep; racial disguise enables him to gain access to private spaces as a socially invisible American. In *Zelica*, a group of White women escape Haitian Revolution violence by painting their skin with tar to disappear into the crowds. In *The Confidence-Man*, steamboat passengers encounter a 'grotesque negro cripple', one of the eponymous figure's many characters. The crowd's debate over whether he is really disabled ignores that the exaggerated Blackness is a performance itself drawn from blackface stereotypes. Brockden Brown, *Ormond, Or the Secret Witness*, ed. Chapman, p. 154; Sansay, *Zelica, the Creole*, vol. 3, p. 232; Melville, *The Confidence-Man: His Masquerade*, ed. Tanner, p. 10.

6. Lott, *Love and Theft*, p. 130.

7. Doty, 'Satire, Minstrelsy, and Embodiment in Sheppard Lee', p. 153.

8. Jones Jr, *The Captive Stage*, p. 51.

9. Bird's notebooks demonstrate that he was interested in creating a set of types, not specific individuals. He lists potential characters by profession alone – 'the genteel forger' and 'the physician' – and others by religious or political views – 'a bigoted Christian' and a 'legislator from Maine' – rather than providing individual names. Bird, notes for *Sheppard Lee*, c. 1836 [Robert Montgomery Bird Papers, Kislak Center for Special Collections, Rare Books and Manuscripts, University of Pennsylvania: Folder 259]. This collection is hereafter cited as *RMBP*. Listed in Looby, 'Introduction', pp. xxvi–xxvii.

10. Turner, *The Forest of Symbols*, p. 93.

11. Bird, journal entry on *The Gladiator*, 29 August 1831 [*RMBP*: Folder 182]; Reed, *Rogue Performances*, p. 162.

12. Bird, journal entry on *The Gladiator*, 26 October 1831 [*RMBP*: Folder 182].

13. Forrest played the eponymous Wampanoag king in John Stone's *Metamora* (1829) as racially ambiguous, 'redding up' with burnt umber and speaking with a muscular and raw eloquence. Hageman, *Hageman's Make-Up Book*, 1898, p. 6, quoted in Rebhorn, *Pioneer Performances*, p. 24. Literally and metaphorically whitening Othello, Forrest portrayed him as a noble Near Eastern figure, 'adjusting his color to a light tawny or a "pale cinnamon" brown'. Collins, 'White-Washing the Black-a-Moor', p. 90.

14. Clipping of review of *The Gladiator*, *New York Standard*, 29 September 1831 [*RMBP*: Folder 199].

15. Bird, *Nick of the Woods or The Jibbenainosay, A Tale of Kentucky*, ed. Dahl, pp. 65, 66, 127.

16. Ibid. p. 342.

17. Ibid. pp. 226, 34.

18. Medina, *Nick of the Woods*, p. 3.

19. Yankee comedies accounted for four of the ten most performed 'legitimate blackface' productions before 1844, in which White performers appeared in place of African American actors. Cockrell, *Demons of Disorder*, pp. 15–16.

20. Woodworth, *The Forest Rose, Or, American Farmers*, p. 30; Bird, *The City Looking Glass*, ed. Quinn, p. 43.
21. W. T. Lhamon Jr provides a thorough biography of the performer's career in his introduction to Rice's works. Lhamon Jr, *Jump Jim Crow*, pp. 1–90.
22. Lott, *Love and Theft*, p. 6.
23. Rice, 'Jim Crow', *c.* 1837–40, in Lhamon Jr, *Jump Jim Crow*, pp. 131–6 (p. 131).
24. Cohen, *The Fabrication of American Literature*, p. 81.
25. Lhamon Jr, *Jump Jim Crow*, p. 35.
26. Rice, 'The Original Jim Crow', 1836, in Ibid. pp. 95–102 (p. 97).
27. Rice, *Virginia Mummy*, *Bone Squash Diavolo*, in Lhamon Jr, *Jump Jim Crow*, pp. 159–209.
28. Rice, 'The Original Jim Crow', pp. 98, 115.
29. Jones Jr, *The Captive Stage*, p. 51.
30. Ibid. pp. 66–7.
31. Playbill for the Bowery Theatre, New York, 1834, in Lhamon Jr, *Jump Jim Crow*, pp. 68–9.
32. Rice, 'The Original Jim Crow', p. 97; Dixon, 'Zip Coon', 1834, *The Library of Congress Music Copyright Database, 1820–1860*, <http://www.loc.gov/item/sm1834.360780> (accessed 9 November 2020).
33. Doty, 'Satire, Minstrelsy, and Embodiment in Sheppard Lee', p. 147.
34. Murison, 'Hypochondria and Racial Interiority in Robert Montgomery Bird's Sheppard Lee', p. 19.
35. Morton, *Crania Americana*, pp. 7, 87.
36. Otter, *Philadelphia Stories*, p. 103.
37. Ibid. p. 107.
38. Bakhtin, 'Discourse in the Novel', in *The Dialogic Imagination*, ed. Holquist, pp. 259–422 (p. 304).
39. Lamb, *The Things Things Say*, p. 230.
40. Additionally, as Siân Silyn Roberts identifies, the novel's opening line of Book I chapter 2 – 'I was born somewhere towards the close of the last century, – but the register-leaf having been torn from the family Bible, and no one remaining who can give me information on the point, I am not certain as to the exact year' – makes the same hazy yet legitimizing genealogical claim as slave narratives. Roberts, *Gothic Subjects*, p. 103; Bird, *Sheppard Lee*, p. 8.
41. Castiglia, *Interior States*, pp. 103, 124.
42. Cohen, *The Fabrication of American Literature*, p. 110.
43. Castiglia, *Interior States*, p. 125.
44. Sklansky, *The Soul's Economy*, p. 37.
45. Doty, 'Satire, Minstrelsy, and Embodiment in Sheppard Lee', p. 144.
46. Kennedy, *Swallow Barn*, vol. 2, p. 228.
47. Roediger, *The Wages of Whiteness*, pp. 65–74.
48. Bird, 'A Night on the Terrapin Rocks', in *Peter Pilgrim*, vol. 2, pp. 13–46 (p. 21).
49. Melville, *Moby Dick*, ed. Tanner, p. 4.
50. Roediger, *The Wages of Whiteness*, p. 66.

51. Trollope, *Domestic Manners of the Americans*, 1839, p. 45, quoted in Roediger, *The Wages of Whiteness*, p. 47. Roediger traces how Northern White workers started using 'helps', 'helpers' or 'hands' instead of 'servant', in order to distinguish themselves from African Americans. Roediger, *The Wages of Whiteness*, p. 49.

52. Bird, 'My Friends in the Madhouse', in *Peter Pilgrim*, vol. 1, pp. 99–177 (pp. 106, 107).

53. In addition, Bird would have been familiar with Edward Williams Clay's cartoon series *Life in Philadelphia*, which lampooned Black dandyism through caricatured appearance and speech. Clay, *Life in Philadelphia*, 1828–30, *Life in Philadelphia Collection*, Library Company of Philadelphia <https://digital.librarycompany.org/islandora/object/Islandora%3ALINP1> (accessed 9 November 2020).

54. Looby, 'Introduction', p. xxxvii.

55. Rice, 'De Original Jim Crow', *c.* 1844, reprinted in Lhamon Jr, *Jump Jim Crow*, pp. 129–31 (p. 131).

56. In addition to Turner, Bird loosely based Governor on enslaved Georgian man Essex, whose story Bird briefly records in a journal entry while visiting Savannah. The escaped Essex 'killed every body (white or black)' and assaulted young women. Leading the slave insurrection, Governor threatens sexual violence and pursues the master's daughters to their deaths. Reinforcing a binary of chaste White women and hypersexual Black men, Sheppard/Tom is struck dumb with horror at the thought of brutal murderers targeting 'innocent, helpless maidens'. Bird, journal entry, 20 April 1833 [*RMBP*: Folder 330]; Bird, *Sheppard Lee*, p. 362.

57. In one such note, Bird calculates the growth of Black and White populations, exclaiming that by 1900, the Black population could number at least '10 of 66 millions!!' Bird, unpublished notes on slavery, *c.* 1840 [*RMBP*: Folder 305].

58. Robert Montgomery Bird to Henry D. Bird, n.d. [*RMBP*: Folder 296]. In another segregationist letter to a friend, an anxious Bird declares that the possibility of Black suffrage in Pennsylvania 'sharpens my desire to be off'. Bird to John C. Groome, 20 January 1837 [*RMBP*: Folder 62].

59. Bird, *The Adventures of Robin Day*, vol. 1, pp. 120, 123.

60. Ibid. pp. 124–5.

61. Turner, *The Forest of Symbols*, p. 102.

# 4

# 'I SAY TO YOU THAT I AM DEAD!': EDGAR ALLAN POE'S PROTESTING CADAVERS

Bricked up in walls, hidden under floorboards or left in unmarked graves, Edgar Allan Poe's dead and dying White bodies suffer continual violation and exploitation. Poe's fascination with inappropriate burial and exhumation reflects pressing early US fears of bodysnatching, a trade in dead bodies to supply medical schools that targeted the corpses of the nation's noncitizens: African Americans, Native Americans, the institutionalised and the itinerant. In this chapter I contend that Poe's tales of human science experiments, framed in the context of medical graverobbing and exploitation, examine marginal states of being that are constructed as beneath the status of full citizenship. Routinely subjecting his White protagonists to near-death or fatal experiences, Poe asks what it means for citizens to lose their self-possession and autonomy and instead become the property of others.

In this chapter I turn to two of Poe's texts that feature medical experiment and dissection, 'Loss of Breath' (1835) and 'The Facts in the Case of M. Valdemar' (1845). In these short stories, dead or dying bodies are subject to the control of the doctor or medical researcher, who threatens or negates their autonomy. The body of medical experiment serves as a stark reminder of the loss of self-ownership and the vulnerability of unprotected bodies after death. Mr Lackofbreath and Ernest Valdemar are liminal figures because they simultaneously appear as both living and dead. Lackofbreath, who inexplicably and suddenly loses his respiration and voice, appears as a dead body and is treated as such because he cannot speak. However, he is a living, conscious man who attempts to escape terrifying yet humorous scenarios when travelling through dissection room, gallows and tomb. Valdemar, a dying man suspended in a mesmeric state, impossibly proclaims his own death after doctors declare him dead, and therefore shows signs of conscious life whilst his body decays. As bodies used for medical education, they share the same fate as the socially dead and marginal groups medical schools usually acquired for dissection and experiment. The two men's proximity to death and states of powerlessness renders them less than White. Under the doctor's gaze, White male citizens are reduced to parts; their bodies are the means to the end of medical discovery. In a context of debates over human dissection in the 1830s and 1840s, Poe's medical experiments reveal anxieties that a White male citizen could be exploited, lose possession of his body and become subject to the volition of another professional White male.

Poe's stories of human experimentation discover the limits of personhood when White male citizens are imperilled. Personhood – the experience of individual autonomy and self-determination – depends on the conscious ability to recognise a 'sense of self' that can make choices and determine actions.[1] Although this is a universal ideal, in the early US only able-bodied White men were afforded the full rights of citizenship – physical, legal and economic freedoms – that allowed them to fully actualise the concept of personhood. In contrast, the enslaved represented the complete absence of autonomy and self-ownership. For Colin Dayan, this 'negative' or erased personhood experienced by the enslaved occurs when 'living, willful, sentient, believing persons' are treated as and transformed into 'inanimate, rightless objects'.[2] She extends this condition of social or civic death to the prisoner, confined and dehumanised by their jailer, and the cadaver, discarded or exploited by the living. In her earlier work on Poe, Dayan asks that critics attend to Poe's characters who inhabit the 'margins of civilisation', where rights and privileges are 'compromised or threatened' – in other words, scenarios in which White characters experience the limits of personhood and become less than White.[3]

Dayan's work enables us to move beyond the redundant scholarly question of a 'racist or nonracist Poe', which Poe studies has previously pursued, to more complex and nuanced issues of racial, civic and legal identity in the antebellum period.[4] This racist/nonracist enquiry borders discussions of the past three decades that often take a binary reading of Poe's Black characters and symbols against White figures. For Toni Morrison in *Playing in the Dark*, 'no early American writer is more important to the concept of African Americanism than Poe'. In situating 'images of impenetrable whiteness' against Africanist presences, she asserts, Poe's work demonstrates that White American writers depend on Blackness simultaneously to threaten and strengthen White character, and to shape national literature.[5] An edited collection entitled *Romancing the Shadow: Poe and Race* (2001), indebted to

Morrison, has furthered her work, discussing how Poe expressed anxieties surrounding White fragility and Black violence through literary form and style. In these readings, black figures – whether enslaved men, Indigenous populations or animals – represent the master–slave relationship and the fear of African American revolt in Poe's tales.[6] As Teresa Goddu notes, however, the danger in taking too literally Morrison's call to pursue a 'singular hunt' for racial figures and non-white signifiers has 'constrained Poe studies', producing scholarship too reliant on Poe's use of symbolism instead of recognising 'the nexus of multiple cultural discourses' that Poe's writing occupies.[7] Although critics pay considerable attention to non-White characters as figures of otherness, they attend less to Poe's White male characters as racial figures themselves, in particular in regards to the formation of the citizen and their personhood.

Recent Poe criticism has returned to Dayan's discussions of personhood. Animal studies works read Poe's texts as limning the threshold of what it means to be a person, a concept delineated along racial lines.[8] Concurrently, scholarship on Poe's prisons and asylums reads them as spaces of exclusion and marginalisation in which White characters transform into less-than-White noncitizens.[9] In 'Loss of Breath' and 'Valdemar', croaks, breathlessness, death rattles and voices that cannot be explained operate outside White public spheres and at the limits of the rational and even the human. This chapter builds on works on Poe's carceral imagination, to focus on medical exploitation as another context that Poe uses to discuss the limits of personhood where men have their ability and autonomy removed. For Rosemarie Garland-Thompson, disability signifies a body subjected to external forces: 'property badly managed, a fortress inadequately defended, a self helplessly violated'. Garland-Thompson's discourse of ownership and estate acknowledges the loss of property-in-oneself the disabled person represents.[10] Poe's dying White men are physically damaged and vulnerable selves shaped by external forces; the scientific professional's manipulation negates their self-possession and self-determination. Employing antebellum medical science as a frame enables us to read Poe's anxieties of fragile citizenship when White male characters lose their abilities, faculties and vitality, and therefore their social rights. When dying White characters become 'slave-like, alarmingly *less white*' or liminally White, they do not operate as symbolic stand-ins for enslaved people, but rather dramatically mark through the decaying body the possibility that White men could lose their Whiteness.[11]

Lackofbreath and Valdemar communicate liminal Whiteness by resisting or protesting the exploitation they experience as dying or dead medical subjects. In searching for their speech or inexplicably talking from beyond the grave, the two men articulate the frightening possibility that anyone, including educated and respectable White men, can encounter the bodysnatcher's shovel or medical student's scalpel. Starting with 'Loss of Breath', I argue that the breathless

Lackofbreath becomes socially dead at the same time as he loses his voice and is mistaken for being physically dead. Throughout the text, Lackofbreath seeks to regain his lost breath, voice and social status by performing White male citizenship in his overly wrought, educated narrative voice, and finally verbally duelling another White man to assert his own self-generating White masculinity. In the second part of the chapter I discuss Valdemar's inexplicable protestations during his mesmeric trance, an analogue for medical dissection and experiment. Speaking of his entrapment and suffering, Valdemar undermines the expectation of a self-possessed antebellum citizen while simultaneously protesting the exploitation he experiences as a dying-then-dead medical subject and seeking to restate his autonomy. The narrator's confounded responses to the misbehaving body mark a failure of rational manhood to assert a civic identity, bolstered by the observation and classification central to medical and scientific phenomena. In these fantastical stories, Poe therefore employs medical experiment to offer a pessimistic and unresolved view of a precarious White male citizenship, one in which an idealised autonomous self is not assured and can be negated by the will of another.

### Antebellum Medicine and the Racial Politics of Graverobbing

In his work, Poe continually blurs the boundary between life and death, asking the reader at what point death truly occurs if the seemingly dead still have coherent voices. In doing so, he charts a growing interest in post-mortem experiment in antebellum medical science. From the late eighteenth century, a drive towards professionalisation in American medicine increased the desire for and procurement of cadavers. By the antebellum period, the doctor had become a figurehead of middle-class masculinity who observed, manipulated and managed the bodies of others. To establish autonomy and power, this group tied itself to discourse of 'scientific, civic management' of the natural world and the human body.[12] As a result of Jacksonian public distrust of educated professionals and elitist qualifications, middle-class doctors feared that medicine could become a classless field, diluted by untrained physicians, quackery and alternative treatments such as homeopathy.[13] In order to distinguish medicine, particularly surgery, as a science rather than a trade, the body – living or dead – became a site of knowledge that could be studied in detail. 'The exemplary methodology of medical science', dissection programmes encouraged professionalism by offering medical students tactile knowledge of human anatomy and providing surgeons with bodies for practice.[14] Students and staff expected schools to provide cadavers for dissection and often criticised shortages in the pages of medical journals. For example, in an 1840 essay, Dr Andrew Boardman of Geneva College, Pennsylvania complained, 'Not *a single subject* was provided for dissection during the *whole session*' of an anatomy course, although students had paid $40 each to secure bodies.[15] In an inaugural lecture to Pennsylvania College medical students, Bird bemoaned the fact that public distaste for dissection and a lack of legislation meant that the anatomist was 'in almost constant fear of the *penitentiary*' for relying on illegal graverobbing to satisfy demand.[16]

To avoid prosecution, graverobbers and medical students (who were sometimes the same people) targeted the poor, the homeless, the institutionalised, itinerant workers, sailors, African Americans, Native Americans and recent immigrants. Ironically, disposable bodies that seemed to be accorded very little importance or respect when alive became incredibly valuable for the medical profession and those who supplied the trade. The practice was public enough in some cities that Harriet Martineau observed in 1838: 'In Baltimore the bodies of coloured people exclusively are taken for dissection "because the whites do not like it, and the coloured people cannot resist".'[17] This illicit trade in bodies was so well known in Baltimore – with reports of disturbed graves and stolen body parts appearing in city newspapers – that Poe channels stories of the city's resourceful dentists into 'Berenice' (1835), in which the obsessive narrator disturbs Berenice's premature grave to extract all her teeth. Beyond city limits, states trafficked socially dead cadavers to provide for medical schools across the nation, including transporting bodies from Northern cities into the South.[18] In the South, this exploitation extended to infirm enslaved people, sold to medical researchers and students as both objects of study to investigate if race affected susceptibility and recovery, and as resources for later dissection. In William Wells Brown's *Clotel; Or, the President's Daughter* (1853), Northerner Carlton asks his Southern host Peck to explain an advert in the *Free Trader* that offers cash for 'negroes affected with scrofula or king's evil, confirmed hypochondriacism, apoplexy, or diseases of the brain, kidneys, spleen, stomach and intestines, bladder and its appendages, diarrhœa, dysentery'.[19] The purchaser boasts running a medical school that has enough cadavers for proper dissections carried on '*without offending any individuals in the community!*' Peck explains that the terminally ill enslaved are on hand at the medical school and when the trainees need to practise dissection, 'they bleed him to death . . . Oh, the doctors are licensed to commit murder, you know.'[20] As human property, the exploitation of enslaved people could be carried out in the open in service of White professionalisation.

The most publicised example of Black medical exploitation is the case of Joice Heth. She illuminates how White male authority continually looked upon the Black body as a site of knowledge. In 1835, P. T. Barnum purchased Heth, an elderly Black woman, and both claimed she was George Washington's 161-year-old 'mammy' at venues across New England. Newspaper reports described her elderly body as 'a mere skeleton covered with skin . . . her whole appearance very much resembles a mummy of the days of the Pharoahs [sic], taken entire from the catacombs of Egypt'.[21] Blind, emaciated and paralysed, but able to converse about her fictional life with the Washingtons, she existed as a talking corpse that

Barnum displayed as a supposed relic of colonial America. As a source of 'sensation among the lovers of the curious and the marvellous' she was also examined by 'the most learned and scientific men' in the country who sought to verify and explain her age.[22] Upon her death in 1836, she was publicly autopsied by Dr David Rogers in Manhattan's City Saloon to 1,500 paying spectators. The report later reached an audience of several thousand through Northern newspapers. The autopsy proved Barnum a liar – Heth 'could not have been more than *seventy-five*, or, at the utmost, *eighty years of age!*' As well as debunking Barnum, the newspapers justified the autopsy and its publication in the service of scientific knowledge because 'the investigation, conducted by a competent hand would doubtless form an instructive and valuable record in anatomical science on the nature of ageing', specifically in the consideration of how race affected ageing.[23] Scientific discovery was not only dependent on easy access to bodies, but centred on the Black body itself as an object of study.

Heth's body was paraded around while she lived, displayed publicly upon her death and further publicised through the print media's detailed descriptions of her corpse being opened up and inspected – details that I will not reprint here. One member of the public commented 'She is the common property of our country' because of her proximity to Washington and Revolutionary history – but more than a public figure of national history, this comment conveys Heth's legal and social position as an enslaved Black woman within a White male knowledge economy.[24] The little agency she had in collaborating on a fake life story was lost when others decided what should happen upon her death. Heth's corpse became a resource for professional men to stake their claim on medical science; in the City Saloon and across the pages of New York newspapers, each scientist and editor 'pick[ed] apart the body to enhance his cultural prestige'.[25] Their respected public spoken and written voices depended on Heth's final silence; they inscribed their racialised medical theories onto her dying then dead body. For Garland-Thompson, Heth is the first American freak, 'the direct antithesis of the able-bodied, white male figure upon which the developing notion of the American normate was predicated'.[26] The White middle-class 'normate' male, such as the doctor, established their own autonomy, self-making and authority on Black and other marginalised cadavers, bodies that the state already denied selfhood to while alive.

In the face of these racialised hierarchies of medical science, a body of literature in the mid-century expresses White anxiety that they could experience this loss of personhood through bodysnatching and dissection. These anxieties deflect onto the Black body in the case of Heth but reflect back onto White bodies in speculative and sensation fiction. Lippard's *The Quaker City* (1845) and J. H. Robinson's *Marietta* (1846) both feature doctors and students reliant on stealing poor and vulnerable bodies of any race. In *The Quaker City*, Devil-Bug stalks Philadelphia to procure fresh cadavers for the mysterious doctor Ravoni, describing with glee 'the jolly business' of 'mash[ing] the coffin lid into small pieces with a blow o' the spade and drag[ging] the stiff corpse out from its restin' place'. In *Marietta*, doctors and graverobbers discuss the best vulnerable bodies to procure for experiment. Medical student Levator cannot bring himself to dissect a female cadaver and pays the bodysnatchers to return her to the grave.[27] Broadly, these snatched bodies were unclaimed by friends or family, left unsecure in municipal spaces or housed by the state, who were considered acceptable for dissection. Ironically, society's dispensable became incredibly indispensable for the medical profession once deceased. In *Sheppard Lee*, Bird satirises the transformation of bodies into economic resources. When searching for a new corpse to inhabit, Sheppard posits that each dead body could be 'converted into five tons of excellent manures; the whole number would therefore produce just one hundred and fifty millions of tons . . . This, therefore, would be a highly profitable way of disposing of the mass of mankind.' Sheppard's scenario positions bodies as raw materials with great usefulness and value for the economic good of the nation.[28] Stolen bodies signal the terrifying possibility that a human being could have more value or worth in death – as educational property or resource – than in life.

In Poe's tales, White men find themselves alone and vulnerable, losing the value and respect they had while healthy and alive. The narrator in 'The Premature Burial' describes the horror of being buried 'as a dog – nailed up in some common coffin . . . some ordinary and nameless *grave*'. Poe emphasises 'grave' but the terror is compounded by 'common', 'ordinary' and 'nameless', which mean he has died among strangers and therefore lost the protection of his friends, and furthermore lost all individualising and humanising characteristics that distinguish him from others.[29] In 'Valdemar', the narrator celebrates the fact that Valdemar has 'no relatives in America who would be likely to interfere' with the experiment, or claim his corpse.[30] His dying and, later, dead body is the narrator's to do with as he pleases. Similarly, in 'Loss of Breath' an opportunistic publican finds the dead Lackofbreath without friends and sells his body to a local surgeon. For White citizens, as these stories imply, the dissection table carried great stigma because it meant they had died without friends or finances to protect their body after death. Furthermore, the intra- and interstate circulation of corpses had frightening resemblances to the slave trade, compounded by the fact that a large number of cadavers were African Americans who 'cannot resist'. To be dissected after death was to be treated in the same way as the noncitizen, thereby negating the rights the White citizen had acquired during life. In a context of debates over human dissection in the 1830s and 1840s, Poe's medical experiments articulate anxieties that a White male citizen could be exploited, lose possession of his body and become subject to volition by another professional White male. Under the doctor or researcher's gaze, White male citizens in

Poe's medical tales are reduced to parts; their bodies are the means to the end of medical discovery.

## Resuscitating White Manhood in 'Loss of Breath'

In 'Loss of Breath', Poe illustrates the unscrupulous desire for cadavers exceeding racial hiearchies with a dead White protagonist who survives dissection. Inexplicably losing his breath whilst shouting insults at his new wife the morning after their wedding, Lackofbreath sets out to regain his breath and falls prey to bodysnatchers and dissectors who believe him to be dead. Alongside 'How to Write a Blackwood Article' and 'A Predicament' (1839), 'Loss of Breath' – subtitled 'A Tale Neither in Nor out of Blackwood's' – clearly parodies the 'extravagancies' of popular sensation tales in *Blackwood's Edinburgh Magazine*.[31] Mr Blackwood in 'How to Write a Blackwood Article' advises aspiring author Zenobia, 'Should you ever be drowned or hung, be sure and make a note of your sensations' in order to create an authentic account, which she duly carries out when narrating her own beheading in 'A Predicament'.[32] Similarly, Lackofbreath comments on being hung that 'to write upon such a theme it is necessary to have been hanged. Every author should confine himself to matters of experience.'[33] Lackofbreath is able to record and narrate multiple fatal situations, exposing the crudeness and absurdity of the literary bodies commonly consumed by American readers in sensational tales and the strange and grotesque cases reprinted in medical journals such as the *American Medical Library and Intelligencer*.[34] Miraculously surviving being hit by a coach, disembowelled and disfigured by an anatomist, mistaken for a fleeing convict and hung from gallows, Lackofbreath perseveres as a revenant, lumbering from one dangerous scenario to the next. Recording their observation and sensations, Zenobia and Lackofbreath's consciousness during these impossible events satirises the medical community's adherence to empiricism and its dismissal of traditional religious or supernatural explanations.

However, although Poe wrote 'Loss of Breath' as satirical fantasy, literary style does not completely obfuscate the real anxieties over fragile White citizenship in the antebellum period. Poe employs the walking dead Lackofbreath to articulate the possibility of White male powerlessness. Lackofbreath captures his liminal state in an early realisation that he is 'alive, with the qualifications of the dead – dead, with the propensities of the living – an anomaly on the face of the earth' (p. 63). His qualifications of the dead are inextricably tied to his lost breath and voice, despite the fact that he remains a walking and thinking person who retains his mental faculties. It is not just being alive that ceases when Lackofbreath loses his voice, but a specific socially privileged life. In a society where the voice marks an autonomous self who can speak for himself and participate in a civic group, Lackofbreath is unable to voice his identity as a citizen and escape these scenarios of manipulation and exploitation. Simultaneously dead and alive, yet unable to speak, Lackofbreath transforms into one of America's routinely disenfranchised noncitizens.

When travelling in the stagecoach into the city, fellow passengers are angered 'that a dead man had been palmed upon them during the night for a living and responsible fellow-traveller' (p. 66). A dead man cannot pay his share of the fare; he cannot fulfil his civic role. If he has been put on the coach already dead, as the passengers assume, he cannot have any friends or family – nobody to speak for him – and so becomes an appropriate dead body to exploit. Beginning the dissection, a local physician 'discover[s] signs of animation', but goes on to remove 'several of my viscera for private dissection'. An apothecary enters, also believing Lackofbreath to be dead, and begins to perform galvanic experiments. When Lackofbreath attempts to show he is living, 'kicking and plunging with all my might and making the most furious contortions', and trying to converse, the apothecary assumes that the reactions are caused by the galvanic battery (p. 67). In this case, the new science intended to increase understanding of life and death in fact prevents the apothecary realising that Lackofbreath has survived breaking his neck, fracturing his skull and being disembowelled. Only the voice will suffice as evidence of life. His body taken to a garret after dissection, Lackofbreath is able to escape, yet a crowd mistakes him for a criminal fleeing execution. Again, unable to speak, Lackofbreath cannot prove his identity. He jokes, 'Of course nothing could be said in my defence' – not just legally, but physically (p. 69). Without the voice, Lackofbreath once again cannot defend himself from becoming another noncitizen, a convict.

Throughout the tale, Lackofbreath endeavours to recuperate his voice and regain his social position through a series of masculine performances that cement the link between the voice and White male citizenship. He attempts to reproduce the civic identity he has lost through different manifestations of White middle-class masculinity – physical prosthesis, oration and a highly educated narrative voice. First, he assumes that he can recapture his breath in tangible form, and searches for a vapory hidden in his closet or drawers. When searching for a supply of breath, he comes across 'a set of false teeth, two pairs of hips, an eye' (p. 64). Through these prostheses, Poe imagines the possibility that social position can be physically rebuilt. Poe returns to this idea in 'The Man That Was Used Up' (1839), in which the severely injured General A. B. C. Smith – whose organic body has been almost completely destroyed by Indigenous violence – rebuilds his reputation as a decorated military leader through prosthetic eyes, teeth, wig, shoulders and limbs. Crucially, by inserting a 'singular looking' mechanical palate, he salvages his vocal 'rich melody and strength'.[35] The force of character that his voice relays can be emulated through this motorised supplement. Although General Smith asserts his reputation through the success of medical technology, he is physically reliant on a Black manservant, Pompey, to literally assemble his White manhood. In this dependency, Poe casts doubt on the idea of a self-generating White masculine power.

Unable to procure synthetic breath, Lackofbreath attempts to find a use for his bizarre breathlessness. Fortunately, he is not completely silenced.

> I discovered that had I, at that interesting crisis, dropped my voice to a singularly deep guttural, I might still have continued to her the communication of my sentiments; this pitch of voice (the guttural) depending, I find, not upon the current of the breath, but upon a certain spasmodic action of the muscles of the throat. (p. 63)

Lackofbreath's muscular production is akin to ventriloquism, a practice that – as discussed in Chapter 1 – had clear connotations of Native American culture. In producing these frog-like and sepulchral tones, Lackofbreath is able to perform the popular Indian drama *Metamora* (1829). He recollects, 'in the accentuation of this drama, or at least of such portion of it as is allotted to her hero, the tones of voice in which I found myself deficient were altogether unnecessary . . . the deep guttural was expected to reign monotonously throughout'. Lackofbreath matches vocal rendition with physicality, performing exaggerated gestures – 'the looking asquint – the showing my teeth – the working my knees – the shuffling my feet' – to successfully hide his breathlessness (p. 65). As discussed in my previous chapter, audiences celebrated Edwin Forrest's muscular and raw performance of the Wampanoag king, in which he created a racially ambiguous yet powerful stage masculinity. William Etter claims that Lackofbreath's acting discloses the 'the threat of skipping across racial boundaries from Anglo American to Native American', further marking Lackofbreath as an impaired antebellum body.[36] Although I agree with Etter, I would add that Lackofbreath's performance is also an attempt to affirm his status as an educated White male. Metamora's dialogue is not the actual voice of a Native American, but White playwright John Augustus Stone's artistic representation. Lackofbreath's recitation divests the play of its original tragic racial meaning, because he transplants Metamora's voice into everyday conversation, finding that 'any portion . . . would apply equally well to any particular subject' (p. 65). Recitation of dramatic passages and recalling cultural references were key markers of eloquent White citizenship. In this context, Native performance and speech therefore contributes to vocal White masculinity rather than detracting from it.

Poe's protagonist blends these discourses of the rough theatrical persona and the well-read gentleman. *Metamora* sits amongst an excess of intellectual and cultural references that Lackofbreath employs in his written narrative. He follows almost every event or thought with a classical, biblical or artistic allusion. For example, after his disembowelling he cites, 'But as the loss of his ears proved the means of elevating to the throne of Cyrus, the Magian or Mige-Gush of Persia, and as the cutting off his nose gave Zopyrus possession of Babylon, so the loss of a few ounces of my countenance proved the salvation of my body' (p. 68). These references simultaneously evince Lackofbreath's familiarity with the *Histories* of Herodotus whilst also ridiculing his self-elevation to a great historical personage. When Lackofbreath is hung, his thoughts rapidly span politics, law, philosophy, art and literature. He is ultimately overcome by these references: 'Then came like a flood, Coleridge, Kant, Fitche, and Pantheism – then like a deluge, the Academie, Pergola, La Scala, San Carlo, Paul, Albert, Noblet, Ronzi Vestris, Fanny Bias, and Taglioni' (p. 79). Throughout the tale, his written voice is a composite. Attempting to assert his intellectual persona and re-establish his autonomous civic identity, he can do so only through listing, referencing and ventriloquising the works and words of others.

Ultimately, Lackofbreath can only regain his voice by taking it from someone else, reasserting his masculine and social dominance. Executed and left in a tomb, he begins to break open caskets and becomes a graverobber himself, picking up and ventriloquising the bodies he finds. Fortunately, he meets his vocal counterpart – Mr Windenough – who has been cursed with too much breath and cannot stop talking. A former suitor to Mrs Lackofbreath, Windenough is desperate to expel his pent-up breath and launches into a long diatribe explaining his circumstances. His loquacious body is another one that does not meet antebellum expectations, and when he has an epileptic fit, he is mistaken for dead like Lackofbreath. Windenough's speech breaks down into contradictory exclamations and meaningless repetitions, 'horrible! – wonderful! – outrageous! – hideous! – incomprehensible! – et cetera – et cetera – et cetera – et cetera – '. This empty language parodies the ideal eloquent male citizen who converses in order to demonstrate that he has something valuable to say, a social expectation I will return to in my next chapter on Melville. Throughout his monologue, he instructs Lackofbreath to be silent, becoming increasingly agitated: 'no reply, I beg you – one person is enough to be speaking at a time . . . not a word I beseech you . . . hold your tongue I tell you' (pp. 73–4). Here, chatting becomes a vocal duel, with each man desperate to talk and silence the other – Windenough because he has to keep talking and Lackofbreath because he wants his faculties to return. Taking control of the dialogue with his sepulchral and croaky tones, Lackofbreath dominates Windenough, harshly castigating him for his choice of words: '"hold my tongue," to be sure! – pretty conversation indeed, to a gentleman with a single breath! – all this, too, when I have it in my power to relieve the calamity under which thou dost so justly suffer'. Wielding this remarkable reparative power, he provokes 'apology upon apology' from Windenough, who submits to Lackofbreath's plans to exchange breath (p. 74).

Lackofbreath dominates Windenough in a competition of who has suffered the most from their respiratory quirks. He directs the exchange of breath, entering into an agreement to create two balanced speaking bodies. The change of ending between two versions of the tale is key here. First published as

'A Decided Loss' in the *Saturday Courier* in November 1832, the original text ends with Lackofbreath facing dissection after being hung, waking up as the apothecary applies the galvanic battery. In contrast, the 1835 version ends with Lackofbreath recovering his voice through his own actions. He regenerates his breath, life and rights by engaging in exchange, an act of White male self-generation. The change of ending attempts to resolve Lackofbreath's prior unmaking by showing him actively regain his social status through a transaction he directs, which Poe frames in economic terms. Lackofbreath recalls, 'my acquaintance delivered me the respiration; for which (having carefully examined it) I gave him afterwards a receipt'. Lackofbreath refuses to supply full details of how this exchange physically occurs, admitting, 'I am aware that by many I shall be held to blame for speaking, in a manner so cursory, of a transaction so impalpable' (p. 74). We are asked to take him at his word for this seemingly impossible end to his fantastical journey. While containing the chaos, Poe leaves residual doubt that these scenarios of vulnerability and manipulation can ever be remedied; it is only through supernatural luck that Lackofbreath returns to full health – considering he has been disembowelled – and full citizenship. Poe's hyperbolic and picaresque style attempts to ridicule and exorcise fears of discorporation: is it likely that a respectable White man would end up in these situations, having to run from premature burial, medical exploitation and the gallows? Of course not. However, Lackofbreath's living death and his liminality, although comical, signals a precariousness in which social rights and privileges can be easily erased or challenged, resulting in the need for White men to reassert their autonomy to others. In Poe's later works, these fears become much harder to contain as Poe refuses to incorporate the liminal White figure back into society.

## Mesmerism and Manipulation in 'The Facts in the Case of M. Valdemar'

In 'The Facts in the Case of M. Valdemar', liminal Whiteness encapsulates a far more pessimistic view of fragile White male citizenship. A text centred on an inexplicable voice, Valdemar is often discussed in regard to Poe's approach to authorship and writing. Poe's mesmerism tales show him exploring how fiction – and writing as a whole – operates amongst new scientific developments. For example, Adam Frank reads animal magnetism as an analogy for the telegraph and contends that '[m]esmerism offered Poe a way to theorize what a medium for writing could be or do' during the emergence of electrical communication.[37] Yet much less attention has been given to the exploitative relationship between narrator P— and Valdemar, or to reading Valdemar as a figure of loss, exclusion and suffering. Within the context of medical science, the mesmerised body serves the same function as the dissected cadaver – Valdemar becomes a powerless less-than-White figure controlled by a professional White male. His proximity to death and states of powerlessness render him, I argue, less than White and less than a person.

'Valdemar' is a strange scientific story about an unnamed narrator inducing a mesmeric state in a dying man, with inexplicable results. Valdemar is another case in the narrator P—'s continuing interest in mesmerism, and it is established early on that this factual account is born of a desire to dispel unscientific and 'unpleasant misrepresentations' of what occurred (p. 1233). Perhaps it is printed in one of the medical journals Poe satirises in 'Loss of Breath'. Although it is unclear what, if any, scientific or medical qualifications the narrator holds, from this opening he establishes himself as a member of the professional, rational, White middle class, who use scientific observation to bolster their claim on civic authority. When the narrator claims that 'there had been a very remarkable and most unaccountable omission: – no person had as yet been mesmerized *in articulo mortis*', he aspires to fill empirically this gap in contemporary studies on mesmerism (p. 1233). Mesmerism, or animal magnetism, originated in the work of German doctor Franz Mesmer (1734–1815). He theorised that magnetic fluid in the body could be controlled to heal illness and mental agitation, such as hysteria. French-Guadeloupean mesmerist Charles Poyen introduced the practice to the United States in the mid-1830s, delivering lectures and writing pieces for the *Boston Medical and Surgical Journal*.[38] By the time Poe's tale was written, mesmerism was increasingly used in America to treat illness and induce altered states of consciousness, including clairvoyance. Having read Charles Hare Townshend's comprehensive *Facts in Mesmerism* (1844) and Rev. Gibson Smith's *Lectures on Clairmativeness, or Human Magnetism* (1845), and attending lectures by prominent mesmerist Andrew Jackson Davis, Poe was well aware of mesmerism as scientific enquiry and medical practice.[39] In 'Mesmeric Revelation' (1844), the narrator employs mesmerism to induce altered states of mind and discover the limits of consciousness. His subject, the dying Vankirk, produces long clairvoyant statements on the nature of God and the soul when hypnotised. Similarly, in 'A Tale of the Ragged Mountains' (1844), the ailing Bedloe experiences past life regression when mesmerised.

Mesmerism became increasingly connected with manipulation of those receptive to the control of another, with clear race, gender and class implications. As Emily Ogden recently writes, 'part of animal magnetism's appeal was that it could bring enchantment over to the cause of management'.[40] Poyen's own interest in mesmerism to prevent slave rebellions on Guadeloupean sugar plantations transferred to an industrial setting when he moved to the East Coast – the susceptible subject widened from the enslaved man or woman to the White factory worker. On his speaking tours, Poyen attracted the attention of the Lowell Mill owners in Massachusetts, who sought to manage and train their mill girls. Ogden's example of a Lowell mill girl who became a more efficient machine operator after Poyen's mesmeric trances – Cynthia Gleason – shows the possibility of mesmerism as 'management strategy' to create pliable and productive workers. Working with Poyen, Gleason would go on to demonstrate clairvoyance to diagnose and treat illnesses when hypnotised.[41] Young White women were viewed as the most passive group, sharing with the enslaved both a weaker will and a 'primitive remnant' of the pre-Enlightenment – in other words, a receptiveness to take in the thoughts and experiences of others and a desire to believe in the seemingly ethereal power of magnetism.[42] For example, Nathaniel Hawthorne's *The House of the Seven Gables* (1851) exposes mesmerism as a threat to young women. Mesmeriser Holgrave is tempted by the exploitative possibilities of controlling and manipulating the passive Phoebe Pyncheon. Concentrating his glance on drowsy Phoebe, Holgrave is aware that with 'one wave of his hand and a corresponding effort of his will, he could complete his mastery over Phoebe's yet free and virgin spirit' and will her to 'live only in his thoughts and emotions'.[43] Holgrave is seduced by the opportunity to direct 'a young girl's destiny' and establish his own autonomy and self-mastery by 'acquiring empire over the human spirit' of another. In this clearly sexualised encounter, Hawthorne positions mesmerism as a threat against autonomy and an abuse of existing social dominance.[44]

Mesmerism worked as a tool of social delineation, marking out and dominating White women and the enslaved. In *The Scarlet Letter* (1850), Hawthorne infuses his depiction of the relationship between Roger Chillingworth and Arthur Dimmesdale with the language of mesmerism to suggest that incapacitated men were also susceptible to influence. After uncovering Dimmesdale's self-inflicted scar by 'thrust[ing] aside' the sleeping man's shirt, physician Chillingworth decides to 'play upon him as he chose'.[45] Weakened by his guilt, which has manifested as nervous temperament, Dimmesdale is vulnerable to manipulation, not through tactile passes but emotional trickery. He is a man 'forever on the rack; it needed only to know the spring that controlled the engine' – Dimmesdale is both the victim and the instrument of his own torture as Chillingworth plays with his emotions, 'arous[ing] him with a throb of agony' and 'startl[ing] him with sudden fear' until his guilt overwhelms him and he imagines 'a thousand phantoms, – in many shapes, of death, or more awful shame, all flocking round about the clergyman, and pointing with their fingers at his breast!'[46]

As a physician 'extensively acquainted with the medical science of the day', Chillingworth is in a position of trust and authority over Dimmesdale the patient.[47] Mesmeric experiment, which depends on the submission of the mesmeric body to the magnetiser's control, mirrors the hierarchical medical relationship as a patient submits to the physician's instructions or manipulations, or as a dissector completely controls a cadaver. In the 1840s, physicians were wary that unqualified practitioners would dilute the class status of professional medicine, but they themselves were increasingly interested in experiments that utilised the body's magnetism. For example, physician Henry Hall Sherwood routinely dismissed Andrew Jackson Davis's medical claims regarding animal magnetism as quackery, but nonetheless developed his own treatments applying 'rotary magnetic' machines to the body.[48] In 'A Tale of the Ragged Mountains', wealthy young man Bedloe pays Doctor Templeton 'a liberal annual allowance . . . to devote his time and medical experience exclusively to the care of the invalid', including mesmeric treatment for his neuralgia.[49] Although the narrator of 'Valdemar' is not a physician himself, he has the full co-operation of Valdemar's doctors; he claims that D— and F— 'opposed no objection' to his experiment. On the contrary, they encourage his mesmerism. Their curiosity is 'greatly excited' and by the latter stages of the experiment, they are in collaboration with the narrator, deciding how to continue (p. 1238).

In these tales, the patient or subject is under complete control of medical figures. Both Bedloe and Valdemar – incapacitated and 'markedly nervous' – are suitable candidates for mesmerism, already placing them alongside receptive White women and enslaved people ('Valdemar', p. 1234). Bedloe's will 'succumbed rapidly to that of the physician . . . sleep was brought about almost instantaneously by the mere volition of the operator'.[50] His will is so receptive that he takes on the past life experience of Templeton's friend Oldeb, recounting the incident of Oldeb's death in an Indian city. Dying in his trance, overwhelmed by a rabble of 'black and yellow men', Bedloe's autonomy is further erased by a deadly poisonous leech that Templeton mistakenly applies.[51] Likewise, Valdemar's body, initially resistant to the narrator's passes, becomes more receptive the closer he is to death, and P— recalls, 'his arm very readily, although feebly, followed every direction I assigned it with mine' ('Valdemar', p. 1238). However, unlike post-mortem exploitation, the men in these tales consent to the experiments performed on them. Integrating himself with the scientific community around him, Valdemar consents to the experiment, stating 'feebly, yet quite audibly, "Yes, I wish to be mesmerized"'. When discussed with P— his interest in the experiment is 'vividly excited'; although previously dismissive of earlier experiments, at the beginning of the tale he shares with the narrator a pursuit of scientific knowledge (pp. 1236, 1234). White male professional pursuit of scientific knowledge depends on controlling and examining the bodies of others: Bedloe and Valdemar are willing participants in an endeavour that results in their own deaths and torture.

Valdemar's position is liminal in the text, shifting from a participant in the experiment to an exploited subject. It is worth paying attention to how Valdemar's Whiteness is delineated in the tale, which compounds his liminality. Valdemar is a recent Polish immigrant but is part of an intellectual community. He is referred to as 'the well-known compiler of the Bibliotheca Forensica, and author (under the *nom de plume* of Issachar Marx) of the Polish versions of Wallenstein and Gargantua', texts originally written in German and French (p. 1234). From this description, the reader can infer he is Jewish, or at least takes on a Jewish pseudonym. Living in Harlem since 1839, bachelor Valdemar has no family or friends to claim his corpse – his dying body is the narrator's to do with as he pleases. Yet, although his ethnic identity places him on the periphery of Whiteness, his authorship and translation work incorporates him into a professional male sphere inhabited by the narrator and his doctors. Through his scholarly pursuits, Valdemar 'becom[es] Caucasian'.[52] In contrast to the perception of African Americans, Valdemar's ethnicity denotes the capacity for autonomy and self-possession, making him White enough to be considered a potential citizen: living in the United States for at least five years, Valdemar would qualify to apply for legal citizenship under the 1802 Naturalization Act.[53] It is this property-in-oneself that is negated through the mesmeric control and exploitation of his body.

Over the course of the story, Valdemar loses possession of his own body and is subsumed into the narrator's research agenda: the mesmeric body loses its autonomy and becomes just as pliable as the cadaver. From the outset the narrator views Valdemar as a dead body – for his '*in articulo mortis*' experiment to succeed, a terminally ill subject is necessary. Approaching death, Valdemar is so thoroughly diseased that he blurs the boundary between a body and a corpse: we could be reading an autopsy. When the narrator sees his friend on the night before his experiment, he describes the dying Valdemar in dense medical detail. The text imitates a pathologist cutting through the body, as the gaze pierces the skin and we read that parts of Valdemar's lungs are in a 'semi-osseous or cartilaginous state' and 'entirely useless for all purposes of vitality', and there are places in which 'permanent adhesion [of the lung] to the ribs had taken place'. The deterioration of his body takes place with 'very unusual rapidity . . . the adhesion had only been observed during the three previous days'. He is decaying in front of the doctors' eyes: his cheekbones break through his skin and his pulse is 'barely perceptible' (p. 1235). Valdemar is subject to not only a medical experiment, but also a kind of living dissection. He is so corpselike that his body functions the same way as a cadaver in medical science: it is there to educate. The emotion that P— may feel in seeing his dying friend is completely absent, replaced by this objective medical surveillance, what Michel Foucault calls the 'medical gaze'.[54] Medical student Mr L—l's presence evinces the pedagogical nature of the experiment. His role is not only as a reliable witness, but also as a note-taker, aiding his own education as well as providing the narrator with a record of events. The body of medical experiment, living or dead, is a source of knowledge that only men of science can comprehend and catalogue.

As the narrator and medical professionals continually survey Valdemar, Poe replicates this process through dense descriptive passages dwelling on the mesmerism's effect. Towards the end of the tale, P— states, 'From this period until the close of last week – *an interval of nearly seven months* – we continued to make daily calls at M. Valdemar's house, accompanied, now and then, by medical and other friends' (p. 1241). Valdemar's peculiar state renders him an entertaining curiosity. Knowing that Valdemar is fixed in a state of dying, the doctors accompanying P— are absolved of their healing responsibility and turn their attention to satisfying professional curiosity about the bodily effects of mesmerism. When he is suspended and observed in this liminal state for several months, he transforms into one of the many marginalised bodies laid open and experimented on in the antebellum period. It is particularly note-worthy that, as he approaches death, Valdemar himself becomes blacker, an effect of his body's decay and disease. He takes on a 'leaden hue', his eyes are 'utterly lustreless' and the ossification turns his internal organs black and putrid (p. 1235). In his proximity to death *and* Blackness, Valdemar is treated by the White, rational community purely as a medical specimen. The image of a group of educated White men surveying and manipulating a prone body is deeply uncomfortable. Anatomised and surveyed, Valdemar is dehumanised and reduced to a utility by and for a community of professional and ratio-nal White men. However, the tale is not a commentary on African American medical slavery, and I avoid a symptomatic reading that would suggest that his darkened body acts as a stand-in for systematically scientifically exploited African Americans. Instead, to read Valdemar's decaying and observed body in this context of publicly known racial exploitation is to recognise a terrify-ing fear for the White male 'normate' citizen – the loss of personal will, self-possession and autonomy. Unlike Joice Heth, Valdemar has the capacity to agree to the experiment, but through his inexplicable voice he withdraws this consent, and with increasingly aggravated speech he challenges the narrator's control and comprehension of his body as a medical specimen.

## An Inexplicable Voice and the Failure of White Rational Manhood

As Valdemar's pale body grows darker in appearance and stranger in action, the narrator's reactions to him notably shift away from the scientific, rational discourse of the text's opening. When the doctors and narrator see Valdemar's emerging blackened tongue, they are repulsed:

> the upper lip, at the same time, writhed itself away from the teeth, which it had previously covered completely; whilst the lower jaw fell with an audible jerk, leaving the mouth widely extended, and dis-closing in full view the swollen and blackened tongue . . . so hideous beyond conception was the appearance of M. Valdemar at this moment, that there was a general shrinking back from the region of the bed. (p. 1239)

At this point in the text, Valdemar begins substantially to unnerve the rational community surrounding him, with his decaying body so unusual (even for those accustomed to death) that it is beyond the narrator's cognitive capability to imagine even something that is so immediately present to his sense. The exposure of the tongue uncovers the universal truth of the body's vulnerability and decomposition after death. Like Valdemar's earlier living autopsy, in which his individuality is stripped away to render him just another cadaver, the extended tongue presents the material self that is vulnerable to manipulation and surveillance by other citizens. When Valdemar apparently begins to speak, and the tongue itself produces hideous utterances, the narrator's alarm increases. Detailed passages describe the voice emanating not from Valdemar's vocal organs, but his extended, vibrating black tongue and distended and motionless jaws:

> In the first place, the voice seemed to reach our ears – at least mine – from a vast distance, or from some deep cavern within the earth. In the second place, it impressed me (I fear, indeed, that it will be impossible to make myself comprehended) as gelatinous or glutinous matters impress the sense of touch. (p. 1240)

The cavernous timbre of Valdemar's voice again suggests a ventriloquial source that cannot be mapped onto the human body and defies the medical community's rational logic. This synaesthesia is the only way the narrator can communicate a sense of what he hears, but this does not provide an explanation of the voice's origin. Again, he struggles to find cognitive rational ability to process the circumstances or the appropriate lexicon to convey events. His medical gaze, which has previously penetrated Valdemar's diseased body, cannot successfully read or comprehend what is now in front of him. In this scene, the discourses of rational observation that bolster White male professional autonomy and authority start to falter.

The speaking blackened tongue is the first sign of Valdemar's body acting independently from the narrator's control and defying his rational approach, in order to voice and protest his liminal state. This rebellious organ lends itself to a symbolic reading of race, but I want to push against a potential reading that sees blackened tongues as a representation of African American voice or violence. Valdemar is a conglomerate of racial signs in the text: his likely Jewishness, 'the whiteness of his whiskers, in violent contrast to the blackness of his hair', his skin shifting from pallid to leaden (p. 1234). This mix of features expresses the potential for liminality and White degeneration I have tracked in this chapter, rather than the introduction of a Black presence. The vibrating blackened tongue itself is reminiscent of ululation – a practice associated with African music – but Valdemar himself does not ululate. The sounds are not open-throated cries produced by the tongue moving back and forth, but, as the narrator takes pains to explain, very clear 'syllabification' (p. 1240). It is this syllabification that marks out Valdemar as human and White – liminally so. Compared with the 'shrill' cries of the orangutan, which lack 'distinct or intelligible syllabification' in 'The Murders in the Rue Morgue' – first denoting a non-White speaker and eventually a non-human speaker – Valdemar's cries are distinguishable and legible as human language.[55] Valdemar's proclamation 'I *have been* sleeping – and now – now – I *am dead*' is beyond rational comprehension in both how it is produced and what it means, but this speech clearly verbalises human consciousness and desire for self-possession against an experiment that negates his personhood. Maintaining a clear – if illogical – voice that speaks of suffering compounds the horror of the text that a White man can become a marginalised, exploited body ('Valdemar', p. 1240).

Valdemar's voice expresses his position: trapped between life and death in a dysfunctional and diseased body; treated as an object, but with an active mind inside. It speaks of a desire to be free from its bondage; Valdemar orders the narrator to end his entrapment in the corpse-body, saying, 'Yes: – asleep now. Do not wake me! – let me die so!' (p. 1238). He wrestles against the limits of personhood that the medical experiment has set. Saying 'I am dead' is Valdemar's attempt at regaining self-determination and articulating his personhood by directing the experiment to its end. The tale portrays White male citizenship as a battle for autonomy from and dominance over other White men, not just non-male non-White figures. Valdemar attempts to recover his personhood by speaking against the narrator's manipulations, while the narrator seeks throughout to assert his power through an authoritative narrative, one that is dependent on his controlling and categorising Valdemar. Whereas Valdemar does articulate his personal torment, P—'s horror cannot be articulated. On hearing the inexplicable voice, the narrator experiences cognitive dissonance manifest in physical form. In other words, confronted by the seemingly impossible talking corpse, who is simultaneously alive and dead, P— cannot rationally comprehend what he encounters, and it provokes an uncontrollable physical response, his 'unutterable shuddering horror' (p. 1240). The detached medical gaze has been overtaken by this subjective visceral response that cannot be processed in the written form on which men of science staked their authority. Valdemar's unexpected and powerful voice breaks through the rational written form to communicate that a White man can no longer be a person, a terrifying realisation for the professional, educated community that the narrator represents.

'The Facts in the Case of M. Valdemar' is not Poe's only tale in which a highly unusual corpse defies a group of professional educated men. In 'Some Words with a Mummy' (1845), a group of Egyptologists reanimate with galvanic batteries the mummy Allamistakeo after thousands of years of entombment. The mummy begins to converse with an unexpected eloquence, shocking the scientists that a 'savage', non-White corpse could not only speak so well, but also profess his culture, science and society greater than theirs, 'gleefully pok[ing] holes in elite white male privilege'.[56] The humour of Allamistakeo's teasing and the White professionals' umbrage is absent in 'Valdemar', replaced with horror. Whereas Allamistakeo's resistant voice is well expressed in its criticism of the White scientific community, Valdemar's inexplicable speech becomes increasingly violent and less eloquent in its articulation. His inexplicable utterances grow in anger towards the end of 'Valdemar', and he shouts, 'For God's sake! – quick! – quick! – put me to sleep – or, quick! – waken me! – quick! – *I say to you that I am dead!*' (p. 1242). The exclamatory voice urges the narrator, who controls Valdemar's physical body, to give him his freedom in death. Valdemar's wishes – to be asleep or awake while being dead – are impossible scenarios and both result in his continued death. For the White educated male, non-existence – a waking or sleeping death – is preferable to an existence manipulated by others. As the experiment reaches its climax, it is clear that his previous autonomous state cannot be recuperated.

Just as the narrator and medical observers attempt to comprehend what they have heard and seen, Poe invites the reader to question if what they read can be possible. Poe continually pushes the limits of what the reader will accept as true. In both 'Loss of Breath' and 'Valdemar', Poe satirises audience expectations of death. Lackofbreath stages his own death on the gallows, bragging, 'My convulsions were said to be extraordinary. My spasms it would have been difficult to beat.' He gives the audience the convincing yet dramatic death they want to see, performing paroxysms that cause gentlemen to swoon and ladies to be 'carried home in hysterics', whilst at the same time he continues to live ('Loss of Breath', pp. 69, 70). In 'Valdemar', Poe exaggerates the grotesque dying body that readers had already enjoyed in previous tales. Although the narrator attempts to avoid sensational garbled and exaggerated accounts, he sets up the gruesome climax as something truly beyond rational comprehension, for which 'it is quite impossible that any human being could have been prepared'. The tale ends:

> As I rapidly made the mesmeric passes, amid ejaculations of 'dead! dead!' absolutely *bursting* from the tongue and not from the lips of the sufferer, his whole frame at once – within the space of a single minute, or even less, shrunk – crumbled – absolutely *rotted* away beneath my hands. Upon the bed, before that whole company, there lay a nearly liquid mass of loathsome – of detestable putridity. (p. 1243)

Here, the narrator continues to attempt descriptive observation, although events have long since departed from the expectations of a medical case study established at the beginning of the account. Valdemar's putrefied remains are, as Jacques Lacan contends, something for which no language has a name.[57] As descriptive terms overlap one another ('shrunk – crumbled – absolutely *rotted*'), the narrator – editing the quick notes of Mr L—l – attempts to portray the state of Valdemar's corpse using a rational observational vocabulary. Once again the rational voice of medical discourse experiences a lexical failure. The narrator's attempts to describe him using any kind of vocabulary, let alone an observational one, are insufficient. Valdemar's protestations are so extreme that they cause the body itself to rupture and disintegrate completely. The body's rapid and grotesque decomposition destroys any post-mortem knowledge the narrator and medical professionals might have hoped to garner, and the experiment is plunged into total chaos as a nearly liquid mass surrounds the onlookers. Whereas the diseased physique earlier served a pedagogical purpose in identifying Valdemar's illness, the liquid body, rotting beyond 'natural' rates of decomposition, prevents the medical gaze from observing, categorising and diagnosing. The body of evidence, in which the rational community invested so much, has perished. There is nothing constructive remaining: in fact, there is only total destruction. Unlike General A. B. C. Smith in 'The Man That was Used Up' – whose body is all but destroyed, but can be supplemented with prosthesis – Valdemar's body is completely obliterated. Whereas Smith's commanding voice is dependent on his mechanical palate and bodily reconstruction, Valdemar's body is contingent on his voice; it is the forceful power of his final utterances that obliterate his body.

This gruesome ending gives voice to fears of discorporation by destroying the White male citizen. Valdemar is an abject, out-of-control body leaking into the world, causing the reader to be both drawn towards him and repelled by his rotted form. Woven into this gore, which is both entertaining and revolting – and entertaining *because* it is revolting – are legitimate fears of exploitation and manipulation, which Poe deliberately chooses not to assuage. The ending provokes an almost physical reaction from the reader, just like the narrator's recoiling in the tale. However, although this body horror can be seen as a distraction in that it provokes a visceral response, instead of a contemplative one, the text's final image of male bodily destruction maps onto anxieties over the erasure of personhood. Valdemar is first reduced to a body, and then reduced to nothing. His attempts to regain self-possession and end the narrator's control come at the expense of his own survival. 'Valdemar' ends without resolution and Poe refuses to reinstate its original societal norms of White male rationality and autonomy. Once the voice erupts through the body, the body cannot be reconstructed and these horrifying exclamations cannot be unarticulated. In the tale's horrific climax, the anxieties about the loss of self-possession, which Valdemar represents, and failed professionalism, which P— represents, hang in the ether like Valdemar's final explosive utterances. After the gruesome ending has faded, the reader is therefore left with the anxiety that White manhood – ostensibly an autonomous and authoritative self, bolstered by rational pursuits – is vulnerable.

In his tales of medical exploitation, Poe discorporates his protagonists to show the limits of White male personhood, lost when self-possession is negated at the hands of fellow White male citizens. Poe depicts consciousness – represented through an enduring voice – as somehow present within a clinically dead body. In doing so, he voices anxieties over White men being reduced purely to bodies and material resources – just like the nation's noncitizens who routinely filled America's dissecting rooms – as opposed to fully autonomous and self-possessed citizens. Whilst in 'Loss of Breath' the voice and selfhood are regained through oral and written performances of masculine citizenship, in 'Valdemar' this loss of selfhood is not recuperated but instead violently protested and destructively uttered. Whereas Lackofbreath asserts his identity through an educated narrative voice, in 'Valdemar' education cannot help the narrator adequately comprehend the dysfunctional body he encounters. Inexplicable utterances defy the professional, middle-class male's empirical worldview and undermine rationality as a tenet of White citizenship. In my next chapter on Melville, I turn to White men drawn increasingly closer to the liminal White figure. Viewing their personal and civic identities through social relations, these men seek to care rather than exploit liminal White men and women to bolster their own autonomous masculinity.

## NOTES

1. Taylor, *Philosophical Papers*, vol. 1: *Human Agency and Language*, p. 97.
2. Dayan, *The Law Is a White Dog*, pp. xii, 33.
3. Dayan, 'Poe, Persons and Property', pp. 408, 405.
4. Ibid. p. 412.
5. Morrison, *Playing in the Dark*, pp. 32, 33.
6. These figures include the emancipated Jupiter in 'The Gold Bug' (1843); enslaved manservants both called Pompey in 'A Predicament' (1838) and 'The Man That Was Used Up' (1839); the Tsalal islanders in *The Narrative of Arthur Gordon Pym* (1838); the orang-utan in 'Murders in the Rue Morgue' (1841), and the eponymous feline in 'The Black Cat' (1843).
7. Goddu, 'Rethinking Race and Slavery in Poe Studies', p. 15.
8. See Boggs, *Animalia Americana*; Mastroianni, 'Hospitality and the Thresholds of the Human in Poe's *The Narrative of Arthur Gordon Pym*'; Peterson, *Bestial Traces*.
9. Erin Forbes tracks depictions of social death, namely incarceration and slavery, in Poe's tale of living death, 'The Premature Burial' (1844). Aaron Matthew Percich reads asylum tale 'The System of Doctor Tarr and Professor Fether' (1845) as a commentary on antebellum prejudice against less-than-White Irish immigrants.

See Forbes, 'From Prison Cell to Slave Ship'; Percich, 'Irish Mouths and English Tea-Pots'.

10. Garland-Thomson, *Extraordinary Bodies*, p. 45.
11. Coviello, *Intimacy in America*, p. 72.
12. Nelson, *National Manhood*, p. 103.
13. Richard Hofstadter summarised Jacksonian anti-intellectualism as a 'distrust of expertise', a 'desire to uproot the entrenched classes' and a doctrine asserting that 'important functions were simple enough to be performed by anyone'. Hofstadter, *Anti-Intellectualism in American Life*, pp. 155–6.
14. Sappol, *A Traffic of Dead Bodies*, p. 53.
15. Boardman, 'An Essay on the Means of Improving Medical Education and Elevating Medical Character', in Brieger (ed.), *Medical America in the Nineteenth Century*, pp. 24–36 (p. 26).
16. Bird, *The Difficulties of Medical Science*, p. 21. There were a number of public riots against medical dissection in New York, Massachusetts, Ohio and Vermont. See Sappol, *A Traffic of Dead Bodies*, p. 106.
17. Martineau, *Retrospects of Western Travel*, vol. 1, p. 231.
18. See Blakely and Harrington (eds), *Bones in the Basement*.
19. Brown, *Clotel; Or, the President's Daughter*, ed. Levine, p. 132. Brown took these details and the advert itself from the *Charleston Mercury*, 12 October 1838, quoted in Weld, *American Slavery As It Is*, p. 171.
20. Brown, *Clotel*, p. 133.
21. 'Longevity', *New York Baptist*, reprinted in *Springfield Gazette*, 16 September 1835, quoted in Reiss, *Showman and the Slave*, p. 2.
22. *The Life of Joice Heth*, pp. 10, 8 <http://docsouth.unc.edu/neh/heth/heth.html> (accessed 9 November 2020).
23. 'Dissection of Joice Heth – Precious Humbug Exposed', *New York Sun*, 26 February 1836, *The Lost Museum Archive*, <http://lostmuseum.cuny.edu/archive/dissection-of-joice-heth-precious-humbug> (accessed 9 November 2020); 'Death of Joice Heth', *New York Sun*, 24 February 1836, *The Lost Museum Archive*, <https://lostmuseum.cuny.edu/archive/death-of-joice-heth-new-york-sun-february-24> (accessed 9 November).
24. Cole, 'To the Editors of the Sun', *New York Sun*, 20 August 1835, *The Lost Museum Archive*, <https://lostmuseum.cuny.edu/archive/joice-heth-new-york-evening-star-and-new-york> (accessed 9 November 2020).
25. Reiss, *The Showman and the Slave*, p. 155.
26. Garland-Thomson, *Extraordinary Bodies*, p. 59.
27. Lippard, *The Quaker City*, ed. Reynolds, p. 358; Robinson, *Marietta*.
28. Bird, *Sheppard Lee*, p. 228.
29. Poe, 'The Premature Burial', in *The Collected Works of Edgar Allan Poe*, ed. Mabbott, vol. 3: *Tales and Sketches, 1843–1849*, pp. 953–72 (p. 967).
30. Poe, 'The Facts in the Case of M. Valdemar', in *Tales and Sketches, 1843–1849*, pp. 1228–44 (p. 1234). Further citations of this edition are given in parentheses in the main text.
31. Poe to John P. Kennedy, 11 February 1836, in *The Letters of Edgar Allan Poe*, ed. Ostrom, vol. 1: *1824–1845*, pp. 83–5 (p. 84).

32. Poe, 'How to Write a Blackwood Article', in *The Collected Works of Edgar Allan Poe*, ed. Mabbott, vol. 2: *Tales and Sketches, 1831–1842*, pp. 334–62 (p. 340).

33. Poe, 'Loss of Breath', in *Tales and Sketches, 1831–1842*, pp. 61–82 (p. 69). Further citations of this edition are given in parentheses in the main text.

34. Etter, '"Tawdry Physical Affrightments"', p. 5. As well as recording routine medical observations and procedures, the *American Medical Library and Intelligencer* featured cases of monstrous births, snakes in stomachs, and people who lived without eating.

35. Poe, 'The Man That Was Used Up', in *Tales and Sketches, 1831–1842*, pp. 376–92 (pp. 388, 389).

36. Etter, 'Tawdry Physical Affrightments', p. 17.

37. Frank, 'Valdemar's Tongue, Poe's Telegraphy', p. 636.

38. Carlson, 'Charles Poyen Brings Mesmerism to America'.

39. Carter, 'A Possible Source for "The Facts in the Case of M. Valdemar"', p. 36.

40. Ogden, *Credulity*, p. 95.

41. Ibid. p. 20. For a discussion of Gleason see Ibid. pp. 75–99.

42. Ibid. p. 17.

43. Hawthorne, *The House of the Seven Gables*, pp. 212, 211.

44. Ibid. p. 212.

45. Hawthorne, *The Scarlet Letter*, pp. 109, 110.

46. Ibid. pp. 110, 111.

47. Ibid. p. 93.

48. Sherwood, *The New-York Dissector*, 4 (1847), p. 247, quoted in Sappol, *A Traffic of Dead Bodies*, p. 156.

49. Poe, 'A Tale of the Ragged Mountains', p. 941.

50. Ibid.

51. Ibid. p. 945.

52. Jacobson, *Whiteness of a Different Color*, p. 8.

53. *Native and Alien. The Naturalization Laws of the United States*, pp. 30–4.

54. Foucault, *The Birth of the Clinic*, p. 9.

55. Poe, 'The Murders in the Rue Morgue', in *Tales and Sketches, 1831–1842*, pp. 521–74 (pp. 542, 558).

56. Nichols, 'Poe's "Some Words with a Mummy" and Blackface Anatomy', p. 2. See also Nelson, *National Manhood*, pp. 204–16.

57. Lacan, 'XVIII – Desire, Life and Death', in *The Seminars of Jacques Lacan: Book II*, ed. Miller, pp. 221–34 (p. 231).

# 5

# 'HOW CAN I SPEAK TO THEE?': HERMAN MELVILLE'S MUTED VOICE

Odd forms of speech permeate Herman Melville's fiction. From the foreign tongues of Polynesian natives in the early *Typee* (1846) to the bizarre mimicry of a trickster conman in *The Confidence-Man* (1857) and the stuttering of his final prose work *Billy Budd* (1888–91), Melville populates his texts with characters possessing unusual and often disruptive voices. In this chapter I examine Melville's use of ineffable and inscrutable speech and trace a move towards muteness to communicate marginality in his later fiction. Many of Melville's prose works attach peculiar vocal utterances to non-White or 'not quite white' liminal protagonists.[1] I narrow my focus on Melville by examining two texts that involve liminal White characters on the interstice between life and death: the incoherently singing Isabel Banford in *Pierre: Or, the Ambiguities* (1852) and the refusing Bartleby in 'Bartleby the Scrivener: A Story of Wall Street' (1853). In their proximity to death and to states of powerlessness, Isabel and Bartleby are less than White. Thinking about these characters as less than White moves away from binary readings of Black versus White to consider characters that are between states of full citizenship and slavery, who exist on the margins of society. Melville uses the liminal figure's voice to communicate this marginality. In *Pierre*, Isabel inhabits a social and spiritual limbo. She is an otherworldly figure who narrates a deprived and excluded upbringing, disconnected from her own history and identity. Meeting her half-brother, she relies upon cries, singing and a spirit-possessed guitar to give voice to her isolation and suffering. In his spectrality, Bartleby effects a haunting upon the lawyer-narrator. His repeated verbal refusals and withdrawals from conversation challenge the narrator's conception of citizenship as tied to sociality and self-making.

Melville writes several texts featuring multiracial environments that lend themselves to readings of interactions between White and non-White characters. In *Moby Dick* (1851), Melville describes the sailors as 'federated along one keel', forming cross-racial partnerships in order to maintain the *Pequod*.[2] At the same time, characters and readers cannot escape the metaphysical horrors of race. Pip, Ahab's Black cabin boy, goes mad from the realisation that, in his native Alabama, his Blackness would mark him as human property worth less than a whale killed on the expedition. After nearly drowning, his speech breaks down into manic cries echoing a fugitive slave advert: 'Pip! Pip! Pip! One hundred pounds of clay reward for Pip; five feet high – looks cowardly – quickest known by that! Ding, dong, ding! Who's seen Pip the coward?' Pip desires to become permanently attached to his White superior; he asks that his hand be riveted to Ahab's and invites the captain to 'use poor me for your one lost leg; only tread upon me, sir; I ask no more, so I remain a part of ye'.[3] Pip's plea for Ahab to physically subsume him conveys the uncomfortable truth that White citizens' freedom and self-determinacy, encapsulated by Ahab's obsessive quest for the whale, is predicated on the subservience of millions of non-White Americans and their exclusion from those rights.

As Whiteness shifts during the antebellum period, Melville's characters on the borders of Whiteness – due to nationality, ethnicity or socio-economic position – 'push against this discourse of whiteness' as a uniting national force. Graham Thompson has argued that Melville's White working bodies cannot appear as fully White because as poor menial and manual workers they are disconnected from middle-class White men. In 'Bartleby' and 'The Tartarus of Maids' (1855), the narrators exclude pallid and pale off-white workers from the idealistic vision that all White men and women are united across the nation.[4] In fact, these not-quite-White working bodies show that Whiteness is stratified by social position and is dependent on excluding and blackening the working class and immigrants. Janine Marie DeLombard takes a similar approach to *White-Jacket* (1850): the flogged sailor is a White figure placed on the limits of Whiteness due to his lowly status in a regimented and hierarchical setting. But rather than make the 'disciplinary degradation of the Caucasian crew' an analogue for slavery, the narrator recognises 'a "scale" of conditions' and 'gradations' between fully enfranchised White citizenship and Black enslavement.[5] Building on this scholarship, I contend that Melville's depiction of off-whiteness extends beyond racialised concepts of the working body itself to a broader model of qualities required to be an antebellum citizen, including autonomy and sociality.

Isabel – an orphaned menial worker not dissimilar to the paper mill girls – and Bartleby – a failure of early white-collar masculinity – are liminal White figures on the edges of Whiteness and Melville renders them as haunting, incorporeal figures between the spiritual and physical worlds. In the eyes of Pierre Glendinning and the lawyer-narrator their not-quite-White counterparts lack property in themselves and the men view Isabel and Bartleby as racially liminal, dependent figures. On Blackness in Melville's fiction, Christopher Freeburg contends: 'Melville correlates the social reality of racial difference with philosophical concerns about mastery: seizing one's destiny, amassing scientific or spiritual knowledge, and perfecting the self.'[6] Isabel and Bartleby are not stand-ins for enslaved people but as liminally White characters they provoke similar reactions in their fully White counterparts. For Pierre and the lawyer, their conceptions of White male selfhood depend on the 'mastery' of these less-than-White figures. Their sense of self is not just tied to autonomy or property-in-themselves, but a sense of ownership over others. In order to recover these lost figures – the sister who has been excluded from the family tree; the office worker who refuses to speak as a self-motivated young man – Pierre and the lawyer create social relations that do not exist in order to establish a familial ownership: Isabel turns from a stranger to a sister and then a wife; Bartleby turns from an employee to a brother and then a son.

Written in the same two-year period, Isabel and Bartleby communicate liminal Whiteness through selective muteness, inscrutable statements or wordless cries. In the first part of this chapter I discuss Isabel Banford as a marginalised figure, born into silence and a world without speech or language. Within her narrative Melville explores how one can move beyond language to testify to suffering. Furthering recent work on connectivity in *Pierre*, I situate Isabel within the early spiritualist movement in the 1850s. Straddling the physical and spiritual worlds, she communicates with her dead mother through a possessed guitar and gives voice to their joint story of suffering and exclusion through unintelligible singing and music. Melville would go on to mock Spiritualism in 'The Apple-Tree Table' (1856), but four years earlier he presents mediumship as an opportunity for alternative means of communication for those on thresholds of society. In response to her utterances, Pierre's conception of the upstanding antebellum citizen unravels. He believes his half-sister depends on him to rescue and legitimise her through marriage, and he attempts to position her into respectable society, of which she has never been a part. Absconding to New York, Pierre increasingly views authorship as a means of self-making and an expression of his autonomy. Isabel's otherworldy cries and periods of wordlessness and Pierre's inability to convey himself through literature put forward a claim that some things cannot be adequately expressed through language and the written form.

In the second part of this chapter I then discuss Bartleby's inscrutable statements and his withdrawals from conversation. Drawing on Sara Ahmed's theory of 'institutional whiteness', I argue that the office is a space of White-coded values, which Bartleby fails to demonstrate.[7] Refusing to work, socialise or even eat, the cadaverous Bartleby's passive resistant rejection – 'I [would] prefer not to' – challenges the narrator's understanding of White citizenship. Specifically, Bartleby fails to embody the values the narrator attaches to the 'model citizen' of antebellum society, the young professional clerk who converses as a means of self-improvement.[8] As a result, the narrator increasingly views the copyist as a dependant whom he must support. I argue that a logic of human ownership pervades this short story. In no longer fitting the expectations of a citizen, the narrator views Bartleby as his ward, his property, and finally as a piece of text. The lawyer in 'Bartleby' attempts to understand Bartleby's refusals by writing the copyist as a dependant character in his own literary sketch, an endeavour that can never be fully realised, as Bartleby's speech remains inscrutable.

Both the lawyer and Pierre are figures of authorship: the narrator in 'Bartleby' uses writing to understand and inscribe the character of others, whereas Pierre attempts self-making and self-expression through Romantic authorship. As well as employing the muted voice as a vehicle for communicating marginality, Melville's use of wordless voices and refusals challenges the literary text. Writing on 'Benito Cereno' (1855), Shari Goldberg contends that Melville's texts 'feature the world's silences as stubborn and unyielding, and they problematize the idea that the text could reverse this essential condition'.[9] This chapter builds on Goldberg's work by considering two texts that show Melville experimenting with language and speech in fiction in relation to resistant and inscrutable voices. Before there is silence there is mutedness, wordlessness and meaninglessness, interrogating whether conversational speech can be a sufficient means of communication.

### 'Behold again how I rave': Expressing Liminality in *Pierre*

In *Pierre*, Isabel Banford appears as if from beyond the grave. A poor seamstress, this sallow and olive-skinned girl first emerges at the Miss Pennies' sewing circle, which Pierre and his mother Mary attend. After haunting Pierre with a piercing shriek upon seeing him, she tells Pierre through a letter and a spoken narrative that she is his father's illegitimate daughter. Melville depicts her as both a 'suffocated' cadaver with a 'death-like beauty' and as a supernatural figure who 'wholly soared out of the realms of mortalness'.[10] In his portrayal of Isabel, Melville draws on transatlantic gothic literature. Her 'death-like beauty' echoes Poe's contention that 'the death, then, of a beautiful woman is unquestionably, the most poetical topic in the world': Isabel is beautiful because she appears dead and unchanging, because she can be appreciated and consumed, as Pierre later does.[11] The claustrophobia and imprisonment of a young woman alludes to Poe's inappropriate burials of Madeleine Usher in 'The Fall of the House of Usher' (1839) and the wife in 'The Black Cat' (1843), as well as the trapped and suffering women in

Charlotte Brontë's *Jane Eyre* (1847) and Emily Brontë's *Wuthering Heights* (1847).[12]

A haunting, incorporeal figure, Isabel fails to embody the model antebellum woman. In Chapter 1 I discussed the ideal republican woman, who was responsible for morally educating her male relatives to engage in civic matters. Clara Wieland and Constantia Davies in *Wieland* and 'Somnambulism' initially serve as prime examples of the rational and constant republican daughter or sister who guides her family through the tumultuous and uncertain new national landscape. By the mid-nineteenth century, gendered distinctions of separate public and private spheres further formalised expectations of female behaviour. Subordinate in civic matters and represented by her husband or father, the antebellum woman did not have the same expectations of self-making, autonomy and industry placed on her as the White male citizen. Instead, manifestos on True Womanhood such as Catharine Beecher's *A Treatise on Domestic Economy* (1841) laid out the female duty to 'have a superior influence' over 'all questions relating to morals or manners' in the family. Women were responsible for 'the formation of the moral and intellectual character of the young'.[13] In providing her family with Christian education, the antebellum True Woman shaped her male relatives into active and engaged citizens who would vote on behalf of her interests. The antebellum woman's gendered citizenship was inextricably tied to the domestic sphere and her identity was shaped through her place in the family, a philosophy inculcated in women since childhood. In *Pierre*, Isabel is a domestic worker but not a homemaker. From the account of her upbringing, it is clear that Isabel is completely disconnected from True Womanhood and the domestic sphere.

Isabel's incomprehension of language and initial inability to vocalise her suffering encapsulates her lack of place within a family structure, and therefore her loss of identity. In her narrative in Books VI and VIII, broken memories of her upbringing emphasise the indeterminacy of her mortal and social status. As if a dream sequence, Isabel's narrative jumps and cuts in time and space as she grapples with her loss of memory – 'the stupor, and the torpor, and the blankness, and the dimness, and the vacant whirlingness of the bewilderingness'. She spends her youth trapped in a nightmare, a gothic dilapidated 'wild dark house' surrounded by 'ghostly pines' that she fears will 'reach out their grim arms to snatch [her] into their horrid shadows', followed by an inhumane asylum. The blankness in Isabel's memory corresponds to the pervading silence of her upbringing. The gothic house – possibly in America, possibly France – is 'dumb as death', as the old man and woman with whom she lives never speak to her (pp. 122, 114, 115). Without speech and the interpersonal connections that come with it, Isabel cannot understand the world around her. In their silence, the man and the woman are the same inscrutable forms as the motionless green foundation stones that trap Isabel in the nightmarish house. When she says of the couple, 'I knew not whence they came, or what cause they had for being there,' she records her lack of comprehension at her own place in the world as well as the other inhabitants of the house, because she defines herself in relation to these figures. In silence, Isabel is an unformed self. Without the voices of the past – 'No name; no scrawled or written thing; no book . . . no one memorial speaking of its former occupants' – Isabel has no place in the world. Orphaned through the death of her French Revolution refugee mother and her father's abandonment, history is lost to her. She says, 'no grave-stone, or mound, or any little hillock around the house, betrayed any past burials of man or child'. In contrast, Pierre's patrilineal history is set down in detail at the beginning of the novel and enshrined in the family estate. Isabel asks, 'What was it to be dead? What is it to be living? Wherein is the difference between the words Death and Life? Had I been ever dead? Was I living?' (pp. 116, 115, 124). These questions encapsulate her liminal state – cut off from her genea-logical ties, she is socially dead and therefore excluded from the freedom and rights of the living.

Isabel struggles with verbal expression throughout the text. We can see this in two ways. The first is her desire for silence. Several times, she acknowl-edges she does not know how to tell Pierre about her upbringing, exclaiming: 'I have no tongue to speak to thee . . . how can I speak to thee?' She repeat-edly tells Pierre to be silent and allow her to be silent, instructing, 'Let me be still again, Do not speak to me' and 'speak not to me; it is too much . . . do not speak to me'. Her feelings overwhelm her ability to verbalise her experi-ence – some things must rename nameless and unexpressed. For example, she refuses to name one of her childhood dwellings as an asylum, saying, 'That word has never passed my lips, even now, when I hear the word, I run from it' (pp. 113, 124, 154, 121). Recalling asylum life, Isabel remembers inmates expressing themselves through 'hand-clappings, shrieks, howls, laughter, bless-ings, prayers, oaths, hymns, and all audible confusions'. One inhabitant simply mutters 'Broken, broken, broken' on meaningless repeat, while others 'could not, or would not speak, or had forgotten how to speak' (p. 120). In this space of exile and disownment, language is insufficient to testify to suffering and marginalisation.

The second way this struggle with language manifests is through the over-wrought way she narrates her story to Pierre. Isabel breaks down language into its smallest components, questioning the very meaning of words. For example, the word 'father' does not carry any familial significance for her because she has been cut off from normative ideas of family. When she does meet Glendinning Sr, she interprets 'father' to mean 'general love and endearment . . . little or nothing more', with no connection to paternity, genealogy or inheritance. Isabel manipu-lates language in her attempts to express her marginality. Before she gives her spoken narrative, Isabel attempts writing, but in her letter to Pierre she likewise struggles with expression, admitting: 'I knew not how to write to thee, nor what to say to thee; and so, behold again how I rave.' She writes: '– Oh, my brother, my dear, dear Pierre, – help me, fly to me; see I perish without thee; – pity, pity, – here I freeze in the wide, wide world; – no father, no mother, no sister, no brother, no living thing in the fair form of humanity, that holds me dear.' In the fragmentation, repetition and exclamation – as if she was speaking through the paper – Isabel's overwhelming outpouring of emotion cannot be contained on the page. Imbued with her broken physical voice, the letter is an embodied document; the paper appears to be bleeding when the ink stained by her tears blurs and runs down the page in a 'strange and reddish hue' (p. 64).

When language is inaccessible or insufficient, music replaces it as a mode of expressing suffering, exclusion and marginalisation. Isabel finds her voice in the séance, in which she channels her mother's spirit through an enchanted guitar, claiming that 'the guitar was speaking to me, the guitar was singing to me, murmuring, and singing to me . . . the guitar was human'. Isabel says of her story, 'for not in words can it be spoken', and instructs Pierre to listen to her guitar, which holds her 'mother's spirit' (pp. 125, 126). The mother-guitar inexplicably responds to Isabel's calls:

> 'Mother – mother – mother!'
> Again, after a preluding silence, the guitar as magically responded before; the sparks quivered along its strings; and again Pierre felt as in the immediate presence of the spirit.
> 'Shall I, mother? – Art thou ready? Wilt thou tell me? – Now? Now?'
> These words were lowly and sweetly murmured in the same way with the word *mother*, being changefully varied in their modulations, till at the last *now*, the magical guitar again responded; and the girl swiftly drew it to her beneath her dark tent of hair . . . Pierre felt himself surrounded by ten thousand sprites and gnomes, and his whole soul was swayed and tossed by supernatural tides; and again he heard the wondrous, rebounding, chanted words
>
> 'Mystery! Mystery!
> Mystery of Isabel!
> Mystery! Mystery!
> Isabel and Mystery!
> Mystery!' (p. 150)

A dark-haired, dark-eyed young woman in a trance-like state, Isabel's appearance fits the image of female mediums in the 1850s, notably the Fox sisters. In March 1848, Rochester teenagers Margaret and Katherine Fox claimed to have communicated with a local dead man through a series of knocks and raps. By 1850, the sisters were on tour and demonstrating their powers to the public.[14] Progressing beyond raps, mediums channelled loved ones and celebrity spirits through writing, speaking, dancing and music. The enchanted guitar was a recurring motif of spiritualist writings, with mediums recording occurrences of spirits playing the instrument to astounded observers. For example, Eliab Capron's October 1849 journal from the Fox house records a guitar 'played by unseen hands, and played so exquisitely too, that it seemed more like far distant music to one just aroused from midnight slumbers, than the music of an instrument a few feet from us'.[15]

At the same time as the fever for Spiritualism gripped the north-east and started to spread west, Melville was intrigued by the Shaker communities near his Arrowhead home. Visiting the Shaker community in Hancock, Massachusetts twice in the summer of 1850, Melville soon after read a Shaker pamphlet describing the members singing 'melodious and heavenly songs' and overcome by 'involuntary operations of singing and dancing' as they channelled spirits.[16] Akin to a Shaker dance, Isabel 'swayed to and fro with a like abandonment, and suddenness, and wantonness', lost in the music of the possessed guitar and her inscrutable lyrics (p. 126). The medium and the Shaker inhabited a liminal position, straddling the boundaries of life and death and exposing that border to be permeable as communication crossed between the material world and the afterlife. Mediums claimed to not only channel the spirits of loved ones through possessed speech, instruments and automatic writing, but also the spirits of celebrity ghosts, including recently deceased presidents and global historical figures. To protest slavery, abolitionist Isaac Post channelled spirits from former enslavers and presidents George Washington, John Calhoun and James Polk, who had all been converted to the antislavery mission in the afterlife. In accounts of spiritualist circles, mediums claimed to be figures such as Mary Stuart, Queen of Scots, while some spiritualist circles witnessed their members speaking in Indigenous tongues.[17] If true, the dead's possession of the medium suggested a dangerous fluidity or 'polymorphousness' of identity across lines of race, religion, class and gender.[18]

It is this loss of individual identity and autonomy, even when identity categories are not crossed, that concerns Hawthorne in *The House of the Seven Gables*, in which he frames characters in the twinned contemporary phenomena of mesmerism and spiritualism. Phoebe Pyncheon is another medium figure, with 'brown ringlets' and skin 'the clear shade of tan', who is able to perceive supernatural presence 'with almost the effect of a spiritual medium'.[19] Her receptivity entrances the mysterious mesmeriser Holgrave, whose temptation to overpower her I discussed in my previous chapter. Like the mesmerised giving up their spirit to the control of another, at spiritualist séances a successful medium surrendered control of their body to fully allow the deceased to enter and control them. In channelling messages from beyond the grave, the medium had to become a passive vessel and lose their personal autonomy. As one member of a Philadelphia spiritualist circle wrote in 1851, 'the person to be prepared must give up all self-control, all resistance, and resign himself to the entire direction and control of the spirits'.[20] We can see this in Isabel's trance-like state as she moves back and forth involuntarily; she loses herself to the power of her mother's spirit – it is not clear whether the 'rebounding, chanted words' are Isabel speaking as herself, ventriloquising her mother, or if the mother-guitar itself has gained a voice (p. 150).

Turning to *Pierre*'s 'companion piece' published in the same summer, *The Blithedale Romance*, Hawthorne continues to treat the interrelated phenomena of mesmerism and spiritualism with scepticism and distaste because of its threats to autonomy and manipulation of the vulnerable.[21] Waif-like 'ghost-child' Priscilla is an archetypal proto-medium figure known as the Veiled Lady, who is rumoured to be held captive by the curse of the veil 'in a bondage which is worse than death'. Dominated by the magician Westervelt, she puts on a performance to paying audiences and floats 'to and fro over the carpet, with the silvery veil covering her from head to foot'.[22] *Pierre* shares many tropes with *The Blithedale Romance*: reunited half-siblings (Isabel/Pierre; Zenobia/Priscilla); non-normative intimacies (Isabel/Pierre; the Blithedale commune); ethereal women involved in quasi-supernatural performances (Isabel; Priscilla). Whereas Hawthorne exposes the potential sexualised dangers of female passivity through Holgrave and Westervelt's thoughts of control, Melville presents Isabel's mediumship as an opportunity for communication, in particularly for young women, who spiritualists viewed as the most 'plausible' vessel for channelling spirits. Ann Braude quotes one 1850s medium who professed, 'the characteristics [of the medium] will be *feminine* – negative and passive': using an electromagnetic frame, women were viewed as receptive and waiting to be charged or filled by a spirit.[23]

Yet spiritualists overturned hierarchies; they 'denounced the authority of churches over believers, of governments over citizens, of doctors over patients, of masters over slaves, and most of all, men over women'.[24] If an individual could access and speak higher truths, then no one could control another and no man could control a woman. As a result, spiritualists spoke in their trances and reflections in favour of radical movements such as abolition and marriage reform. Spiritualism proposed a radical merging of identities and non-normative intimacies. Female spiritualists paradoxically employed passivity to claim agency, taking on the equivalent of preaching roles denied to them in traditional Christian denominations. Isabel's spiritualist performance is radical in that her murmuring, singing and playing gives voice to both her and her mother's stories of suffering and marginalisation; her mediumship is an effective medium to communicate a collective as well as individual trauma. However, in her wantonness she does not claim agency or autonomy as female mediums did, but instead asks for ownership. Isabel tells Pierre of her 'immense longings for some one of my blood to know me, and to own me' and asks 'Tell me, by loving me, by owning me, publicly or secretly, – tell me, doth it involve any vital hurt to thee?' (pp. 158, 159). Her pathetic performance is an attempt to sway Pierre to acknowledge and possess his newfound sister and rescue her from her current life of genealogical and social loss.

In giving up herself, Isabel paradoxically wields an 'extraordinary physical magnetism' that draws in Pierre (p. 151). The séance emphasises what Pierre has felt since his first encounter with Isabel. Her 'long-drawn, unearthly, girlish shriek' at the sewing circle causes an emotional reaction framed through touch. Isabel's voice 'split[s] its way clean through his heart' and has 'taken hold of the deepest roots and subtlest fibres of his being' (pp. 45, 48). In her spirit pieces Isabel conjures an intensely charged supernatural environment. Her 'rebounding' and resonant chants and murmurs, as well as the vibration of the guitar strings, create an 'architectonics' that again, Pierre perceives through touch.[25] In these synesthetic moments, Pierre mirrors Isabel's physical movements psychologically, feeling 'swayed and tossed' by her cries (p. 150). Entranced by her song, Pierre becomes

> vaguely sensible of a certain still more marvelous power in the girl over himself and his most interior thoughts and motions; – a power so hovering upon the confines of the invisible world, that it seemed more inclined that way than this; – a power which not only seemed irresistibly to draw him toward Isabel, but to draw him away from another quarter ... Often, in after-times with her, did he recall this first magnetic night, and would seem to see that she then had bound him to her by an extraordinary atmospheric spell – both physical and spiritual – which henceforth it had become impossible for him to break, but whose full potency he never recognized till long after he had become habituated to its sway. (p. 151)

The powerless girl now has a 'marvellous power' that like Holgrave, shapes and directs the 'most interior thoughts and motions' (p. 151). Pierre's response to her calls to be loved and owned is outside consciousness, he cannot resist her, he is bound to her. Thinking about *Pierre* as a telegraphic novel shaping characters through electromagnetic forces, Paul Gilmore writes that the connection Pierre feels is marred by 'miscommunication'. If everyone could experience this connection, as the development of the telegraph suggests, then there would be too much 'dissonance' and 'noise', leading to misinterpretations.[26] The fault in Pierre's reaction to Isabel is not that he has misinterpreted her – he feels a deep connection with her that she explicitly asks for – but what he does afterwards. The radical action he takes in response to Isabel's hazy claim is in service to his new conception of autonomous masculinity, which requires a reshaping of familial structures.

The 'infinite significancies' Pierre invests in Isabel's shrieks, singing and murmurs entirely alter his perception of his place in the world (p. 126). After reading her embodied letter – which speaks to him not just in Isabel's voice, but also reanimates his father's mysterious dying cry 'My daughter! My daughter!' – his 'whole previous moral being was overturned' and he is aware, through Isabel's revelation, 'that for him the fair structure of the world must, in some then unknown way, be entirely rebuilded again, from the lowermost cornerstone up' (p. 87). His long-held belief that his father was a respectable gentleman is undone. Depicted through pure white imagery, Pierre's father represents an unattainably untainted ideal of antebellum citizenship. A notable example is his shrine on the family estate. Within 'stood the perfect marble form of his departed father, without blemish, unclouded, snow-white, and serene, Pierre's fond personification of perfect human goodness and virtue'. In his static stone form, the dead father represents the abstracted body of the ideal antebellum citizen; he retains his 'reputation as a gentleman and a Christian', a devoted husband and 'virtuous' father. Unchanging, he can only be 'uncorruptibly sainted in heaven' after being 'so beautiful on earth' (pp. 68, 69). However, after reading Isabel's letter, Pierre recognises that the pure marble is a façade and that behind the perfect statue are the 'specks and flaws' in his father's character that resulted in his adultery and abandonment of Isabel and her mother (p. 68).

In his new perception of the world, Pierre's resolve that the world must be 'entirely rebuilded' centres on remaking himself through a new social role. He disowns his late father – saying 'I will no more have a father' – by becoming him, refashioning himself as a fatherless independent young man who owns and protects his own new dependant (p. 87). He determines to rewrite family history, sacrificing his respectability by abandoning his fiancée Lucy Tartan and foreclosing Isabel's illegitimacy within a new narrative of marriage. This plan intends to remedy Isabel's exclusion from her father's inheritance by giving her claim on the Glendinning name and its Saddle Meadows estate. In doing so he will rescue Isabel from her menial wage labour and insert her into the True Woman's domestic economy from which she has been excluded. Pierre becomes not only a husband to his half-sister, but also a father, making up for Glendinning Sr's lack of financial and social care. As brother, husband and father, he will 'own her boldly and lovingly' (p. 170). Pierre's marriage to Isabel compounds the collapsed and corrupt relations running throughout the novel, in which blood relations are inescapable and confused, as he often calls his mother 'sister' and Lucy 'cousin'. This intra-family marriage turns Pierre into a father figure, replacing Pierre Sr as benefactor and protector, but it simultaneously terminates the genealogical line and thwarts the transferral of property between generations when Mrs Glendinning ends his inheritance.

Mary Glendinning is appalled at the elopement, not only because Pierre has broken his promise to Lucy, but also because his choice of bride is so lowly.

Not knowing Isabel's true identity, Mary mutters to herself, 'Oh! oh! oh! Thus ruthlessly to cut off, at one gross sensual dash, the fair succession of an honorable race! Mixing the choicest wine with filthy water from the plebeian pool, and so turning all to undistinguishable rankness!' (p. 194). Her fear of dilution and the crossed and collapsed bloodlines in the novel clearly have racial connotations. As Jeffory Clymer and Robert Levine have argued, the emergence of natally alienated, racially ambiguous offspring reflects abolitionist campaigns against the moral stain of sexual violence and family corruption in the South.[27] Isabel has 'dark, olive' skin but at no point is her racial identity explicitly discovered (p. 46). Rather, the logic of human ownership and the destruction of traditional family structures perpetrated in slavery translates into anxieties about property relations between the elite Glendinning family and the less-than-White marginal Isabel. Mary uses the language of miscegenation to discuss class, exemplifying how White people on the thresholds of society due to low socio-economic status and vague nationality could exist on the boundaries of Whiteness. In order to preserve his father's reputation and at the same time afford Isabel the privileges of the Glendinning name, Pierre's new narrative of cross-class elopement mars the respectable Whiteness of the elite White family.

As Freeburg writes, Blackness is both a racial marker and psychological concept for Melville, and White protagonists experience 'psychic and physical disruptions' when encountering it.[28] Blackened – not just racialised as Black – characters provoke these reactions. The 'Nubian power' of Isabel's eyes is a black marker of the dependency and lack of property-in-oneself she experiences as a deprived woman outside society and family (p. 145). Pierre sees this in Isabel's story of abandonment and in response to this dark, socially powerless yet hypnotising girl, he positions her as a dependant who relies on him for security and prosperity. Attempting to master Isabel and himself, Pierre bolsters his self-image as the model White male citizen who cares and provides for his dependants and sees himself returning Isabel to the family structure needed for her to fulfil her White gendered civic role. At the same time, the discovery of his father's adultery spurs Pierre to attempt to redefine himself as an independent, self-made man in the city. However, this self-making is at odds with the urban marketplace he encounters. Absconding to New York with Isabel, Pierre endeavours to forge his identity away from the market economy; this is exemplified in his dramatic change in attitude towards writing. Just as he rewrites family history to forge a respectable narrative for Isabel, a key facet of Pierre's self-making and autonomy is attached to writing itself – writing that becomes increasingly divorced from the marketplace Pierre relies on after losing his inheritance. Hershel Parker makes a case for excluding the authorship 'subplot' from the novel, arguing that Melville added these strands later in a deliberate attempt to create a failed novel and to attack the unkind literary marketplace.[29] However, Pierre's changing conception of authorship is a necessary component because it is inextricably linked to his new perception of the world after he encounters Isabel. For Pierre, authorship transforms from a means of cultivating gentlemanly accomplishment into a Romantic calling, while avoiding putting himself in the literary marketplace.

Critics praise Pierre's earlier works for their genteel taste, such as a 'long and beautifully written review' that claims, 'This writer is unquestionably a highly respectable youth.' He is happy to supply sonnets for ladies' scrapbooks and write pieces for magazine publication, such as 'The Tropical Summer', that display his 'Perfect Taste' (p. 245). Once in New York, Pierre begins to see authorship as a transcendental calling and a means of expressing higher truths. This self-expression is a marker of his complete autonomy and independence as an antebellum citizen. Pierre has several moments of solitary contemplation in which he examines his relationship with the literary marketplace. He seeks to disengage from expectations of the professional writer, declining invitations to speak in public and refusing to provide a daguerreotype because 'when every body has his portrait published, true distinction lies in not having yours published at all'. The idea that everything – even artistic persona – is for sale in the city horrifies Pierre. In a radical conversion, he detests his previous writing as 'Trash! Dross! Dirt!' Viewing himself as an artist following a higher calling, he commits himself to conveying the truth through literature. He intends to 'gospelize the world anew, and show them deeper secrets than the Apocalypse! – I will write it, I will write it!' (pp. 254, 272, 273). In seeking an autonomy that rejects the marketplace, his writing, like Isabel's spiritualist song, seeks to transcend the material world itself.

By finding an individual and authentic authorial voice, Pierre stakes a claim as a self-made – or self-written – man. Uncomfortable with both his previous life as landed gentry and his new independent life in the city, Pierre actively seeks to write himself as an autonomous man, but one who is defined outside of economic exchange. He is instead consumed by 'the primitive elementalizing of the strange stuff, which in the act of attempting that book, have upheaved and upgushed in his soul'. In the scenes of writing in the New York Apostles apartment, Pierre increasingly struggles to write anything that adequately expresses his pursuit of higher truths. In his effort to write, his body is in turmoil. It unconsciously repels the written page itself as '[t]he pupils of his eyes rolled away from him in their own orbits' (pp. 304, 341). What Isabel's narrative has demonstrated to Pierre and the reader is the insufficiency of language. The further Pierre retreats into his own trance-like state – 'suspended, motionless, blank' – the more he sees 'the everlasting elusiveness of Truth, the universal lurking insincerity of even the greatest and purest written thoughts' (pp. 341, 339). Like Bartleby, to whom I turn shortly, Pierre transforms into a silent figure who can no longer write and barely speak. Haunting the text since Isabel's introduction, silence and wordlessness pervade, until by the end of the novel Pierre can no longer express himself.

He cannot escape the genealogical mess he has created. On first appearance, Isabel's 'death-like' attractiveness seems to draw on Poe's philosophy of poetical beauty. However, by the end of the novel she transforms into Poe's motif of the undying madwoman who haunts the male protagonist. Offering up her body parts – 'take out these eyes, and use them for glasses' – Isabel moves away from the civic womanhood Pierre has imagined for her and back towards the ostracised girl with no sense of self (p. 349). Contemplating the impossible situation of living with both Isabel and Lucy, who has left Saddle Meadows to join them and further complicate the novel's intimacies, Pierre retreats into silence. Pierre has reached a dead end as his modes of masculinity fail: the self-replicating father figure has been unsuccessful at providing for his dependant, the autonomous Romantic artist has been unproductive in expressing higher truths. He is ultimately left without language, his feelings 'entirely untranslatable into any words that can be used' (p. 353).

Throughout *Pierre*, Melville reflects his protagonists' struggle with expression by testing the capabilities of language itself. He continually invents new words in *Pierre* but the majority are formed through adding prefixes and suffixes, creating plurals or making gerunds: 'upheaved', 'upgushed', 'significancies', 'rebuilded', 'blurrings' and 'whirlingness'.[30] Melville breaks language down into its smallest linguistic units of meaning, experimenting with different combinations. In this sense, these words are not entirely new forms of expression, but instead syllables deliberately manipulated to show the limitations of language. Furthermore, the written word becomes redundant as etymologically related words or synonyms in close proximity on the page 'pile up without accreting meaning'.[31] In his move to short fiction, Melville continues to experiment with the boundaries of language and the meaning of speech. Turning to 'Bartleby the Scrivener', Melville writes another character with inscrutable vocal utterances. In willingly restricting his speech, limiting his vocabulary to repeated statements and rejecting conversation, Bartleby disavows expectations of the professional male citizen, and as a result the patriarchal narrator turns him into a dependent figure.

## REFUSING INSTITUTIONAL WHITENESS IN 'BARTLEBY THE SCRIVENER'

In her 2007 essay 'A Phenomenology of Whiteness', Sara Ahmed terms Whiteness a 'straightening device' that takes hold in institutionalised spaces and workplaces through everyday habits, in order to delineate who does or does not belong. Specific ways of being that she terms 'styles, capacities, aspirations, techniques, habits' become White. These codes and habits are made to be so natural and invisible that, as with all aspects of Whiteness, White people take them for granted and do not think of them as constructed. Whiteness promises a sense of ownership over the self and by extension, access to spaces – for example, the assumption that White people are at home in professional spaces, as Ahmed illustrates through her own experience as a woman of colour in the university. 'The effect of this "around whiteness"', she writes, 'is the institutionalization of a certain "likeness", which makes non-white bodies feel uncomfortable, exposed, visible, different, when they take up this space'.[32] Ahmed's theory works in spaces where all the inhabitants appear as White, and yet White people can be marked and policed for not embodying these codes of White behaviour. These codes must be constructed and naturalised in White-only spaces so that, as Ahmed discusses, non-White people have something to stand out against. We can see the origins of institutional Whiteness in 'Bartleby the Scrivener'. I read the Wall Street office as a White-encoded institutional space, in which workers must conform to a set of identity expectations. As Whiteness became an *enforced* identification' in the antebellum period, the workplace was significant as a space for professional men to demonstrate White civic qualities, namely a sense of self-improvement culti-vated through socialising.[33] Through his polite refusals to engage in workplace conversational habits, Bartleby challenges the demands of cohesive sociality for White professionals: this is what institutional Whiteness looks like. Unable to 'straighten' Bartleby into these habits, the narrator marks him out as a less-than-White figure, transforming him into a dependent and spectral noncitizen who must be exorcised.

Bartleby is an otherworldly figure, a copyist whom the Wall Street lawyer-narrator describes as 'the strangest I ever saw or heard of'.[34] He is an apparition, one day appearing in the Wall Street office to respond to the narrator's job advert. Hiring Bartleby after his own promotion, the narrator hopes the copyist – 'a man of so singularly sedate an aspect' – will be a calming and regulating influence on his existing inefficient clerks, Turkey and Nippers. At first Bartleby 'gorge[s] himself' on copying, working 'silently, palely, mechanically' day and night on the lawyer's documents. But when asked to check his copies against the other clerks, Bartleby responds 'in a singularly mild, firm voice . . . "I would prefer not to"' (pp. 24, 25). From that moment, Bartleby repeats 'prefer not to' and variations of this polite refusal at nearly every request, question or instruction, ceasing work yet not leaving the office when eventually fired by the narrator.

Figured as a dying man, a corpse and ghost, Bartleby evades categorisation as either living or dead as he occupies the interstice between these two states. Withdrawn from work, sociality and physical sustenance – his only meals consisting of ginger biscuits – Bartleby is slowly dying. At the same time, the narrator frequently refers to Bartleby as already dead. He appears with a 'cadaverously gentlemanly *nonchalance*' and like a dead body 'laid out . . . in its shivering winding sheet'. Later the lawyer corrects himself, calling Bartleby 'this man, or rather ghost' (pp. 32, 33, 43). Convinced the copyist will never leave, the narrator briefly imagines bricking up Bartleby's corpse in the office. This image – which I return to in more detail later – reinforces a sense of the space as haunted; in the future, Bartleby's corpse could remain in the office and he would repeat his occupation as a literal ghost. Like a poltergeist, Bartleby refuses to leave and, according to a tenant, 'persists in haunting the building generally, sitting upon the bannisters of the stairs by day, and sleeping in the entry by night'. The Wall Street office becomes a haunted house containing a ghost who cannot be reasoned with, and who forces out the living residents. Unable to remove the scrivener through reasoning, bribes or demands, the narrator flees to a new office instead of having Bartleby arrested, whilst the same remaining tenant complains that 'Every body is concerned; clients are leaving the offices,' unnerved and dissuaded by Bartleby's immovable, wan presence (p. 45).

In his inscrutability, Bartleby is open to many divergent yet coexisting critical approaches. In *Passive Constitutions* (2007), Branka Arsić layers interpretation upon interpretation to provide seven and a half different analyses of Bartleby.[35] Arsić is comfortable in offering these sometimes contradictory readings at the same time, which leave Bartleby as a somewhat empty, floating signifier instead of a figure rooted in the antebellum world. In these multiple discussions of Bartleby, Arsić and other critics have tended not to give much consideration to race and its relationship with the voice. I argue that returning to the voice – the perplexingly absent centre of the text – makes Bartleby more than simply empty. A literary successor of Frank Carwin in *Wieland* (discussed in Chapter 1), Bartleby is liminal and evades categorisation because he refuses to explain his actions. However, whereas Carwin's voice is disruptive because it is so limitless, as shown through his ventriloquism that transgresses boundaries of gender, race and class, Bartleby deliberately limits his voice, perplexing and frustrating those around him. Carwin's mimicry presents an overflowing of identity, whereas Bartleby clearly lacks identity. In his refusals, which are polite variations of saying 'no', Bartleby is a negative entity. His continual silences negate sociality and community, to the extent that the narrator starts to erase his Whiteness.

Bartleby's statement 'I would prefer not to' is a declaration of two possible futures. It means 'I do not want to but I will' or 'I do not want to and I will not.' In the words of Gilles Deleuze, Bartleby's ambiguous opinion 'ravages language as a whole'.[36] Crucially, Bartleby destroys meaning by using the polite 'prefer' instead of angry or aggressive language to voice his refusal and resistance. 'Prefer', a 'queer word' according to Turkey, is a strange piece of vocabulary that is out of place in the office (p. 36). It is a polite declaration of opinion, unexpected in a space where set tasks are carried out by those paid to follow instructions and orders. It denotes personal choice where choice should be irrelevant. For the employer, it is irrelevant whether an employee prefers one task or another; he expects the worker to do what he has been paid to do, or to leave. The text's narrator is unnerved because he expects that any refusal to work would be voiced in 'anger, impatience or impertinence', not mildness (p. 25). As a striking worker, Bartleby should say 'I will not' forthrightly instead of 'I would prefer not to.'

Bartleby's polite expression of preference, telling us that he has the choice to work or not, is an act of 'passive resistance'. As a veil for 'no', it shuts down any further conversation. The narrator always gets the same answer behind each response and he cannot advance in understanding why Bartleby refuses. When the lawyer asks, '*Why* do you refuse?' the response 'I would prefer not to' is again ambiguous, as it can mean either 'I do not want to tell you' or 'I do not want to refuse' (pp. 28, 26). This polite, illogical response prevents the conversation progressing. Its politeness suggests a positive face in a conversation (having his desires appreciated), but by offering no alternative (what he would like to do instead) his negative face is revealed. He does not placate the listener, nor give them a way forward in the conversation. These negative-facing statements are declarations of independence, disengagement and disregard for how the other participant in the conversation feels.[37] Sociality at a basic conversational level is thwarted. For Bartleby, all statements are vocal detractions from the narrator and the workplace, and their repetition shows that he is unaltered by how the listener receives his opinion. Even one positive variation of this declaration ('I would prefer to be left alone here') displays his negative face and is another way of saying 'go away', heedless of the narrator's response (p. 36). In presenting an emotional blank face, 'leanly composed', 'dimly calm' and without 'a wrinkle of agitation', Bartleby's choice not to emote compounds his vocal disengagement from the feelings of those around him (p. 25).

This 'queer word' infects the office, until the narrator and his other clerks import the word into their own speech. Turning the word into a threat of violence, Nippers irascibly responds to Bartleby, 'I'd *prefer* him; I'd give him preferences, the stubborn mule!' This transference is not lost on the employer and his staff, who comment on the phenomenon of Bartleby having 'turned the tongues' of the office (pp. 36, 37). Turkey parrots Bartleby, facetiously replying to one request, 'Oh certainly sir, if you prefer that I should.' The narrator 'tremble[s]' at the thought of having 'involuntarily' used the word 'upon all sorts of not exactly suitable occasions', as if infected with a contagion that could turn him into another Bartleby (p. 36). Similar to the cries of 'broken' in the asylum in *Pierre*, in its repetition 'prefer' becomes meaningless; it is a virus that spreads around the office.

As his refusals announce, albeit without explanation, Bartleby withdraws from work, community and life itself. As a figure of both productivity and unproductivity – switching from rapid, excessive copying to complete cessation – Bartleby exists at both extremes of the working spectrum.[38] Just like his perplexing refusals, he perplexes the capitalist logic that depends on the exchange of requested labour for income. However, Bartleby's inaction and the failure of a White working body is only one aspect of a broader concern regarding White citizenship in the professional environment. Turning to Melville's other tale of off-white working bodies, 'The Paradise of Bachelors and the Tartarus of Maids' delineates between different types of White workers. Both Bartleby and the paper mill girls are 'pallid' and 'blank' workers who each carry out repetitive labour: Bartleby copying documents by hand; the 'girls' processing and folding paper for hours at a time in the New England factory.[39] However, at the paper mill the workers are silent: 'not a syllable was breathed' as 'the human voice was banished from the spot'. The women are reduced to 'cogs to the wheels' of the factory machinery and in order to maintain the mechanical efficiency of the paper mill, speech is unnecessary.[40] The conditions of the Wall Street office as an institution differ greatly from the paper mill. Whereas the factory owner silences the girls and rarely interacts with them, the lawyer attempts to make the office a site of kinship and intimacy. For professional antebellum White men, the office was significant because it was a space of institutionalised Whiteness that involved a broader model of civic qualities than work alone, where workers were encouraged to cultivate and demonstrate qualities tied to citizenship, namely self-improvement and autonomy.

In the mid-century, thousands of young men travelled to the nation's urban centres in order to pursue careers in offices, banks and shops. These professions required a level of formal education and skills in arithmetic, reading and writing that set this class of men above factory workers or labourers. However, the clerk was not simply a professional figure but a representation of a number of personal attributes and characteristics. Clerks saw themselves as figures of self-sufficiency, who were 'persistently seeking self-advancement, self-improvement, or self-gratification'.[41] Leaving home to work in the city amongst strangers, clerks were the epitome of independent male citizenship. They strove to be seen by employers, clients and new acquaintances as respectable men. The office was therefore a social institution, where it mattered just as much what you did when you were not working as how much work you did.

Reading Bartleby against Nippers, the other young scrivener in the Wall Street office, shows two extreme formations of the clerk-citizen. Nippers is ambitious and focused on self-gratification. In the eyes of the narrator, he displays 'a certain impatience of the duties of a mere copyist' and is keen to make extra money at the Justices' courts. He epitomises Brian Luskey's description of young office and shop workers as 'on the make'. Rankled by having to take on Bartleby's work, he hisses to the narrator that 'this was the first and the last time he would do another man's business without pay'. Although convinced that Nippers' ambition and focus on money makes him irascible, the narrator praises him for dressing 'in a gentlemanly sort of way . . . reflecting credit upon my chambers' (pp. 21, 27, 22). From the outset of 'Bartleby', the unnamed narrator constructs an image of himself as a successful lawyer who prides himself on the quality of his work and the financial remuneration he receives. By name-dropping John Jacob Astor's praise, the lawyer emphasises the importance of reputation and respectability, a concern filtered through the rest of his narrative.[42] He expects his employees to follow suit. Having bribed Bartleby to leave the office with an extra twenty dollars' final pay, the narrator congratulates himself on dismissing him in such a respectable and agreeable manner. He is proud of his 'masterly management' of the situation and of carrying out a gentlemanly 'procedure' with 'no vulgar bullying, no bravado of any sort, no choleric hectoring' (p. 39). When he returns the next day to find Bartleby still present, he berates him for breaking their agreement, stating that he thought the copyist was of a 'gentlemanly organization' and would respectably acquiesce to the narrator's request (p. 40).

Bartleby has little regard for whether people respect him or not. His lack of self-regard and aspiration challenges the narrator's vision of an educated working male citizen. Whilst the lawyer deprecatingly calls himself 'one of those unambitious lawyers', he does so after having already secured financial success, and he expects Bartleby to wish to do the same (p. 18). Offering to help Bartleby find new work, he suggests a number of careers – a merchant clerkship, bartending, collecting bills or accompanying men travelling in Europe – all met with Bartleby's refusals: 'I would prefer not to,' 'I would not like it at all' and 'I would prefer to be doing something else' (p. 46). When presented with these options, Bartleby is ultimately ambivalent about the prospects of a career – he does not like the confinement of a store nor the travel required of a gentleman's companion. His desire to be stationary and withdraw from these career options rejects ideologies of self-making found in young professional men of the antebellum period.

Work itself was only one facet of the clerk's role as an antebellum citizen. Office and store workers saw themselves embarking on a project of self-improvement that revolved around social interactions. Societies such as the Mercantile Library Association provided opportunities for self-improvement through offering public lectures (like the ones Pierre declines), organising evening classes and hosting discussion spaces. Conversation and speaking were means of 'fostering sociability' and cultivating and displaying 'moral properties of middle-class taste'.[43] For example, George Nayes, a clerk writing for the *Mercantile Library Reporter* in 1856, explained why he preferred conversation to reading:

> The manner, the expression, the tone, the gesture, the lively anecdote, the brilliant wit, the sharp repartee, the well-conducted argument, the workings of different minds, the animation depicted on the countenance of the speakers, the natural eloquence flowing from the heart, excite a deeper interest, and make more lasting impressions of pleasure on the mind than the perusing of a book in solitude, however elegant or agreeable be the style, and however exciting or instructive be the theme.[44]

Nayes' exuberant and overflowing description of conversation reflects the excitement of young professional men who viewed conversation as both an art in itself and a performance of cultural taste and education. Eloquence was a key marker of respectability: these young professional men wished their acquaintances to see them as men who had something valuable to say. We could think of this as a 'White voice' – a voice that communicates confidence, ease and independence and attempts to garner respect.

The office was a professional space in which to practise conversation and form bonds of affiliation, as it brought together individuals in 'close *psychological* proximity'.[45] For the narrator in 'Bartleby', the office is an intimate space that provides opportunities for connection and refuge in a city of crowds and disconnection. When Bartleby first arrives, the narrator is pleased by the tranquillity he offers in opposition to Nippers and Turkey. He instals Bartleby in his room, separated by a 'high green folding screen' that removes the scrivener from the narrator's sight but not from his voice; privacy and society are 'conjoined' (p. 24). In this partitioned chamber, with only a screen between them, conversation is always possible and the narrator has the opportunity to talk to Bartleby. The office becomes a space that provides relative tranquillity away from the bustle outside and is therefore open to intimate human interaction and communication. When Bartleby begins to refuse tasks, the narrator sees himself and Bartleby inextricably linked by a 'fraternal melancholy!' as two isolated souls in the impersonal city (p. 33). This connection leads him to attempt to forge a familial relationship – at times fraternal, at times paternal – with the copyist, a relationship that is not reciprocated.

However, Bartleby is a man who has given up not just on work but, inexplicably, on everyday human interactions. His utterances are only in response to the narrator; he does not initiate conversation. His silences reject the 'intimate attachment and affiliation' White citizens formed through conversation.[46] It is absurd that Bartleby could have a career as a 'companion to Europe, to entertain some young gentleman' with conversation when he continually rejects the bonds of familiarity and intimacy offered to him that connect citizens across the nation (p. 46). With no intention to use the Wall Street office as a space of self-improvement, Bartleby has no reason to talk. Never venturing outside the office or interacting with the world through newspapers and magazines, unlike the clerks visiting the Mercantile Library Association, Bartleby has nothing to talk about. His refusals and silences are in opposition to both the bustle of capitalism and the professional social interactions expected in the workplace. He rejects expectations of the clerk-citizen in his disengagement from the workplace community and his muteness regarding his personal life and history. Exasperated by Bartleby's desire for privacy, the narrator enquires:

'Will you tell me, Bartleby, where you were born?'
'I would prefer not to.'
'Will you tell me *any thing* about yourself?'
'I would prefer not to.'
'But what reasonable objection can you have to speak to me? I feel friendly towards you.' (p. 35)

From his initial introduction of the scrivener, the narrator admits, 'While of other law-copyists I might write the complete life, of Bartleby nothing of that sort can be done' (p. 18). Bartleby arrives without a history and with no connections to the world outside of the office. Arsić and Deleuze call him an original because he is formless and undecipherable.[47] Part of that unreadability for the narrator and the reader is because his personal or family history – his formation – cannot be traced. Over the course of Bartleby's short employment and lengthy severance, the narrator seeks to know more about the copyist's past, to both understand Bartleby's inaction and forge a bond with him beyond that of employer–employee.

Bartleby rejects the narrator's demand for conversation, his expectation of collegiality and his larger desire to be 'friendly'. He blocks the ease of the narrator and marks himself as not comfortable in taking up this space where a collegial intimacy is expected. Unlike Isabel in *Pierre*, Bartleby inhabits a relatively socially privileged position afforded by his gender and profession: he is not the paper mill girl or the seamstress; he exists within the professional White male realm of the office. His refusal to speak – either to explain his behaviour or engage in societal acts expected in the office – challenges the ideal that White male citizens can and should speak for themselves. He is the most discomfiting character in this book because he refuses to use his voice to demonstrate the qualities of cultural citizenship ascribed to White professional men, qualities that the narrator repeatedly encourages and expects. His continuing presence poses the question of what should happen if someone does not want to speak for themselves or withdraws from cultural expectations of citizenship. In 'Bartleby', the narrator transforms Bartleby into a dependant, no longer viewing him as a citizen because he refuses to act or speak as one.

Like Pierre, the lawyer collapses his relations into intimate ones, and he increasingly views Bartleby as a dependant who must be looked after because he fails to embody the autonomy and self-improvement expected of the clerk-citizen. In the eyes of the narrator Bartleby is a 'poor, pale, passive mortal' who 'prefers to cling' to him, recalling the image of Pip riveting himself to Ahab (p. 44). Bartleby becomes a helpless creature who is clearly dependent on the lawyer's goodwill – in the lawyer's mind – to save him from a life on the streets. Bartleby is a 'millstone' around the lawyer's neck and at the same time a pitiable creature that the narrator can claim as his own (p. 37). Hearing the scrivener's unreasonable and inexplicable utterances, the narrator views Bartleby as a spiritual challenge sent to better him. As in *Pierre*, ownership of others bolsters claims of self-possession and autonomy. Driven by self-interest, the lawyer converts Bartleby into a spiritual prop. He has been sent by 'an all-wise Providence' to test the lawyer, so that his 'mission in this world' is to house the copyist. Again, this relationship is predicated on a bond between the two men that the narrator assumes to exist: that because Bartleby does not feel at home in the office space like a fraternal employee, he must be cared for like a child. In considering their association 'predestinated from eternity' the narrator firmly binds himself and Bartleby together in a relationship beyond the workplace (p. 42).

The narrator's assumed ownership of Bartleby clearly marks the copyist as a racialised figure. This is not to say that Bartleby is a slave analogue or that his resistance to his occupation represents a slave revolt but that, like *Pierre*, the text exists within a pervading logic in which people can be turned into property, a state of dependency occupied to different extents by White women, children and the enslaved. It is clear that Bartleby is a figure of independence, disruptively voicing his opinion, and as a liminally White man there is always the possibility that his Whiteness could be re-established if he ascribed to the correct professional and cultural values the narrator encourages. However, because he is not interested in self-improvement either in the office or in a new position, the narrator takes on an increasingly paternal role, reducing Bartleby to a creature who must be looked after. In a period in which the figure of the White man connoted independence and the non-White and non-male occupied a state of dependence, a man who cannot be responsible for himself is no longer a citizen and loses his Whiteness. Ahmed argues that if a body cannot perform White behaviours it loses its capabilities and access: 'When someone's whiteness is in dispute, then they come under "stress", which in turns threatens body motility, or what the body "can do".'[48] The narrator starts to shape Bartleby into different postures, marking him out as something to be possessed and positioned.

The narrator's paternalist attempt to possess Bartleby as a dependant can be seen in the connection Melville draws between the copyist and physical property. In lacking property in himself, Bartleby becomes a piece of property. Bartleby is a fixture in the office, and Melville closely associates him with the empty White wall at which he stares, because they are both immovable and blank. The narrator likens him to furniture, thinking he is as 'harmless and noiseless as any of these old chairs'. Later, he becomes an extension of the staircase, sitting on the banisters stilly and silently. However, perturbed by Bartleby's immovability, the narrator imagines a scenario of inheritance in which Bartleby could 'perhaps outlive me, and claim possession of my office by right of his perpetual occupancy'. The narrator not only fears becoming like

Bartleby himself, as shown in his copying of Bartleby's language, but that the reverse could also be true and Bartleby could usurp his social position. The prospect of a dependant – someone who now very clearly does not belong in the institutional space – taking over this professional space and 'scandalizing' the narrator's reputation deeply troubles the lawyer (pp. 42, 43).

This fear abates by the narrator rapidly killing off the seemingly immortal Bartleby in his mind. It's not only Bartleby's motility that is affected, but his imagined, and later real, *mortality*. Instead of inheriting the office, Bartleby will die there, and the narrator briefly fantasises that he will 'mason up his remains in the wall' (p. 44). The image of a corpse subsumed into the built environment resonates with Poe's stories of entombment, for example 'The Fall of the House of Usher', 'The Tell-Tale Heart' (1843), 'The Black Cat' and 'The Cask of Amontillado' (1846). The proximity of the buried body in Poe's stories sends the murderers mad because they cannot distance themselves from the victim. Similarly, Melville's narrator imagines Bartleby's death and burial to negate his clinging threat of inheritance. However, at the same time, he continues to make a genealogical claim on Bartleby as his ward and inextricably tied to him. Assuming that Bartleby has no friends or family, the narrator takes control of Bartleby's body as his own property and a part of the real estate he leases. Having failed to make inroads using an argument of self-improvement, he turns Bartleby into a dependant rather than face the reality that Bartleby is disengaging from work and self-development, yet is still an autonomous man. In a last-ditch attempt to save him, the narrator explicitly invites a familial relationship, asking Bartleby to return to his house: 'Will you go home with me now – not to my office, but my dwelling' (p. 47). He does not specify what would happen there, but a paternal desire to care for Bartleby as a dependant – even temporarily – is patent.

The narrator's final step in making the copyist a dependant is to turn Bartleby into text itself. Throughout the short story, the lawyer attempts to understand Bartleby's inscrutable statements by reading his facial expressions, his movements and his possessions. For example, he invades Bartleby's desk in order to find clues of the scrivener's personal life, but finds only a handkerchief containing his small savings. On realising that Bartleby is a blank space and that neither his possessions nor his statements will reveal why he refuses, the narrator finds the impetus to fill in the blank space with his own narrative. This is most apparent in the narrator's postscript to the story, in which he relays a rumour about Bartleby's previous employment. The narrator invests in this rumour because it provides a form of closure and explanation; it makes Bartleby's character and history legible and easier to comprehend. If Bartleby will not speak for himself in order to demonstrate his character or explain his behaviour, then the rumour will speak for him. This 'vague report' claims that before coming to Wall Street, Bartleby previously worked at the Dead Letter Office in Washington, DC, sorting unopened lost mail. This rumour holds a 'strange suggestive interest' for the lawyer because it enables him, finally, to understand Bartleby's inaction and inexplicable voice. The narrator constructs a narrative in which Bartleby's dealing with those hopeless correspondences heightens his own 'pallid hopelessness', causing him to withdraw from work, human interactions and life itself (p. 51).

In the narrator's eyes, these letters reinforce Bartleby's position outside the community. When the narrator asks, 'Dead letters! does it not sound like dead men?' he believes the answer to be yes (p. 51). Dead letters can sound like – or denote – dead men because of the continual importance the narrator places on communication. Saturated in thousands of cut-off correspondences from tragically foreshortened relationships, the Dead Letter Office comes to symbolise disconnection, missed opportunities and the severance of bonds of affection. Men who do not participate in forming these bonds of affection, like Bartleby, who refuses to use his voice to converse with the narrator, fail to meet the expectations of the antebellum White male citizen. The narrator turns Bartleby into a character in his own literary sketch, fashioning an affecting backstory for the scrivener in order to explain Bartleby's muted and inscrutable voice. Of course he would become 'a little deranged' (p. 49). The postscript is a rationalising fiction that explains why people like Bartleby can't be in society and professional spaces and must belong in a different institution: the jail, the asylum and eventually the grave. However, Melville ultimately makes the truth unattainable. The narrator and the reader can never truly know Bartleby's reasons. The lawyer's final exclamation – 'Ah Bartleby! Ah humanity!' – is again, just like Bartleby's polite preferences, an ambiguous statement. It can mean either that Bartleby is the epitome of the human condition or that he is in fact the opposite (p. 51). Bartleby's silence has become a contagion itself, disavowing explanation or closure. Like the ending of *Pierre*, the lawyer is left with his own silence, as language cannot fully explain or testify to experience.

In his fantastical examples of people on the edges of society – the shrieking, otherworldly illegitimate girl, the refusing, cadaverous clerk – Melville presents muteness and wordlessness as ways of communicating marginality. Melville returns to the possibility of silence as a tool of resistance in 'Benito Cereno'. Unable to explicitly tell Delano of the slave revolt aboard the *San Dominick*, both Don Benito and the enslaved men communicate this exchange of power through looks, gestures and conversation.[49] Don Benito's vocal interactions with his personal manservant, the enslaved Babo, demonstrate the reversal of racial hierarchy. Benito's failing speech, described as 'husky whisper[s]', mutterings and 'vacant response[s]', in contrast to the 'conversational familiarities' of the loquacious Babo, reveals to the reader the failure of White mastery.[50] Delano, blinkered by his belief in racial science and the subservience of Africans, is unable to see that Babo's deferential language is not a sign of ultimate devotion to his enslaver but of dominion over the captain. Babo interjects, speaking for Benito when the cadaverous captain cannot talk, such as apologising for the captain's poor state of health and mind: 'His mind wanders. He was thinking of the plague that followed the gales . . . my poor, poor master!'[51] Babo's sympathetic statement creates a new narrative of shipwreck and illness and contributes to his performance of devoted slave, which conceals the truth of the revolt. Just as he attends to the captain's physical needs, Babo's control of the conversation signifies his control over the captain. What appears as submission is a veil for resistance. This cross-racial encounter challenges White citizenship by overturning ideologies of racial hierarchy – White people as benevolent masters, Black people as subservient servants. As I turn to in my final chapter on *The Garies and their Friends*, Frank J. Webb equally overturns expectations of White and Black behaviour through discourses of Black respectability, and Whiteness itself is shown to be an arbitrary yet fiercely guarded construct.

'Benito Cereno' ends with periods of extended silence after Delano's crew crush the revolt. Benito, unable to reconcile the murder of his friend Aranda at the hands of the enslaved, dies shortly after providing a legal testimony. A Spanish notary mediates the account in several pages of third-person legal narrative, which renders Benito voiceless once more. White power is violently restored but Benito has no response to the shadow cast over him by Babo's seizure of the ship. At the same time Babo, captured and sentenced to death for leading the uprising, 'uttered no sound, and could not be forced to'. Babo's 'unabashed' wordless gaze is a deliberate refusal to testify before his execution. His 'voiceless end' resists the White hegemony's need for a narrative.[52] Like Bartleby, in not speaking he declines to provide an explanation for his actions and disavows closure. The two men and Isabel offer the possibility that for people on the margins or excluded from society, their experiences could exist and be most powerfully expressed 'in a voice-less state'.[53] Although White supremacy has been reinstated, 'Benito Cereno' ends equally as pessimistically as 'Bartleby' and *Pierre*. Babo's final resounding silence leaves the failure of White mastery and self-mastery hanging over the White community and the reader.

## NOTES

1. Wray, *Not Quite White*, p. 2.
2. Melville, *Moby Dick*, ed. Tanner, p. 106.
3. Ibid. pp. 461–2, 471.
4. Thompson, '"Through Consumptive Pallors of This Blank, Raggy Life"', p. 40.
5. Melville, *White-Jacket or The World in a Man-of-War*, ed. Hayford, Parker and Tanselle, p. 379; DeLombard, 'White-Jacket: Telling Who Is – and Aint – a Slave', in Levine (ed.), *The New Cambridge Companion to Herman Melville*, pp. 51–67 (p. 57).
6. Freeburg, *Melville and the Idea of Blackness*, p. 4.

7. Ahmed, 'A Phenomenology of Whiteness', p. 157.
8. Zakim, 'Producing Capitalism', in Zakim and Kornblith (eds), *Capitalism Takes Command*, pp. 223–48 (p. 224).
9. Goldberg, *Quiet Testimony*, p. 88.
10. Melville, *Pierre: Or The Ambiguities*, pp. 112, 142. Further citations of this edition are given in parentheses in the main text.
11. Poe, 'The Philosophy of Composition', in *Essays and Reviews*, pp. 13–25 (p. 19).
12. Melville's friend Evert Duyckinck reviewed *Jane Eyre* and *Wuthering Heights* in *The Literary World*. Hershel Parker suggests that Melville translated Duyckinck's comments on the 'hideous inhumanities' of *Wuthering Heights* into the 'horrible and inscrutable humanities' of Isabel's gothic childhood. Parker, *Herman Melville*, vol. 2, pp. 55–6.
13. Beecher, *A Treatise on Domestic Economy, For the Use of Young Ladies at Home, and at School*, p. 33.
14. The sisters held private and public séances in New York in 1850, attracting writers such as James Fenimore Cooper and William Cullen Bryant. Braude, *Radical Spirits*, p. 16.
15. Capron and Barron, *Explanation and History of the Mysterious Communion with Spirits*, p. 70. See also Coggeshall, *The Signs of the Times*, pp. 98–9; Tiffany, *Lectures on Spiritualism*, p. 205.
16. *A Summary View of the Millennial Church*, p. 88. See Sealts, 'Melville and the Shakers'.
17. Post, *Voices from the Spirit World*; Brittan (ed.), *Spiritual Telegraph*, vol. 1, pp. 177–8. For discussions of 'Indian' spirits see Bennett, *Transatlantic Spiritualism and Nineteenth-Century American Literature*, pp. 83–113; McGarry, *Ghosts of Futures Past*, pp. 66–93.
18. Brooks, *Bodies in Dissent*, p. 21.
19. Hawthorne, *The House of the Seven Gables*, p. 96.
20. *A History of the Recent Developments in Spiritual Manifestations, in the City of Philadelphia*, p. 11.
21. Mueller, *The Infinite Fraternity of Feeling*, p. 24.
22. Hawthorne, *The Blithedale Romance*, pp. 187, 112–13, 111.
23. Braude, *Radical Spirits*, p. 23.
24. Ibid. p. 56.
25. Jonik, *Herman Melville and the Politics of the Inhuman*, p. 76.
26. Gilmore, *Aesthetic Materialism*, p. 89.
27. Jeffory Clymer states that *Pierre* 'reprises the interracial incest plots that filled anti-slavery novels and stories'. Robert Levine contends that the novel's 'miscegenated (and unknown) genealogies' from Pierre's slaveowning grandfather extend beyond Isabel to Pierre himself, locating Blackness at the heart of the model antebellum family. In addition, Carolyn Karcher argues the suggestion of Pierre's blood relation to his grandfather's horses represents 'the illegitimate mulatto children fathered by slaveholders' which precursors the warped familial relations throughout the novel. Clymer, *Family Money*, p. 74; Levine, 'Pierre's Blackened Hand', p. 34; Karcher, *Shadow over the Promised Land*, p. 101.

28. Freeburg, *Melville and the Idea of Blackness*, p. 3.
29. After signing a book contract with Harper Brothers in February 1852, Parker contends that Melville then 'added many wholly unplanned pages on his hero as a juvenile author' plot to the novel. In the 1995 Kraken edition, Parker restores the text to its original shorter state. Parker, 'Introduction', in Melville, *Pierre, Or, The Ambiguities: The Kraken Edition*, ed. Parker, pp. xi–xlvi (p. xi).
30. Faulkner, 'The Ambiguousnesses', pp. 44–7.
31. Weinstein, 'We Are Family', p. 22.
32. Ahmed, 'A Phenomenology of Whiteness', pp. 159, 154, 157.
33. Coviello, *Intimacy in America*, p. 11.
34. Melville, 'Bartleby the Scrivener', in *The Complete Shorter Fiction*, pp. 18–51 (p. 18). Further citations of this edition are given in parentheses in the main text.
35. Arsić, *Passive Constitutions, Or 7½ Times Bartleby*.
36. Deleuze, 'Bartleby; or, The Formula', in *Essays Critical and Clinical*, pp. 68–90 (p. 73).
37. 'Positive face is defined as the individual's desire that her/his wants be appreciated and approved of in social interaction, whereas negative face is the desire for freedom of action and freedom from imposition.' Watts, *Politeness*, p. 86.
38. Knighton, *Idle Threats*, p. 33.
39. Thompson, '"Through Consumptive Pallors of This Blank, Raggy Life"', p. 25.
40. Melville, 'The Paradise of Bachelors and The Tartarus of Maids', in *The Complete Shorter Fiction*, pp. 313–32 (pp. 325–6).
41. Luskey, *On the Make*, p. 2.
42. Ibid. Even a small detail like his attendance at Trinity Church implies his investment in others viewing him as respectable. Newly rebuilt in 1846, Trinity Church was a pillar of prosperity and one of the most powerful landlords in Manhattan. Burrows and Wallace, *Gotham*, pp. 726, 767.
43. Augst, *The Clerk's Tale*, pp. 95, 102.
44. Nayes, 'Good Conversation and Prose Writing', *Mercantile Library Reporter* 2 (1856), pp. 69–70, quoted in Ibid. p. 99.
45. Augst, *The Clerk's Tale*, p. 227.
46. Coviello, *Intimacy in America*, p. 10.
47. Arsić, *Passive Constitutions*, p. 7; Deleuze, 'Bartleby; or, The Formula', p. 83.
48. Ahmed, 'A Phenomenology of Whiteness', p. 160.
49. For a discussion of reading signs in 'Benito Cereno', see Goldberg, *Quiet Testimony*, pp. 105–9.
50. Melville, 'Benito Cereno', in *The Complete Shorter Fiction*, pp. 52–126 (pp. 58, 66, 69).
51. Ibid. p. 62.
52. Ibid. p. 126.
53. Goldberg, *Quiet Testimony*, p. 101.

# 6

# 'I'M MAKING A WHITE MAN OF HIM': MAKING AND BREAKING WHITENESS IN *THE GARIES AND THEIR FRIENDS*

While writing his debut novel, Frank J. Webb took to the stage. Following his wife's lauded performances of Harriet Beecher Stowe's dramatisation of *Uncle Tom's Cabin* (1852), *The Christian Slave* (1855), on both sides of the Atlantic, in May 1857 the African American couple returned with a new sketch, 'The Linford Studio', at Camden House in Kensington:

> Mr. and Mrs. Linford are a young married couple in difficulties. Linford is by profession an artist, . . . At length the idea of 'getting up' an entertainment occurs to the ingenious little wife, and as her husband has informed her that a Mr. Timkinsi is shortly coming to have his portrait photographed in a variety of characters in which he, the said Timkinsi, thinks that he is a proficient, she determines to disguise herself as the expected Timkinsi, and to see whether she cannot astonish her husband in the particular line in which the 'coming man' considers himself so great. . . . but before she puts her plan into execution she and her husband sing together one or two charming little American melodies full of sweetness and simplicity – two of which, 'The Old Kentucky Home' and 'The Old Folk at Home,' would become very popular if known.[1]

The following entertainment came from fair-skinned Mary E. Webb, wearing a variety of costumes and emulating voices to sing from 'Meyerbeer's opera', give Othello's 'Most potent, grave' speech, and later appear as 'an Indian woman, a

Chinaman, a Frenchman', a cross-racial and cross-gender performance she had already perfected in her dramatic readings of Stowe's antislavery novel, which I return to later.[2] Performing national and racial types in comic fashion, Mary Webb is a Black woman putting on a one-woman minstrel show.

What I find most striking here is the couple's choice of music in the scene, which complements and extends Mary Webb's transgression of the colour line. The two songs were written by White songwriter Stephen Foster and encapsulate his changing attitudes to slavery. Foster wrote in exaggerated African American vernacular the earlier 'The Old Folks at Home' (1851), about an enslaved man longing for the plantation, and sold it to the Christy Minstrels blackface troupe, who sang it in their lampooning of *Uncle Tom's Cabin*. The later 'My Old Kentucky Home, Good-Night!' (1852) continued to romanticise the South but without Ebonics and was praised by Frederick Douglass for 'awaken[ing] the sympathies for the slave, in which anti-slavery principles take root, grow, and flourish'.[3] Bringing these two songs together from opposing positions on slavery, the Webbs perform a double racial transformation. In the newspaper account it is not specified what race the Linfords are – only that when Mary Webb appears as Timinski she is a 'dark man' – but this lack of attention from a White reporter suggests that the Webbs are acting as a White couple who sing a sympathetic abolitionist song in unmarked voices before switching to perform in a blackface dialect.[4] Through the voice alone, the African American couple on stage temporarily become blackface minstrels. In singing as a Black couple constructed through a White minstrelised mouthpiece, the Webbs paradoxically reinforce the prior Whiteness of the Linfords and their own access to Whiteness in portraying them. Frank and Mary Webb's sketch and song shows Whiteness to be a performance that can be made through speech and gesture, and at the same time, in the very act of putting on these domestic scenes and White oratory to a genteel White audience, they cross the boundaries of Whiteness to claim respectability, talent and taste as no longer virtues exclusive to White men and women.

I start this chapter with such a seemingly small episode because it captures the performativity and permeability of Whiteness at work in the quotidian encounters of Webb's fiction. Returning to the origin of critical Whiteness studies, African American writing, this chapter examines how tenets of Whiteness are constructed and arbitrary in Webb's *The Garies and their Friends* (1857). Assembling a cast of respectable free African American families and cunning and dishonest White men in Philadelphia, Webb demonstrates that civic values coded as White are not intrinsic to people coded as White, but yet the rights Whiteness affords are not extended to Black Americans who embody those tenets. Influenced by the cross-racial oratory of his wife, Webb conveys the permeability of the colour line through episodes of African American passing and White racial transformation.

The second novel published by an African American, after William Wells Brown's *Clotel* (1853), sentimental novel *The Garies* follows interracial couple Clarence and Emily, who leave Georgia for Philadelphia, where they can freely marry. In Philadelphia the reader meets working-class Black family the Ellises (Charles, Ellen and their three children, Esther, Caddy and Charlie), wealthy Black businessman Walters, and 'Slippery' George Stevens, an estranged relative and neighbour of Clarence who orchestrates a murderous lynch mob and shoots Clarence in order to inherit his wealth. After the murder of Clarence and Emily, their children grow up on different sides of the colour line, as daughter Emily remains in the Black community but her brother Clary passes for White, a performance that is tragically uncovered at the end of the novel. Moving away from the plantation, Webb thinks beyond the issue of emancipation for Black Americans. Therefore, *The Garies* is not primarily an antislavery novel – it is an antiracist novel. Asking what free Black life can look like after slavery, Webb draws the reader's attention to the legal structures and extra-legal violence in a 'free' Northern city that prohibit Black safety and success. Through several literal and rhetorical episodes of racial transformation, Webb shows Whiteness itself to be a construct, permeable and therefore fiercely guarded by a White supremacist society.

Although receiving high praise from Stowe in her British preface, the novel's shift from Savannah to Philadelphia explains why *The Garies* did not make it to an American press for over a century.[5] Webb's focus on free Black life did not fit the literary marketplace's expectation that African American writers would narrate uplifting journeys from slavery to emancipation.[6] After the text's rediscovery and republication, 1970s and 1980s Black literary scholars were disappointed in Webb's seeming disinterest in abolition and radicalism. Certainly, Webb's opening chapters, which I discuss later, present a kindly White master amongst a group of devoted enslaved men and women, suggesting at the outset a diminishing of slavery's cruelty and its role in Black American life. Furthermore, both Addison Gayle Jr and Bernard Bell critique Webb for claiming wealth as the necessary path to securing racial equality. In the figure of entrepreneur Walters, Bell sees Webb promoting 'green power' over religion or radicalism to end racism, and Gayle calls the novel 'the *Poor Richard's Almanack* of the black middle class'.[7] Criticism from the 1990s onwards has been more sympathetic to Webb's choice of location and politics. Robert Levine argues the text attends to the 'contradictions and vulnerabilities of black middle-class life in Philadelphia' in a much more realistic mode than previous criticism suggests. Recent scholarship has considered specific ways Black characters navigate a White supremacist society in Philadelphia, and the more complex articulations of race and class at work in the novel.[8] Meticulous historical work by critics such as Mary Maillard has established detailed autobiographical connections between Frank Webb's extended family and characters in *The Garies* – in this chapter I focus on how Mary Webb's performance career illuminates her husband's depiction of race and Whiteness in the novel and structure the chapter through sets of characters who index the arbitrariness of Whiteness and its exclusive yet threatened status.[9] In the first part of the chapter I discuss the multiple movements across the colour line that Mary Webb makes in her readings of *The Christian Slave* and in 'The Linford Studio', movements that evinced that the talent of performing as another race was not limited to those with pale skin. In *The Garies*, Webb stakes a claim on 'white' values to show Black men and women worthy of respect and success. In Black businessman Walters and White-passing characters George Winston and Emily Garie – who display all the values of White citizenship but are bound and excluded by a structurally White supremacist society – Webb writes a critical Whiteness studies novel.

Further to characters becoming White, Webb presents a number of White characters who figuratively or physically lose Whiteness, becoming liminally White and placed on the borders of society. In the second part of the chapter I discuss how Whiteness is under threat from cross-racial kinship – extending from abolitionism to interracial marriage in the case of Clarence Garie – and that physical blackening marks out those who fail to demonstrate White civic values. Webb's understanding of Whiteness is prescient of how critical Whiteness studies operates at the end of the twentieth century – to show Whiteness as a set of privileges and rights that can be removed if someone fails its values. Robert Nowatzki writes that 'Webb's novel anticipates recent theoretical discussions about the constructed nature of race'; beyond showing that Whiteness can be both made and partially or fully erased, I argue that Webb engages in the second aim of critical Whiteness studies as raised in the Introduction – to be critical of Whiteness and White supremacy.[10] In concert with his episodes of blackening, in his scenes of White death and the tragic end to Clary Garie's passing, Webb shows White supremacy as a significantly damaging enterprise that poisons and warps those who seek to uphold it, Black or White. Throughout the novel Webb breaks Whiteness by showing it as fragile and permeable, but his resounding critique is that Whiteness breaks others. At the end of the chapter I turn to scenes of White death and decay in other works of early Black fiction. These episodes across sentimental and gothic genres show Black writers reversing the White gaze to use White pain as a creative and emotional resource, and they offer the first glimpses of a possible world without White supremacy.

### 'THE BLACK SIDDONS': MARY WEBB'S CROSS-RACIAL ORATORY AND BLACK RESPECTABILITY

Born into a free Black family in Philadelphia in 1828, Frank J. Webb grew up in the city's flourishing Black community and worked there as a commercial designer. After his business failed, he moved to writing and speaking on Black civil rights and emigration schemes, before supporting his wife's performance tours. Married to Frank in 1845, Mary Webb (née Espartero) was the daughter of a fugitive enslaved woman in New Bedford and the White 'Spanish gentleman of wealth' who unsuccessfully attempted to purchase her freedom.[11] Supported at first by her estranged father's income and later by her mother's labour, Mary enjoyed 'all those educational advantages which the influence of friends managed to secure for her, despite the prevailing prejudice against persons of African extraction' and developed 'marked elocutionary powers'.[12] Applauded for her performances of Shakespeare and Longfellow in Philadelphia and Boston, she attracted the attention of Stowe, who dramatised *Uncle Tom's Cabin* specifically for Webb. Following performances in Northern cities with a tour of the UK at the invitation of Stowe, the Webbs lived in London from June 1856 to shortly after the September 1857 publication of *The Garies*.[13]

More than a mouthpiece for Stowe's abolitionism, Webb's dramatic readings show two clear points on Whiteness that appear in *The Garies* – one, that race can be constructed and the colour line can be transgressed, and two, that Black performers utilised the 'White' virtue of respectability to challenge White supremacy and its denial of Black civil rights. Reviews of her performances pay close attention to her voice. In speaking as several characters from *Uncle Tom's Cabin* she becomes Black or White, and by extension through her respectable talent she gains access to Whiteness. In her performances of *The Christian Slave* Webb had to switch between characters of different races using only her voice and gesture. Her skill was well regarded, with *The New York Times* responding, 'the different tones of the different characters so well sustained throughout, that with the eyes closed one would have been sure that different readers were engaged upon the parts'.[14] Like Frank Carwin, Webb was able to create vocalic bodies of different races, moving in and out of African American vernacular dialect and taking on different tones to perform a variety of characters from Tom to Eva to Topsy. Crucially, reports lauded these performances as authentic renderings, 'as nearly natural as it is possible for an imitator to give them'. The New York *Evening Telegraph* praised how she was 'delineating with graphic truthfulness all the varied intonations of the many characters', while *The New York Tribune* applauded her ability to 'intonate through the range of extensive and sympathetic voice according to the characters' demonstrating she has 'evidently taken much pains to qualify herself for the task'.[15]

This praise for authentic yet clearly studied and imitated speech throws up the question of Webb's perceived and shifting racial identity in the North and in London. Before the readings, reviewers commented on both Webb's fair skin and her unquestionable status as a Black woman. She was 'mistaken for an "Anglo-Saxon" who was "a deep brunette"', yet newspapers labelled her 'Black Siddons' or 'Coloured Siddons' to distinguish her from White English actress Sarah Siddons and emphasise her Blackness, and the one illustration of her speaking in London depicts darker skin.[16] The *Illustrated London News* review took pains to clarify that 'Mrs. Webb is not a "nigger",' even though within the pages of *Uncle Tom's Cabin* and *The Garies* she would have undoubtedly faced this slur. For the *News*, Webb's parentage – 'but her father was a European' – elevates her to 'a lady of colour'.[17] Her Blackness was noted in all accounts of her readings and despite being endorsed by Stowe and British aristocratic abolitionists, she faced slights in London based on her race. For example, she was denied use of Charles Dickens's theatre because he disapproved of the influx of Black performers to London theatres and did not want 'Uncle Tom (or Aunt Tomasina) to expound King Lear to me'.[18] Passing for White but having refined Blackness as a social status legible on the pages of newspapers, Webb straddled the colour line.

Throughout the reports of Webb's performances, her Blackness is commented on to mark out talent but not discussed when the individual speeches themselves are appraised. The responses to the readings seem to position her as outside Blackness and as having needed to study and practise what a Black character would sound like. Due to social attitudes against actors of colour, performing Blackness was a White undertaking. Othello – who Webb briefly performed in 'The Linford Studio' – remained a White act, in spite of Ira Aldridge's success in the 1820s and 30s. Therefore, performing Blackness and taking ownership of a non-White character is itself an act of Whiteness. The dark-skinned characters Webb voiced in *The Christian Slave* further erased her own Blackness. Reviews pick out that 'Her imitation of Topsey [sic] was particularly good' and that her 'hoarse negro voice' and particular 'negro intonation' for Tom's hymn singing created 'a mixture of solemnity and pathos quite indescribable'.[19] It's not clear which scene of hymn singing Webb performed, but in III.vi Stowe strangely has Tom open Isaac Watt's hymn 'When I Can Read my Title Clear' (1707) with two verses from the Foster/Christy Minstrels' song 'The Old Folks at Home'.[20] This inclusion further minstrelised Tom, evincing, as Saidiya Hartman has claimed, that Black characters in White antislavery melodramas bore 'a striking resemblance' to the blackface minstrels they countered, and the two opposite portraits of Blackness both served as creative material for White writers and performers.[21] With the Webbs singing 'The Old Folks at Home' in May 1857 while *The Christian Slave* still toured – as discussed at the start of this chapter – it's likely that Webb included this scene when reading. Therefore a quadrupling of racial performance takes place: Webb reads a White-authored text, which voices a flattened portrait of an enslaved Black man, who sings a White-penned song, itself written in blackface dialect and performed by minstrels, themselves engaged in racial transformation. In simultaneously crossing the colour line in both directions but doing so through taking on two White performances – the sentimental antislavery play, the minstrel show – Webb became Whiter by taking on White-authored constructions of Blackness.

Not much is reported on *The Christian Slave*'s White characters in newspaper reviews, but returning to 'The Linford Studio', Webb lays claim on imitating Whiteness with a satiric purpose. After the sketch, Webb continues a solo performance with a repertoire of characters, including an 'excellent illustration' of 'Precilla [sic] P. Bedott, a Yankee lady, from Boonville, Connecticut'.[22] A rural White character mocked for her pretentious speech, Priscilla Bedott appeared in Frances M. Whitcher's *The Widow Bedott Papers* (1855) – earlier serialised in *Godey's Lady Book* – an epistolary satire of the widow Priscilla attempting to find a new husband. Attending to this small detail, like the Foster songs, shows how Black racial performance critiques and gains access to Whiteness. In speaking as this White woman, Webb performs whiteface, the satirising of pretentious White groups by African American performers and enslaved people, and a reversal of the blackface minstrelsy and caricature that mocked the Black dandy, as seen in George Washington Dixon's Zip Coon and Edward Clay's *Life in Philadelphia*. As Marvin McAllister argues, whiteface performances render 'whiteness as usable property', drawing on Cheryl L. Harris's 'whiteness as property' that frames Whiteness as a tool of social domination and ownership over Black and Indigenous groups. In whiteface performances, Whiteness is taken on as artistic material to demonstrate Black self-ownership and their demeaning of – often rural or poor – pretentious White men and women.[23] At the same time as making a comedic statement by mocking a White character as a Black performer, Webb gains further access to Whiteness. She joins in with McWhitcher's satire, claiming that she as a Black woman is more respectable than bumpkin Bedott, but she does so through a White authorial mouthpiece, aligning and even dissolving herself – albeit temporarily – into the White author. In these performances, Webb continually oscillates between operating outside and operating along the edges of Whiteness.

In the biographical sketch of his wife, Frank Webb makes clear the aims of Mary's cross-racial performances. Praising her 'elocution and oratory talent', Webb argues that her 'genius has come the conqueror of prejudice'.

> It will prove that the right which has been claimed for us, by the friends of our race, to stand side by side with our fair-skinned oppressors, that our claim for the right to compete with them in the world of art for the prizes it offers, is not made without strong foundation for its support.[24]

Here, Webb makes an antislavery argument, clearly complementing the content of *The Christian Slave* and the broader arguments other touring American and British abolitionists made. At the same time, he thinks beyond emancipation to questions of equality, success and being recognised for the genius of their endeavours. As Tavia Nyong'o writes, Black activists 'claimed respect in the face of its quotidian denial on both sides of the Atlantic'.[25] In his wife's biography,

Webb forcefully demands this respect, claiming that Mary will 'wring from the unwilling lips of the despisers of her race a confession of her merit'.[26] *The Era* reviewer of 'The Linford Studio' was completely convinced by Webb's case, remarking that 'the marvel . . . arises from a consideration of *who the persons are* that present this entertainment to us'. Although incorrectly stating that the Webbs had formerly been enslaved, the reviewer speaks to broader appreciation that this oppressed group of people could demonstrate 'thought, intellect, possessions, labour, skill, all the property of a master!' as represented by Mary Webb's sophisticated performance.[27] Crossing genders, races and nationalities, Mary Webb's flexibility, in the words of Laura Mielke, 'showcased the genius of a representative African American performer'.[28] In bringing together multiple performance modes – Shakespearean tragedy, Stowe's sentimental drama and the comedic sketch – she simultaneously spoke as a White writer and amply proved her skill as a Black actor.

Genius, talent, thought, skill: these are all markers of respectability that Black men and women in the early US employed to demand abolition and civil rights. As Emma Lapsansky discusses, when Webb was growing up in a free family in 1830s Philadelphia, 'a black elite emerged, defined at first simply by stable employment, circumspect moral behaviour, and participation in local black community affairs'.[29] In their construction of local businesses, social venues, churches and schools, and advocacy of uplift and increased rights – essentially in just living normal lives in the city – they demonstrated all the values prescribed to White citizenship, but without the reward of suffrage or respect. In a structurally White supremacist city, 'success and the "good life" involved opportunity for prominence, but little chance for power'.[30] In 1838 the Pennsylvania congress added 'White' to new suffrage legislation, allowing all White men to vote but excluding all Black men, and Black men were barred from almost all higher education, instead relying on alternative careers in retail and real estate.[31] Mr Balch, Garie's lawyer in *The Garies*, summarises these limitations: 'White boys can go to better schools, and they can enter college and become professional men, lawyers, doctors, &c, or they may be merchants . . . Coloured people can enjoy none of these advantages; they are shut out from them entirely.'[32] Respectable Black families repeatedly came up against virulent anti-Blackness, examples of which we see in *The Garies*: being thrown out of segregated train carriages, being denied schooling in White classrooms or jobs with White employers, being subjected to physical violence and property damage from White rioters. For a sympathetic British antislavery audience, the respectable Black families in *The Garies* affirmatively answer Stowe's preface question: 'Are the race at present held as slaves capable of freedom, self-government, and progress?' (p. 41). At the same time, one initial British review criticised Webb for 'insensibly' endowing his Black characters 'with attributes which in Europe are found only in the most intellectual and refined classes', disbelieving that such a respectable Black community and individuals existed.[33] In this context, Black respectability in the novel critiques the structures and strictures of Whiteness that drove legal exclusions and extra-legal violence, by showing Whiteness itself to be a constructed set of values – not an innate essentialist condition – that could be embodied by those not White, and therefore demands that Black men and women be seen as citizens, not subjects, the same demands Webb makes for himself and his wife during their tour.

Walters is the prime example of Black respectability and success in the novel. The physically darkest character, he stands

> above six feet in height, and exceedingly well-proportioned; of jet-black complexion, and smooth glossy skin. . . . The neatness and care with which he was dressed added to the attractiveness of his appearance. His linen was the perfection of whiteness, and his snowy vest lost nothing by its contact therewith. A long black frock coat, black pants, and highly-polished boots, completed his attire. (p. 144)

His physical dominance comes without a trace of sexualised threat that would be found in racial caricature and anti-abolition writings. In fact, Webb seems to be teasing a White audience uneasy with the prospect of a prominent, attractive Black man by guaranteeing that the 'snowy white vest' will remain undiminished – not from contact with his black clothing but his white, thereby inverting the expected threat. Walters's respectable appearance is matched by his respectable wealth as a real estate dealer 'worth half a million dollars' who owns 'one hundred brick houses' to rent in the city. From Charles Ellis's description of his success, his friend George Winston asks 'oh, then he is a white man?' – even though George has been passing as White himself, he cannot fathom a Black man being afforded this success in a White society (p. 84). Walters' function in the text is to disprove anti-Black sentiment, and as *The Morning Post* of London review of the novel feared, to 'prove the superiority of the coloured population over their white-faced brethren'.[34] Webb elevates the Black population above White Philadelphia, using Walters as an example of many African Americans who outshine 'whites in wealth and general intelligence: for whilst it was one in fifteen amongst the whites unable to read and write, it was but one in eighteen amongst the coloured'. Black wealth from men such as Walters disproportionately maintains the city's welfare; they pay 'in the shape of taxes upon our real estate, more than our proportion for the support of paupers, insane, convicts, &c' according to Charles. Indeed, figures on Black social conditions quoted in the novel counter 'the most distressing tales of our destitution' and dependency put forward by segregationist Northerners such as the local Colonization Society, proving that Black residents are not only equal to but exceed the civic behaviours of their White antagonists (pp. 84, 83).

In an anti-Black society, Walters is derided for his respectable, moneyed masculinity. Stevens's virulent hatred for him is specifically due to Walters's 'grand airs' and his replication of elite Whiteness in disrespecting a middling white man – 'it is bad enough to be treated with *hauteur* by a white man, but contempt from a nigger is almost unendurable' (p. 147). In print and performance culture, the Black gentleman figure attracted ridicule from minstrels and cartoonists because they dared to cross the colour line in their behaviour. Clay's *Life in Philadelphia* lithographs mock Black social mobility and interest in respectable fashion and socialising. Clay distorts these men and women into exaggerated physical caricatures who are lampooned by their own foolish dialogue. For example, when a gentleman asks in one print, 'How you find yourself dis hot weader Miss Chloe?' the young woman responds with the malapropism 'I aspire too much!' In this pun Clay shuts down Black social aspirations and claims on White public and private spheres.[35] While Walters embodies middle-class gentility coded as White, he never diminishes his Blackness, further compounding the shame and anger Stevens feels. In a challenge to racist caricature, Webb draws the reader's attention to a single work of Black portraiture hanging on Walters's wall that captures Clarence's eye. Walters responds to his glance:

> 'So you, too, are attracted by that picture . . . All white men look at it with interest. A black man in the uniform of a general officer is something so unusual that they cannot pass it with a glance . . . That is Toussaint l'Ouverture . . . and I have every reason to believe it to be a correct likeness. . . . [He] looks like a man of intelligence. It is entirely different from any likeness I ever saw of him. The portraits generally represent him as a monkey-faced person, with a handkerchief about his head.' (p. 145)

The picture he proudly displays is likely modelled after Nicholas Eustache Maurin's sketch depicting the general in military uniform and neoclassical profile. Composed in the 1820s before appearing in Joseph Saint-Rémy's 1853 biography, Maurin's drawing copied a now lost portrait the Haitian leader gave a French official in 1801, suggesting that unknown artist and therefore Maurin achieved 'a correct likeness' of which Toussaint approved.[36] This respectable work of art showing Toussaint as an intelligent and attractive military leader takes ownership of and undoes the White gaze of Clay's caricature and impresses on the reader how Walters wishes to be seen. Taking in this resplendent and powerful Black subject, Clarence comments that the portrait 'gives me an idea of the man that accords with his actions' – a quiet moment of support for Black self-determination and leadership and a further demonstration of Webb's aim to demand respect for Black citizens shut out by Whiteness (p. 145).

In concert with prominent figures of Black respectability, Webb depicts acts of inadvertent and deliberate passing to furthermore reinforce Whiteness as an arbitrary construct not intrinsic to White bodies but that is permeable to those who look, act or sound 'White' enough. Emily Garie is mistaken as White by Jule, the wife of George Stevens, during an encounter in the Garies' darkened parlour. Just as *The Christian Slave* audience member could close their eyes and imagine Mary Webb manifesting a White or Black character, Emily could be anyone in the dark. Having met Emily's White husband and her White-passing 'sweet' and 'so very affectionate' daughter, and hearing from her own daughter that Emily is 'a pretty lady, with large great eyes', Jule assumes the well-spoken and genteel woman must be White. Feeling secure in her racial detection, Jule launches unprovoked into a complaint about the possibility of having Black neighbours, and she calls for emancipated people to be sent back to Africa for being 'the most ignorant, idle, miserable set I ever saw' (p. 150). When Clarence brings a lamp close to Emily's face, 'their visitor saw that she belonged to the very class that she had been abusing in such unmeasured terms'. In this revelation, Jule is 'completely demolished' as her assumptions of White and Black behaviour and virtue are overturned – a hierarchy she re-establishes by immediately banishing Clary from their house and seeking to have the Garie children expelled from the local White school (p. 151).

Emily's cousin – George Winston – does not require the dark to convince White men he is White. Winston successfully passes for White on many occasions as his behaviours stop White men and women from questioning his heritage. Working as a clerk while enslaved in New Orleans,

> his manners and person improved with his circumstances; and at the time he occupied the chief-clerk's desk, no one would have suspected him to be a slave, and few who did not know his history would have dreamed that he had a drop of African blood in his veins. He was unremitting in his attention to the duties of his station, and gained, by his assiduity and amiable deportment, the highest regard of his employer. (p. 51)

Industrious and respectable, Winston escapes categorisation as Black by White society and enters into Whiteness by embodying the behaviours valued in White citizens. Webb's separating out of physical appearance, heritage and behaviour demonstrates once again how Whiteness is a construct that can be secured by those who appear to be 'White' enough and demonstrate expected behaviours. Manumitted as a young man and inheriting significant funds from his enslaver, Winston visits the North to consider opening a business there. On his return to Savannah at the opening of the novel, he regales Emily and Clarence with his experience of passing in Philadelphia, going to 'the opera, the theatre, to museums, concerts, and I can't tell where all' at the invitation of Clarence's acquaintance Mr Priestly, who believes 'the existence of a "gentleman" with African blood in his veins, is a moral and physical impossibility' (pp. 45, 46). If Black men cannot be gentlemen, but a Black man is treated as a gentleman, then he must be White, exposing the colour line as a social construct. Amused by this hoodwinking, Clarence intends to write to the segregationist Priestly to reveal Winston's identity and demolish his preconceived prejudices. Webb excludes this letter-writing from the novel, but if Clarence were to proceed, he would expose Winston to denigration and exclusion on any return to Philadelphia. Whiteness can be gained through behaviour and virtue, but it can be quickly and violently removed from White-passing characters when their heritage is revealed. It is this fear alongside not wanting to experience the 'isolation and contumely' Black residents face that – in a nod to Webb's own emancipation schemes – propels Winston to leave the US and seek success in South America 'without the additional embarrassments that would be thrown in his way in his native land, solely because he belonged to an oppressed race' (p. 54). Even when characters such as Jule Stevens and Mr Priestly are comically incorrect, Webb reveals Whiteness as a state carefully delineating between 'a drop of African blood' or none – a policing that extends to and operates against White characters.

### 'I WISH THERE WERE NO WHITE FOLKS': LOSING WHITENESS IN *THE GARIES*

While White-passing Black characters fear their heritage could be uncovered, a group of White characters socially, rhetorically and physically cross the colour line to become less than or liminally White. Clarence Garie suffers the most dramatic change of circumstances in crossing the colour line, moving from plantation owner on the outskirts of Savannah to the victim of mob violence on the streets of Philadelphia. Clarence is violently punished for breaking the borders of Whiteness by living with a Black woman and attempting to secure legal rights for her and their children. In doing so, he falls outside these borders by tainting his own Whiteness. He finds himself punished for one interpretation of respectability – a masculinity that cares for and protects its dependents – by another – a Whiteness that abhors cross-racial kinship. Reading the idyllic Savannah scenes in the novel sets out the respectability in which Clarence invests. On the plantation, the reader is confronted by the conflict between legal frameworks and personal relationships. Emily is an enslaved woman and Clarence her enslaver, yet repeatedly feelings trump structural realities. Slavery, which has the potential 'for many evils', is instead a familial institution, one in which the owner can show kindness to those enslaved; the narrator describes Clarence as 'the most kind and affectionate fellow in the world', 'a very kind master', 'the kindest of owners' (pp. 78, 91, 130). As Jeffory Clymer identifies, the view on display 'remarkably resembles proslavery ideology that represented bondage as a cluster of personal relationships rather than a legal system of domination', with enslaved and enslaver working together harmoniously to pursue economic goals, and enslaver treating the enslaved as personal rather than legal relations.[37] Slavery is not a structural or social problem in this novel, only a personal cruelty if practised without paternalism.

However, Webb opens in this plantation romance mode, in which a 'kind' slavery unites everyone into a working family, not to defend slavery, but – as Mary Webb had done in voicing minstrelised Blackness to encourage abolitionism – to use seemingly adversarial material to frame his argument on White respectability. When Emily begs Clarence to take the family North to secure freedom, he is not swayed by the immorality of slavery, but paternalism. For Clarence, slavery is a just system and as 'a Southerner in almost all his feelings . . . [he] had never had a scruple respecting the ownership of slaves' (p. 89). What is important to him is being a providing and protecting husband and father and creating a respectable and comfortable life for the one enslaved woman he has elevated above the others who serve him. He is offended when Emily reminds him of their enslaver/enslaved relationship because of his care – 'What have I done to revive the recollection that any such relation existed between us? Am I not always kind and affectionate?' – and only agrees to move North after she recounts an emotional story of legal separation affecting a similar interracial family. Horrified, he realises that his own children 'might be seized and sold by his heirs' if he suddenly died, and acts on the risk of these familial bonds being severed (pp. 87, 89).

Webb critiques the system of slavery that results in 'unclean (southern) interracialism' but focalises the narrative through Clarence to show that his personal idea of respectability sits against both the moral argument of abolition and segregationist ideals of Whiteness.[38] In moving the narrative north, Webb punishes Clarence for his racial innocence but does so through segregationist violence, showing Clarence failing both abolitionist and anti-abolitionist ideals of respectable Whiteness. When the family does move to Philadelphia, the Garies find hostility from their White neighbours. Clarence expects to receive 'ill-natured comments' and 'sneering remarks' from former friends, but he underestimates White Northern reactions – the Garies face a febrile atmosphere of virulent anti-Blackness that includes segregation in employment and schooling, lack of police protection and extra-legal violence (pp. 122, 169). As Tess Chakkalakal writes, 'Clarence naively believes his marriage to be a matter of personal right and preference without considering its social consequences or legal ramifications'; his statement in marrying an enslaved woman in service of respectability demonstrates ignorance of how his personal relationships figure in the larger social and legal context.[39] In marrying a Black woman, free or unfree, Clarence is disreputable in transgressing the colour line and tainting his own Whiteness, resulting in his, Emily's and their newborn child's deaths at the hands of an incensed mob and Stevens's pistol.

Webb models the White riot against the Garies and the Ellises on the 1842 Lombard Street riot, one example of mass White violence against Black residents and abolitionists in the city.[40] As the mob approaches, Clarence hears their threatening shouts:

> 'Down with the Abolitionist – down with the Amalgamationist! give them tar and feathers!'
>     'It's a mob – and that word Amalgamationist – can it be pointed at me? It hardly seems possible; and yet I have a fear that there is something wrong.' (pp. 226–7)

Clarence does not understand the extent of the crime against Whiteness he has committed. This confusion is a sign of his occasional colour-blindness in the novel; at times he simply does not register Emily's social position as a woman of colour – as suggested by his unhappiness when she reminds him of her legal status – nor the perceived threat this relationship poses to White society. Viewing his interracial relationship as a personal matter that may aggrieve people but not provoke violence, the 'amalgamationist' comment cannot be directed at him. While abolitionists saw interracial sex as a sign of slavery's White sexual violence and moral stain, Northern segregationists and anti-abolitionists wielded the prospect of amalgamation to suppress Black social mobility and political power. The multiple petitions that called for Pennsylvanian suffrage to be limited to White men in 1838 did not largely focus on the question of the vote, but rather demanded an opposition to '"racial amalgamation", suggesting to the signatories that the [legislative] convention was encouraging sexual intermixture'.[41] In the mob's shouts, 'abolitionist' is not limited to the opposition of slavery (a position to which Clarence does not subscribe) but is a synonym for amalgamation and Black advancement at the expense of White workers. Repeatedly in the novel, 'abolitionist' appears as a slur, reflecting the widespread segregationist sentiment in the North, and as Nowatzki explains, 'even *accusing* a white person of abolitionism was to question his or her whiteness' and loyalty to the White community.[42] Talking of the working-class mob he will whip up against the Garies, Stevens comments that 'a very strong feeling exists in the community against the Abolitionists, and very properly too', because their support of Black rights was seen to undermine the tenuous political and economic rights of White workers – an argument David Roediger makes in *The Wages of Whiteness*, which I discussed in Chapter 3 (p. 181). Abolitionists such as William Lloyd Garrison were seen as disreputable, disruptive and dangerous fanatics promoting immediate emancipation and amalgamation; abolitionism was anti-White work and White abolitionists were met with White violence in Northern cities. Clarence joins Garrison – himself threatened with tar and feathers during a Boston riot in 1835 – as White men whose threats to Whiteness are met by forceful expulsion across the colour line through painful Blackening.[43] His fears of failing to protect his family come true when Clarence is further Blackened in death. He loses control over his own property – both financial and human – when his genealogical ties to his children as heirs is broken and his inheritance passes to his legal White beneficiary, Stevens.

The White riot sits in a wider context of respectable White Northerners who, while against violence and sympathetic to the city's Black population, hesitate in taking antiracist action. A group of minor White characters in the novel shy away from 'abolitionism' and, like Clarence, only involve themselves in helping Black people whom they personally know when provoked by personal sympathies. For example, George Burell comes across dejected teen Charlie Ellis, who has been refused work by Burrell's friend due to fears of angering White workers. After relaying the incident to his wife, she responds:

> 'I was trying to imagine, Burrell, how I should feel if you, I, and baby were coloured; I was trying to place myself in such a situation. Now we know that our boy, if he is honest and upright – is blest with great talent or genius – may aspire to any station in society that he wishes to obtain. How different it would be if he were coloured! – there would be nothing bright in the prospective for him.' (p. 294)

In imagining their own child suffering the indignities of racism, the Burrells rely on empathy and identification, a common tactic of abolitionist writers. *Uncle Tom's Cabin* is a more familiar example, when she directly asks the White reader to identify with the fleeing Eliza: 'If it were *your* Harry, mother, or your Willie, that were going to be torn from you by a brutal trader, tomorrow morning . . . how fast could *you* walk?'[44] Here, maternal instinct and love transcends the boundaries of race in order to convince the White reader of slavery's brutality. In *The Garies*, George teases his wife that women 'let your hearts run away with your heads', but it is this emotive and maternal imaginative leap that engenders the Burrells' charity and encourages George to employ Charlie himself (p. 293).

The Burrells engage in a form of transracial empathic imagination, which, as I discussed in Chapter 3, was prominent in antislavery literature to encourage White Americans to see a shared civic and emotional connection with currently enslaved Black potential citizens. However, in order to come to the realisation that everyone is the same, Black or White, Black suffering is transferred onto White observers. In this respect, the Burrells embody the 'repressive effects of empathy' Hartman observes in White accounts of brutality against enslaved people, which make the captive body 'a vessel for the uses, thoughts, and feelings of others'.[45] In speaking, Mrs Burrell crosses the colour line to imagine experiencing the discrimination Black Philadelphians faced, but in supplanting Charlie's body with her family's she imagines their own suffering, how wrong it would be for them – or their 'honest and upright' and talented son – to be treated in this way. Black pain, whether physical or emotional, offers a moment to meditate on White feelings and imagine a specific suffering that White families would never experience. Like Clarence, the Burrells do the right thing, but rely on the emotive and empathic power of the family to do so – it is unclear if they would extend this charity to a complete stranger, and they certainly would not engage in broader calls for societal change. The Burrells are respectable White middle-class Northerners, and they reject the label of 'abolitionist', even if they do support abolition, because of its connotations of tainted Whiteness. George admits 'some little prejudice . . . against coloured people' but is shocked that 'sensible men' such as his friend would prevent a young Black man from bettering his life (p. 292). He condemns the actions around him but also cannot understand that his own views, while sympathetic to individual African Americans he encounters, are another part of a systematically anti-Black society that is expressed through discrimination and violence by other White Philadelphians. Similarly, in the South, Clarence can be against physical violence against enslaved people on his plantation while upholding a slave system that engenders violence. Away from structural change, doing a good deed boosts the Burrells' own conception of themselves as charitable, respectable, upstanding White citizens. After informing the Ellises, Mrs Burrell remarks, 'how easy it is . . . to make the hearts of others as light as our own' and feels 'heartfelt gratification' at becoming a benefactor (p. 298). The livelihoods and wellbeing of their Black fellow Philadelphians become material for them to feel better about themselves, while they continue to refuse the anti-White label of abolitionist. Serving no further purpose, the Burrells are not heard from again apart from a brief mention at Charlie's wedding in the final chapters.

The Burrells' moment of transracial imagination shows how Whiteness can be bolstered through temporarily imagining its loss in service of White respectability. In the figure of George Stevens, Whiteness itself is rendered disreputable as White supremacist characters strive to keep the privileges and exclusivity of Whiteness for themselves. Affronted by Walters' bankrupting of a White businessman who denied him service, Stevens admits, 'if I was a black . . . living in a country like this, I'd sacrifice conscience and everything else to the acquisition of wealth' (p. 148). The irony, of course, is that Stevens does not need to turn Black to sacrifice his conscience in pursuit of social mobility. The son of a genteel woman (Clarence's aunt) who has married below her station, Stevens is from a lowly background but carries himself as a gentleman. His designs to rise from a 'pettifogging attorney' to a wealthly and respectable gentleman he perceives himself to be rest on violence, bribing political candidates, gerrymandering and property speculation (p. 146). Telling his friend Mr Morton of his plan to whip up a White working-class mob, Stevens hopes to force Black residents out and 'render the district so unsafe, that property will be greatly lessened in value', meaning that he and Morton can buy up the property and sell 'at an immense advantage' once the violence stops. Intending to 'control the elections in the district . . . as to place in office only such persons as will wink at the disturbances', Stevens knows White corruption and immorality will face no consequences if it is in service to anti-Blackness (p. 181).

Webb undercuts this cunning villainy with a scene in which Stevens himself is subjected to racist violence. While organising the mob violence, he disguises himself in dilapidated clothing to blend in with the largely Irish drunken group of rioters at a tavern. Immediately he crosses the class line and has his Whiteness partially erased. Putting on ill-fitting items in a second-hand clothing store, 'he seemed completely robbed of all appearance of respectability', and the Black shopkeeper remarks, 'Why, you don't look a bit like a gentleman now, sir' (p. 195). Leaving the tavern wearing the coat of a firefighting group – a front for a working-class gang – he is set upon by a rival gang, who beat and tar him. A second group of young men then appears, mistaking him for an African American as Mr Morton walks by:

> 'What have you got here?' he [Morton] asked, pressing forward, until he saw the battered form of Mr. Stevens; 'oh, let the poor darkey go,' he continued, compassionately, for he had just drunk enough to make him feel humane; 'let the poor fellow go, it's a shame to treat him in this manner.'
>
> As he spoke, he endeavoured to take from the hands of one of the party a piece of chip, with which he was industriously engaged in streaking the face of Mr. Stevens with lime, 'Let me alone, Morton – let me alone; I'm making a white man of him, I'm going to make him a glorious fellow-citizen, and have him run for Congress. Let me alone, I say.' (p. 201)

Only by revealing his identity to Morton, a passing acquaintance, can Stevens end the violence. In the space of a few minutes Stevens has undergone a double racial transformation. He is blackened as a sign of disrespect against his perceived specific working-class politics in the form of the coat, then whitened as a sign of disrespect against his perceived Blackness. In Stevens's misfortune of crossing between racial groups in one evening, Webb tells his readers that racial violence is deeply intertwined with the expression of White class identity. Blackness 'is a mask imposed upon Stevens because of his perceived class position'.[46] To establish the dominance of one White working-class group over another, a White 'working-class' man is made no longer White; to establish the dominance of White working-class men over African Americans, a 'Black' man is taunted with the political freedoms he can never possess. In instances of White racial transformation, Webb conveys the permeability of the colour line, and in the speed and ease in which this violence occurs, he marks out on the White body White male anxieties that they could lose the privileges of Whiteness themselves.

As I have discussed throughout this book, authors employ markers of Blackness and indigeneity to distinguish White men perceived to be (or who feel themselves to be) on the borders of Whiteness. Episodes of physical racial transformation have the potential to engender cross-racial empathy, but most authors reject this possibility and instead use Blackness and indigeneity to express White insecurity. In Stevens's blackening, Webb depicts an act of anti-Black violence as a manifestation of precarious Whiteness but denies him the sympathy extended to Clarence in his death. Unlike the discrimination Charlie faces as a young Black man, which provokes identification from the Burrells, there is no call to readers – White or Black – to put themselves in the position of Stevens. The only sympathetic description Webb gives of Stevens after the tarring is 'he was, indeed, a pitiable object to look upon':

> The countenance beneath [his hat] would . . . have absorbed the gazer's whole attention. His lips were swelled to a size that would have been regarded as large even on the face of a Congo negro, and one eye was puffed out to an alarming extent; whilst the coating of tar he had received rendered him such an object as the reader can but faintly picture to himself. (p. 200)

Webb turns Stevens into an exaggerated Black figure from Clay's prints, an object of racial grotesquery. Who is the gazer in this moment? An antagonistic or sympathetic White city dweller walking past, an abolitionist White reader, but possibly also passing Black residents, a smaller group of Black readers, and the Black author himself. As a Black author, Webb reverses the White gaze of anti-abolitionist media that makes Blackness a source of amusement. In depicting a White man's racial transformation, Webb does not mock Blackness but the White man underneath, subjecting his White villain to a temporary experience of the violence to which Black Americans are subjected. In concert with challenging the White gaze and arbitrary Whiteness through depictions of Black respectability, Webb inverts this gaze and critiques White supremacy by making Whiteness itself the grotesque Other.

## Last Words: White Death

Webb makes Whiteness a comic spectacle through the act of blackening, but away from the tar he depicts White supremacy as a corrupting force on the White body. A figure of living death while only middle-aged, Webb maps Stevens' moral deviancy onto his body. Stevens is introduced as 'a person from whom you would instinctively shrink', possessing 'cunning-looking grey eyes' and high cheekbones with 'cadaverous skin . . . so tightly drawn across them, as to give it a very parchment-like appearance' (p. 146). Without colour – without life – in his skin, the vampiric nature of Stevens's property speculation plan is amplified. The off-whiteness of Stevens's skin reflects his place on the borders of Whiteness – not for his downwardly mobile origins, but for his disreputable behaviour. Decades after his murderous usurpation, Stevens complains to McCloskey, the man keeping his murderous secret:

> 'haven't I suffered – look at my grey hairs and half-palsied frame, decrepit before I'm old – sinking into the tomb with a weight of guilt and sin upon me that will crush me down to the lowest depth of hell. . . . every piece of gold I count out, I see his hands outstretched over it, and hear him whisper "Mine!" He gives me no peace night or day; he is always by me; I have no rest.' (p. 307)

Avarice has destroyed Stevens's body and mind, rendering him a living revenant – not haunting others, but haunted by the vision of Clarence reclaiming his stolen property. His expulsion of Clarence from Whiteness in order to gain wealth and respectability for himself torments him. As the identity of Clarence's murderer is finally revealed, Stevens chooses death over accountability. A warrant out for his arrest, his daughter Lizzie finds 'lying on the pavement . . . the mangled form of her father, who had desperately sprung from the balcony above' to escape a magistrate (pp. 347–8). Webb refuses Stevens a good death; for his destruction of Black families he is not bestowed forgiveness or resolution.

Likewise McCloskey – an Irish criminal paid at first to lead the mob, and then to keep Stevens's secret – is punished in death for both his direct and intermediated violence against Black families. In making a full confession from his hospital bed – 'how he agreed to murder Mr. Garie – of his failure when the time of action arrived, and how, in consequence, Stevens had committed the deed, and how he had paid him time after time to keep his secret' – McCloskey sets in motion the chain of events that returns Clarence's bequest to his adult children, offering them resolution (p. 356). For Webb and his readers, however, this confession does not absolve McCloskey, and he lies on his deathbed haunted by 'the phantoms of his victims', dying the opposite of a good death 'with distorted face, clenched hands, and gnashing teeth' (p. 357). McCloskey's Irish immigrant status positions him on the edges of Whiteness but he refuses cross-racial solidarity with Black Philadelphians and instead both he and Stevens cling to the structures of Whiteness that place them above Black men and women. Although McCloskey does not support murdering Clarence, he has no qualms about carrying out Stevens's broader plan 'to convince [Black residents] that they were still negroes, and to teach them to remain in their proper place in the body politic' by violently attacking people and property (p. 189). In the unsentimental endings of his White villains, Webb enacts a potent critique of White supremacy as a deathly force itself – a corrupting power that makes its followers crooked, decrepit and ultimately excluded from the good death afforded to respectable men.

In Webb's conclusion, Whiteness breaks those who seek to uphold its exclusionary borders, and this extends to Clary Garie, who hides his Black heritage as a young man. Instructed by Balch to *'never, never* tell' anyone about his mother, passing as White offers Clary a world of educational, economic and romantic opportunities that would be denied if his parentage were to be revealed (p. 275). At the same time, he acknowledges a contradiction in his racial identity, not due to physical markers but social:

> 'I can't be white and coloured at the same time; the two don't mingle, and I must consequently be one or the other. My education, habits, and ideas, all unfit me for associating with the latter; . . . I don't avoid coloured people because I esteem them my inferiors in refinement, education, or intelligence; but because they are subjected to degradations that I shall be compelled to share by too freely associating with them.' (p. 311)

In passing as White, Clary must choose Whiteness and disavow his Blackness, including his sister Emily, who has remained in Black society. As with White anxieties of being labelled an 'abolitionist', Clary too must distance himself from Black life and community in case it threatens his own precarious claim on Whiteness, including his relationship with the White Anna 'Birdie' Bates. At the opening of the novel, Clarence Garie considers disclosing Winston's race to segregationist Priestly and the daughter Winston has escorted, imagining: 'The old man will swear till everything turns blue; and as for Clara, what will become of her?' which produces a 'burst of laughter so side-shaking and merry' (p. 45). In a tragic mirror to this imagined episode, when Clary's racial identity is revealed to his White fiancé's family, the father exclaims, 'I'll kill him, the infernal hypocrite! Oh! the impostor to . . . steal the affections of my daughter – the devilish villain! a bastard! a contemptible black-hearted nigger' and banishes him from further contact. Nothing has changed in Clary's character or appearance, but he loses everything because of 'a few drops of negro blood' (pp. 334, 336). The unnamed threat of amalgamation and the shame it would bring White women means that Whiteness, anxious over its own potential for permeability and dilution, fiercely guards itself.

In his self-enforced identification as White and sudden exclusion from Whiteness, Clary has lost part of himself twice, and in a version of the 'tragic mulatto' storyline, he succumbs to illness and early death. Clary is killed by White supremacy – a 'poor victim of prejudice to thy colour! . . . that malignant sentiment that persecuted thee' – becoming sick and frail after losing his White fiancé (p. 367). Although the intra-Black marriage between Charlie and Emily provides the novel's happy ending in contrast to Clary's death and his parents' murder, I do not believe Webb is critical of interracial relationships in and of themselves, as Robert Reid-Pharr claims. Webb wants to 'reiterat[e] "black" distinctiveness' and he does so through the multiple examples of Black respectability and sociality. He exorcises the 'unclean (southern) interracialism' of the Garie parents, who are products of the slave system, but in the North, his target of critique is White America, which both enforces the loss of Black identity through passing and punishes those men and women when uncovered for entering Whiteness.[47] Indeed, Webb hopes that Anna and Clary's relationship may one day be possible – he looks favourably towards their union in the afterlife, as a few years after Clary's death Anna 'passed away to join her lover, where distinctions in race or colour are unknown, and where the prejudices of earth cannot mar their happiness' (p. 366). Throughout the novel, Webb attacks 'the injustice of society' that has made concealing and disidentifying with Black heritage necessary to secure a life free from discrimination (p. 336). Clary's passing is a consequence of his passing, itself a consequence of White segregation. In killing Clarence, Stevens, McCloskey and Clary, Webb's antiracist novel offers a searing critique of Whiteness and its poisonous and violent anxiety, a prescient reading experience for today.

In early Black fiction, the White gaze towards the dying or imperilled White body is further inverted as Black writers critique White supremacy and use White death as a creative and emotional resource. In *The Curse of Caste* by Julia C. Collins (1865), White men face injury and death for both starting interracial families and thwarting them, the same as in *The Garies*. Here the Philadelphia riot that confronts Clarence Garie is replaced by Louisianan domestic violence – Colonel Frank Tracy shoots his son Richard for purchasing and marrying one-eighth Black Lina Neville. Richard survives, but during his long convalescence separated from his wife, Lina gives birth to a daughter and dies. Both Richard and his daughter Claire are kept ignorant of each other's existence by Richard's friend George Manville, who hides news of Richard's survival, encourages him to move to Europe and sends Claire to the North to be educated as a White woman. As this serialised novel was left unfinished owing to Collins's death, it remains unclear why Manville would deceive his friend, but he clearly fears the risk from or *to* an interracial family enough to break it apart. Although Frank Tracy later reverses his anti-miscegenation stance and serendipitously employs Claire as a governess before reuniting her with Richard, Manville is not redeemed. As a novel centred on recovering blood ties, a father or grandfather can be recuperated but a friend cannot. After nearly twenty years of guilt, Manville's moral failings are marked out on his body and he is 'slowly dragging out the remainder of his life, a miserable cripple' in New Orleans, living 'with the attending horrors of an accusing conscience'; he dies shortly after atoning and receiving Claire's forgiveness.[48] With the novel open-ended, it is possible that Collins planned to conclude with Claire's acceptance in White society, inverting the tragic mulatto storyline and punishing her White male characters who orchestrated the destruction of interracial families.

Harriet E. Wilson's *Our Nig* (1859) employs episodes of White death to demonstrate a Black woman's emotional complexity. Mercilessly exploited, castigated and beaten by the Bellmonts, free Black adolescent Frado finds her closest relationship with son James. A White Christian character proselytising to a Black servant, James's deathbed speech halfway through the novel emulates Eva's in *Uncle Tom's Cabin* in promising eternal cross-racial kinship in an interracial Heaven. James consoles Frado, 'if you will be a good girl, and love and serve God, it will be but a short time before we are in a *heavenly home together*'.[49] Inverting racial gendered roles, Wilson gives Frado's emotional reaction to James's death more space than his own wife's. She takes up the mourning role, 'sinking on her knees at the foot of his bed', burying 'her face in the clothes', weeping 'like one inconsolable' and returning the next day 'as often as she could, to weep over his remains, and ponder his last words to her'.[50] Frado initially appears as one of many Black men and women weeping over deceased White people, for example those on the St Clare plantation in *Uncle Tom's Cabin*, whom White writers frame as dependent on and enriched by the familial attention of kind enslavers. However, in replacing the White wife, Frado becomes the complex, feeling subject in this novel rather than the traditional protagonist and reader of sentimental fiction, the White woman.

White death is a vehicle for Frado's emotional development as a fully realised human subject. She disavows the Christianity that James preaches and refuses to extend her sympathy to other members of the Bellmont family. For example, when she hears that her racist childhood tormentor, Mary Bellmont, has died, Frado is giddy with glee. Rejecting the assumption that a 'good' church-going White woman will go to Heaven, she exclaims, 'S'posen she goes to hell, she'll be as black as I am. Wouldn't mistress be mad to see her a "nigger!"'[51] In this brief imagined blackening, Wilson does not condemn Blackness, but like Webb, she employs racial transformation to break Whiteness and subject White villains to exclusion and discrimination to mark out their moral failings. Wilson employs sentimental White death and mourning as a creative resource for Frado to develop her own close cross-racial connections and demonstrate multifaceted emotional responses, challenging segregationist society and White portrayals of flattened and passive Blackness.

The feebleness of White male death as seen in Collins and Wilson is hyperbolised in William J. 'Ethiop' Wilson's 'The Afric-American Picture Gallery' (1861). In the third paper, Ethiop visits Black sculptor Bernice's lodge, and comes across a historical narrative, 'Year 4,000. The Amecans, or Milk White

Race'. This speculative document imagines the rise, fall and disappearance of the Ame(ri)cans, describing the race with

> *milk white skins*, and their faces were like the chalk of foreign hills, yea like unto the evil spirit; and their hair was long and straight and uncomely; . . . And their faces were long and narrow, and their noses sharp and angular, and their nostrils thin; so also were the lips of their sunken mouths, . . . They had sharp white teeth.[52]

The Ame(ri)cans are very white, and very ugly. Reversing the ethnographic gaze, Ethiop makes Whiteness monstrous and grotesque, a startling contrast to the beautiful sculpture Bernice produces. White skin and European features are the markings of Ame(ri)can moral degeneracy in trading the writer's forefathers as human property. Proud and lazy, 'their hearts became more and more filled with the world and the lust thereof' until 'a great physical and mental weakness came over them'. Fading, 'their hair darkened, so also did their eyes and their skins' until the Ame(ri)cans appear the same as the people they have enslaved. Rather than equalising, this blackening is one step to the Ame(ri)cans' final fall as they 'dwindled at last to leanness; and their minds became feeble, . . . and finally they disappeared from among the children of men'.[53] The Ame(ri)cans decay and die through their own misdeeds framed as evolutionary failure. In the death of the Ame(ri)cans, Wilson 'consigns the Americans to ancient history in an inversion of the settler-colonial narrative of the disappearing native'.[54] However, unlike Irving or Cooper, who make the White man a vanishing Indian to refocus sympathy towards specific types of White men, Wilson offers no sympathy and makes the Ame(ri)cans a lost Indigenous group to eradicate White supremacy. He takes to the extreme episodes in *The Garies* where Whiteness is temporarily lost or erased, asking if Whiteness and its attendant hierarchies can be eradicated. Whereas many writers in this book return their characters to Whiteness, in Wilson's short story there is nothing to return to, as Whiteness – represented through the White body – dies out.

Bernice's historical document of a future yet to pass is a fiction constructed to cover his individual reckoning against White supremacy. After Ethiop reads the 'The Year 4,000', Bernice reveals his own decaying, 'pale and shriveled' Ame(ri)can – Felix – chained up in a subterranean cell.

> Was it a man, was it even human? . . . his mouth was white with foam. He soon commenced an incoherent muttering the only words distinguishable was *Bernice, Bernice!* . . . he raved, he shrieked, he tore his hair; . . . then he bounded the length of his chains, then he stamped them in the earth, then he gnawed at their links, then he begged, then he pled incoherently for something.[55]

In this Poe-esque, horrific climax, the gothic scene of chattel slavery is reversed. Revealing that Felix is his former enslaver, who murdered his son, Bernice justifies his vengeance outside the law: '*Laws!!* what laws, what justice is there for the oppressed of our *class?*' Not 'harm[ing] a hair on his head', Bernice's denial of Felix's freedom is a racial role reversal and in his mind, a fitting punishment for one who deprived others of liberty. Ethiop and the reader are left with the powerful image of the White 'wretched fiend' trembling with fear as Bernice nonchalantly 'drew himself up to his full height, and with a commanding gesture waved me to retire'.[56] Read by an unintended White audience, the revenge against White masters and an imagined lost White race is a horrific threat of lost rights, a threat which returns in contemporary fears of White loss and genocide. Published in an African American magazine, however, Wilson's story of Black dominance is ambivalent; both the individual detainment of a White man and White erasure in two and half millennia are enticing and even rewarding thought experiments for the Black reader, but they are not practically or physically possible in the US in 1861. What this speculative gothic tale does offer is an imaginative space where Whiteness no longer has its destructive hold. With Ame(ri)can characteristics of avarice, enslavement and violence overcome, what could Ame(ri)ca look like for Black and White residents? Early Black fiction attends to Whiteness as a site of critique, criticises Whiteness's poison and starts to imagine a world where Whiteness decays and dies.

## NOTES

1. 'Mr. and Mrs. Webb at Camden House', *The Era*, 31 May 1857, p. 10.
2. Ibid.
3. Douglass, *My Bondage and My Freedom*, ed. Bernier, p. 329.
4. 'Mr. and Mrs. Webb at Camden House'.
5. When Webb's short fiction was published in Frederick Douglass's *New Era* in 1870, the by-line refers to Webb as the author of *The Garies*, 'extensively read in England and this country', suggesting that some American readers had encountered the novel through import. *New Era*, 13 January 1870, p. 3, quoted in Crockett, 'The Garies and Their Friends: A Study of Frank J. Webb and His Novel', p. 2.
6. Golemba, 'Frank Webb's The Garies and Their Friends Contextualized within African American Slave Narratives', in Habich (ed.), *Lives out of Letters*, pp. 114–42.
7. Bell, *The Afro-American Novel and Its Tradition*, p. 43; Gayle Jr, *The Way of the New World*, p. 13.
8. Levine, 'Disturbing Boundaries', p. 351. See Stockton, 'The Property of Blackness'; Clymer, *Family Money*; Kohl, 'Frank Webb's "The Garies and Their Friends" and the Struggle over Black Education in the Antebellum North'; Sbriglia, 'Specters of Marxism in Frank J. Webb's The Garies and Their Friends'.
9. Maillard, '"Faithfully Drawn from Real Life"'.
10. Nowatzki, 'Blurring the Color Line', p. 29.

11. Webb, 'Biographical Sketch', in Stowe, *The Christian Slave* (1856 edition), <http://utc.iath.virginia.edu/uncletom/xianslav/xsesfjwat.html> (accessed 9 November 2020).

12. Ibid.

13. Maillard, '"Faithfully Drawn from Real Life"', p. 290.

14. Quote from *The New York Times* in 'Mrs Webb's Reading', *The National Anti-Slavery Standard*, 22 December 1855, <http://utc.iath.virginia.edu/uncletom/xianslav/xsno08ot.html> (accessed 9 November 2020).

15. Quote from *Daily Plain Dealer* in Mielke, *Provocative Eloquence*, p. 62; 'Special Notices', *New York Times*, 18 December 1855, <http://utc.iath.virginia.edu/uncletom/xianslav/xsno05at.html> (accessed 9 November 2020); 'Mrs Webb's Reading'.

16. 'The Black Siddons', *Provincial Freeman*, 12 May 1855, quoted in Joyce, 'Creating a Living Historiography', p. 434; 'Special Notices'; 'Dramatic Reading by a Coloured Native of Philadelphia', *The Illustrated London News*, p. 12.

17. 'Dramatic Reading', p. 11.

18. Laura Korobkin performs a meticulous close reading of the Dickens–Webb missed encounter as an example of the private racism faced by Black Americans visiting Victorian Britain. Charles Dickens to Lord Carlisle, 15 April 1857, quoted in Korobkin, 'Avoiding "Aunt Thomasina"', p. 119.

19. *The Tribune*, quoted in 'Mrs Webb's Reading'; 'Dramatic Reading', p. 12.

20. Stowe, *The Christian Slave, A Drama* (1855 edition), pp. 61–2.

21. Hartman, *Scenes of Subjection*, p. 28.

22. 'Mr. and Mrs. Webb at Camden House'.

23. McAllister, *Whiting Up*, p. 45; Harris, 'Whiteness as Property', pp. 1721, 1718.

24. Webb, 'Biographical Sketch'.

25. Nyong'o, *The Amalgamation Waltz*, p. 118.

26. Webb, 'Biographical Sketch'.

27. 'Mr. and Mrs. Webb at Camden House'.

28. Mielke, *Provocative Eloquence*, p. 67.

29. Lapsansky, 'Friends, Wives, and Strivings', p. 23.

30. Ibid. p. 6.

31. Bateman, *Disenfranchising Democracy*, p. 195.

32. Webb, *The Garies and Their Friends*, ed. Walsh and Howell, p. 275. Further citations of this edition are given in parentheses in the main text.

33. 'The Garies and Their Friends', *The Literary Gazette, and Journal of Archaeology, Science, and Art*, 26 September 1857, p. 918.

34. 'Review: The Garies and Their Friends', *The Morning Post*, 6 October 1857, p. 7.

35. Clay, *Life in Philadelphia, Plate 4* (1830), <https://digital.librarycompany.org/islandora/object/Islandora%3A60203> (accessed 9 November 2020).

36. In Walters's account, the portrait is 'presented to an American merchant by Touissant himself' – rather than a French official – before Walters purchases it, which cements an even stronger link between himself and Touissant as respectable Black leaders. Webb, *The Garies*, p. 145; Saint-Rémy, *Mémoires Du Général Toussaint-L'Ouverture*, front matter.

37. Clymer, *Family Money*, p. 30.

38. Reid-Pharr, *Conjugal Union*, p. 71.

39. Chakkalakal, *Novel Bondage*, p. 55.
40. See Maillard, '"Faithfully Drawn from Real Life"'.
41. *Proceedings and Debates of the Convention of Pennsylvania*, I, pp. 423–4, quoted in Bateman, *Disenfranchising Democracy*, p. 191.
42. Nowatzki, 'Blurring the Color Line', p. 43.
43. Yerrinton, *The Boston Mob of 'Gentlemen of Property and Standing'*, p. 26.
44. Stowe, *Uncle Tom's Cabin*, ed. Yellin, p. 55.
45. Hartman, *Scenes of Subjection*, p. 19.
46. Engle, 'Depiction of the Irish in Frank Webb's "The Garies and Their Friends" and Frances E. W. Harper's "Trial and Triumph"', p. 161.
47. Reid-Pharr, *Conjugal Union*, pp. 76, 71.
48. Collins, *The Curse of Caste*, ed. Andrews and Kachum, p. 62.
49. Wilson, *Our Nig*, p. 53.
50. Ibid. p. 54.
51. Ibid. p. 59.
52. Ethiop, 'Afric-American Picture Gallery: Third Paper', *Anglo-African Magazine*, 1.6 (April 1859), p. 175.
53. Ibid. pp. 175–6.
54. Spires, *The Practice of Citizenship*, p. 192.
55. Ethiop, 'Afric-American Picture Gallery: Third Paper', p. 176.
56. Ibid. p. 177.

# CODA: THE RESURRECTION OF WHITENESS

What race is Melville's confidence man? This seems to be a straightforward question, but in the multiplicious novel of the same name, race – like all aspects of identity – is unstable. Aboard the *Fidèle* steamboat there is 'no lack of variety' of people across profession ('men of business and men of pleasure; parlor men and backwoodsmen'), nationality ('English, Irish, German, Scotch, Danes'), ethnicity ('slaves, black, mulatto, quadroon; modish young Spanish Creoles, and old-fashioned French Jews') and religion ('Mormons and Papists; Dives and Lazarus').[1] Amongst this 'piebald of parliaments' on the Mississippi, Melville clearly delineates one group from another using physical markers – an observer would be able to tell a 'Quaker in full drab' apart from a 'solider in full regimentals', and a 'grinning negro' apart from a 'Sioux chief' due to their appearance.[2] However, as soon as Melville introduces this list of identifiable types, he asks how certain we can be that people are who they say they are, as the confidence man appears in a whirlwind of disguises across class, profession and race in this plotless novel of conversation and encounter. In a frantic, crowded society of strangers, it is not enough to be able to distinguish people as types if those types can be assembled and dissembled through masquerade.

In the early chapters of the novel, Melville destabilises race by opening with two opposing yet linked characters: the White mute and the talkative Black cripple. *The Confidence-Man* (1857) opens with the deaf mute man dressed 'in cream colours', with a 'fair' cheek, 'flaxen' hair and a white fur hat. When this vision of white purity goes to sleep on the ship, he 'lay[s] motionless, as some sugar-snow in March, which, softly stealing down over night, with its white placidity startles the brown farmer peering out from his threshold at daybreak'.[3] Moving from white to brown to black, the next character given a portrait is Black Guinea, the Black cripple, in chapter 3; this gradation tells us that the two men are masquerades of the same person. Black Guinea is an audacious portrait of a beggar,

> a grotesque negro cripple, in tow-cloth attire and an old coal-sifter of a tambourine in his hand, who, owing to something wrong about his legs, was, in effect, cut down to the stature of a Newfoundland dog; his knotted black fleece and good-natured, honest black face rubbing against the upper part of people's thighs as he made shift to shuffle about, making music, such as it was, and raising a smile even from the gravest.[4]

Asking for charity in the form of coins he catches in his mouth 'like an elephant for tossed apples at a menagerie', Black Guinea is a grotesque version of the abolitionist image of a kneeling supplicant enslaved man asking 'Am I not a man and a brother?'[5] This excessive playfulness lends itself to a blackface reading of Black Guinea, as put forward by Eric Lott: Black Guinea is one of the confidence man's guises and Melville, through recognisable signs of the minstrel show, wants his readers to see through this performance.[6] The *Fidèle* passengers are not as savvy as the attentive reader, not doubting Black Guinea's Blackness and more concerned that his disability is fraudulent, with the exception of the man 'with the wooden leg' who claims, 'He's some white operator, betwisted and painted up for a decoy. He and his friends are all humbugs.'[7] Unlike Rice's teasing double-voiced lyrics, blackface performance that does not let its audience in on the act is a con.

The Blackness of blackface minstrelsy is a construct, but who is doing the constructing? It is possible that the confidence man is himself Black, performing an exaggerated Blackness as Black Guinea, and then whiteface for the mute and a series of other characters, as an audacious racial confidence trick to hoodwink White America and show the colour line as meaningless. Carolyn Karcher suggests that with no description of the confidence man out of character, his race is a mystery: 'There is no way of knowing, and that is precisely the point. Nothing could more radically discredit the concept of race.'[8] In his putting on and taking off of different racial characters to cross the boundaries of race, I argue the trickster is a liminally White man who exploits a powerful ordering system marking out and making different groups of people legible to one another.

Circulating through the steamboat in a number of guises, often appearing as disembodied voices in disconnected conversations, we could read the confidence man as a spiritualist and *The Confidence-Man* as a séance. The séance emulated the crowded city or the populous steamboat, bringing together multiple spirits into one intimate space – not only departed loved ones from across the social spectrum, but also celebrity ghosts from across geography and history. At a séance mediums and audiences could encounter 'men of business and men of pleasure; parlor men and backwoodsmen . . . English, Irish, German, Scotch, Danes . . . slaves, black, mulatto, quadroon; modish young Spanish Creoles, and old-fashioned French Jews; Mormons and Papists; Dives and Lazarus', if those spirits wished to communicate.[9] Spiritualism offered the potential for radical cross-racial consciousness with the possibility that spirits of colour, namely 'Indian' spirit guides, could enter into and speak through passive White women and men. The 'polymorphousness' of spiritualism suggested 'a culture with no borders at all' between individuals, classes, races or genders.[10] Spiritualism threatened autonomy by allowing others to control thoughts, speech, writing and gestures. Just as one medium could channel multiple spirits in one evening, the confidence man fragments himself into multiple circulating parts, negating the ideal of the self-contained, autonomous White man with an identity rooted in his race, class, gender, nationality.

Reorienting spiritualism to be a taking on as well as taking in of otherness, the choice of spirits across racial borders indulged fantasies for a temporary self-induced excursion outside of Whiteness. White spiritualists channelling 'Indian' spirit guides were involved in a vocalic redface, creating a set of stoic and sage Native figures as 'powerful spiritual predecessors' for their own radical higher connections with the afterlife.[11] Like blackface minstrelsy, spiritualism suggested the erasure of racial boundaries through the potential to become someone of another race, but it also made non-White figures creative and emotional resources for White speakers. Blackface, spiritualism, the confidence trick: in this novel of dispersed counterfeit identity, Melville invites us to hold two positions on Whiteness at the same time. Through identity crossing, Whiteness is emptied out of meaning, yet this transgression enacts the pinnacle of social freedom afforded to Whiteness. In other words, the ultimate privilege of Whiteness is to be able to take it off by co-opting other identities. One month after the Supreme Court denied African Americans citizenship and limited enslaved peoples' ability to move freely in the free states, the White confidence man completely exploits his freedom to the point where he repeatedly absconds from his own identity. It is not that the conman has 'no "real" race' or that race does not exist, but rather that his repeated dissemblance is Whiteness itself.[12] In Melville's novel, Whiteness is the confidence trick.

Philip Roth recommended reading *The Confidence-Man* as 'the relevant book about [Donald] Trump's American forebear'. Roth found Trump's dissembling and fraud predicted in Melville's novel – it 'could just as well have been called "The Art of the Scam"'.[13] What Roth did not mention, but commentators such as Ta-Nehisi Coates have done, is that the cover of Whiteness enables Trump's confidence trick. As a candidate and president, Whiteness affords Trump the protection to act without impunity because he is not Obama and because he acts against Obama, which is why Coates calls him the 'first white president'.[14] As I have discussed throughout this book, Whiteness in the early US consisted of a set of personal and civic values for Anglo-American men that if negated or challenged could result in liminal Whiteness. Over the course of the nineteenth and early twentieth centuries, Whiteness expanded to admit more people of European heritage as Germans, the Irish, Italians, Eastern Europeans and Jews gradually became White through changing attitudes that non-Anglo populations could possess White-coded values. The Fourteenth Amendment expanded legal citizenship beyond the colour line, but the cultural ideology of citizenship – a set of rights and responsibilities predicated on autonomy, rationality, industry, respectability and sociality – still upheld racial hierarchies and White social dominance. Whiteness still finds and maintains borders against Black people, Indigenous people and people of colour, still translating physical appearance and heritage into character. As Tressie McMillan Cottom writes, 'Whiteness defends itself. Against change, against progress, against hope, against black dignity, against black lives, against reason, against truth, against facts, against native claims, and against its own laws and customs.'[15] A repeat of Bird and Webb's 1830s and 1850s narratives, Whiteness snaps back to protect itself against Black social mobility or the advancement of minority rights.

The campaign and election of Trump unites two ideas and ideals of Whiteness that I have been gesturing at through discussions of liminality in the early United States. At the end of *White* (1997), Richard Dyer frames these two Whitenesses as 'extreme' and 'ordinary'. Extreme Whiteness is the pure Whiteness that adheres to and demonstrates all White civic and personal values, whereas ordinary Whiteness is all other people with pale skin and European heritage who see themselves in a 'way of being that is not marked as white' when not achieving these values. In other words, ordinary Whiteness is liminal Whiteness, a Whiteness that is less-than and on the edge. Dyer continues:

> The combination of extreme whiteness with plain, unwhite whiteness means that white people can both lay claim to the spirit that aspires to the heights of humanity and yet supposedly speak and act disinterestedly as humanity's most average and unremarkable representatives.[16]

Whiteness is exclusive and elevated, but it is also universal and average. Both modes – Whiteness as superior and Whiteness as normal – meet in the middle to claim White victimhood. In the Trump campaign, the re-emergence of this White identity politics renders White Americans the average representative American but more so, the forgotten people, the victims of a system that discriminates against them in favour of minority groups. After his election and inauguration, Trump tweeted: 'The forgotten men and women of our country will be forgotten no longer. From this moment on, it's going to be #AmericaFirst.'[17] For Trump and his ardent supporters, both 'forgotten' and 'America' are White – Whiteness is both the only valid representation of the nation and what needs to be rescued or Made Great Again.

Carol Anderson calls the White America first policy and law enacted since Emancipation 'white rage'. White rage 'wreaks havoc subtly, almost imperceptibly'; it is unseen and structural, 'work[ing] its way through the courts, the legislatures, and a range of government bureaucracies' to prevent Black equality and advancement in suffrage, housing, education, finance.[18] Without spectacle or noise, White rage does however have an accompanying soundtrack – the language of White victimhood. We can see this in the language of Trump's acolytes, such as former Maine governor Paul LePage. On the possibility that the US could abolish the electoral college, LePage commented the change would make him and other White Americans – as Trump had lamented – 'a forgotten people':

> 'Actually what would happen if they do what they say they're gonna do is white people will not have anything to say . . . It's only going to be the minorities that would elect. It would be California, Texas, Florida.'[19]

For the nineteenth-centuryist, LePage's language is reminiscent of Irving's vanishing Indians in *The Sketch Book*, who 'will vanish like a vapor from the face of the earth; their very history will be lost in forgetfulness . . . the places that now know them will know them no more forever'.[20] White people become the minority themselves, but rather than facing extermination from widespread expansionist violence, LePage's forgotten people are imperilled and silenced by Latino/a Americans through a democratic process that would more accurately represent American voters. Rather than embracing democracy, LePage and others embrace Whiteness because they perceive the prospect of equality as oppression. More broadly, nearly half of White Americans polled in a 2017 survey agreed or strongly agreed with the statement 'White people are currently under attack in this country.'[21] Forgotten and attacked – in this figurative language of oppression and violence, a significant percentage of White Americans feel similarly to Robin Day, jostled and denigrated on the streets of Philadelphia, in Bird's *The Adventures of Robin Day*.

Throughout this book, the texts I have discussed suggest the possibility that White citizens could be treated or feel they are treated in the same way as non-White noncitizens: excluded, marginalised, disenfranchised, oppressed, subjugated, objectified, dehumanised. They co-opt the language and signs of oppression levelled against Black and Indigenous people through playing

Indian, wage slavery, blackface, the White slave narrative, to amplify liminal White characters' own positions on the periphery of White communities. Rather than killing off Whiteness itself as a coercive identity, they imagine White physical death to exorcise liminal White men from Whiteness, or they inexplicably avoid White physical death to return them to Whiteness. Making their liminal White men ghostly or cadaverous, akin to socially dead groups, is a potent way to express and attempt to allay imagined fears of lost White rights while citizenship is under development. This book challenges the persistent belief that because Whiteness is considered the normate or default position for citizenship, White able-bodied men do not ascribe to or practise identity politics. These authors and texts evince the opposite – they continually and actively discuss a specific racial and gender identity, either by questioning the tenets and values of White citizenship or by voicing anxieties that the privileges of White citizenship can be negated, each resulting in liminal Whiteness.

Reading the liminal White voice in early US fiction enables us to examine this sustained and still prevalent racialised cultural ideology of American citizenship. Repeatedly, the fear of being treated as a minority in the early US finds form in the language of White exclusion, subjugation and replacement, continuing today. These are not new narratives and the victimhood language of contemporary White supremacy is a continuum, not an aberration, but the resurgence and prominence of this language is why critical Whiteness studies is of urgent importance to nineteenth-century American studies today, both in our research and teaching. A return to White authors that foregrounds Whiteness as a constructed identity – expressed in places through literal and figurative erasures of Whiteness – rather than an absence or abstraction will help confront the genealogy of White supremacist imaginaries in early US fiction.

## Notes

1. Melville, *The Confidence-Man: His Masquerade*, ed. Tanner, p. 8.
2. Ibid. pp. 8–9.
3. Ibid. pp. 1, 5.
4. Ibid. p. 10.
5. Ibid. pp. 11–12; Ryan, *The Grammar of Good Intentions*, p. 63.
6. Lott, *Love and Theft*, pp. 63–4.
7. Melville, *The Confidence-Man*, p. 15.
8. Karcher, *Shadow Over the Promised Land*, p. 220.
9. Melville, *The Confidence-Man*, p. 8.
10. Brooks, *Bodies in Dissent*, pp. 21, 17.
11. McGarry, *Ghosts of Futures Past*, p. 67.
12. Ryan, *The Grammar of Good Intentions*, p. 65.
13. Thurman, 'Philip Roth E-Mails on Trump', *The New Yorker*, 30 January 2017, <https://www.newyorker.com/magazine/2017/01/30/philip-roth-e-mails-on-trump> (accessed 9 November 2020).

14. Coates, 'The First White President', *The Atlantic*, October 2017, <https://www.theatlantic.com/magazine/archive/2017/10/the-first-white-president-ta-nehisi-coates/537909/> (accessed 9 November 2020).

15. McMillan Cottom, 'The Problem with Obama's Faith in White America', *The Atlantic*, 13 December 2016, <https://www.theatlantic.com/politics/archive/2016/12/obamas-faith-in-white-america/510503/> (accessed 9 November 2020).

16. Dyer, *White*, p. 223.

17. Trump, 'The forgotten men and women of our country will be forgotten no longer. From this moment on, it's going to be #AmericaFirst' [*Twitter post*] (@realDonaldTrump, 20 January 2017), <https://twitter.com/realdonaldtrump/status/822502450007515137?lang=en> (accessed 9 November 2020). See also Trump, 'Such a beautiful and important evening! The forgotten man and woman will never be forgotten again. We will all come together as never before' [*Twitter post*] (@realDonaldTrump, 9 November 2016), <https://twitter.com/realdonaldtrump/status/796315640307060738?lang=en> (accessed 9 November 2020).

18. Anderson, *White Rage*, p. 3.

19. Riga, 'LePage: Eliminating Electoral College Would Make Whites "A Forgotten People"', *Talking Points Memo*, 28 February 2019, <https://talkingpointsmemo.com/news/lepage-eliminating-electoral-college-whites-forgotten-people> (accessed 9 November 2020).

20. Irving, *The Sketch Book of Geoffrey Crayon, Gent.*, ed. Bradbury, p. 238.

21. 'New Poll: Some Americans Express Troubling Racial Attitudes Even as Majority Oppose White Supremacists', *University of Virginia Center for Politics*, 14 September 2017, <http://centerforpolitics.org/crystalball/articles/new-poll-some-americans-express-troubling-racial-attitudes-even-as-majority-oppose-white-supremacists/> (accessed 9 November 2020). We can also think of the false corrective 'White Lives Matter Too/All Lives Matter' as another expression of White victimhood in the face of calls for Black equality. 'Black Lives Matter' is already a corrective statement – meaning 'Black Lives Matter Too/As Much as White Lives'. 'White Lives Matter Too/All Lives Matter' reads 'Black Lives Matter' as 'Only Black Lives Matter/Black Lives Matter More' and assumes White subjugation rather than racial justice.

# BIBLIOGRAPHY

Archive Collections

Robert Montgomery Bird Papers, Kislak Center for Special Collections, Rare Books and Manuscripts, University of Pennsylvania, Philadelphia.

Primary and Secondary Material

*A History of the Recent Developments in Spiritual Manifestations, in the City of Philadelphia* (Philadelphia: G. S. Harris, 1851).

*A Summary View of the Millennial Church, or United Society of Believers, Commonly Called Shakers*, 2nd edn (Albany, NY: C. Van Benthuysen, 1848).

Adams, John, *A Defence of the Constitutions of Government of the United States of America* (London: C. Dilly, 1787).

Ahmed, Sara, 'A Phenomenology of Whiteness', *Feminist Theory*, 8.2 (2007): 149–68.

Altschuler, Sari, 'From Empathy to Epistemology: Robert Montgomery Bird and the Future of the Medical Humanities', *American Literary History*, 28.1 (2016): 1–26.

Altschuler, Sari, and Cristobal Silva, 'Early American Disability Studies', *Early American Literature*, 52.1 Special Issue: Early American Disability Studies (2017): 1–27.

'An Instance of Ventriloquism', *The Weekly Magazine of Original Essays, Fugitive Pieces, and Interesting Intelligence*, 2.22 (30 June 1798): 277–8.

Anderson, Carol, *White Rage: The Unspoken Truth of Our Racial Divide*, paperback edn (New York: Bloomsbury, 2017).

Anthony, David, *Paper Money Men: Commerce, Manhood, and the Sensational Public Sphere in Antebellum America* (Columbus: The Ohio State University Press, 2009).

Arsić, Branka, *Passive Constitutions, Or 7½ Times Bartleby* (Stanford: Stanford University Press, 2007).

Augst, Thomas, *The Clerk's Tale: Young Men and Moral Life in Nineteenth-Century America* (Chicago; London: The University of Chicago Press, 2003).

Bakhtin, Mikhail M., 'Discourse in the Novel', in *The Dialogic Imagination: Four Essays*, ed. Michael Holquist, trans. Caryl Emerson and Michael Holquist (Austin: University of Texas Press, 1981), pp. 259–422.

Baldwin, James, *The Cross of Redemption: Uncollected Writings*, ed. Randall Kenan (New York: Pantheon Books, 2010).

Bateman, David A., *Disenfranchising Democracy: Constructing the Electorate in the United States, the United Kingdom, and France* (Cambridge: Cambridge University Press, 2018).

Bebout, Lee, *Whiteness on the Border: Mapping the US Racial Imagination in Brown and White* (New York: NYU Press, 2016).

Beecher, Catharine E., *A Treatise on Domestic Economy, For the Use of Young Ladies at Home, and at School*, 3rd edn (New York: Harper & Brothers, 1848).

Bellion, Wendy, *Citizen Spectator: Art, Illusion, and Visual Perception in Early National America* (Chapel Hill: University of North Carolina Press, 2011).

Bennett, Bridget, *Transatlantic Spiritualism and Nineteenth-Century American Literature* (New York: Palgrave Macmillan, 2007).

Berger, James, *The Disarticulate: Language, Disability, and the Narratives of Modernity* (New York; London: NYU Press, 2014).

Bergland, Renée L., *The National Uncanny: Indian Ghosts and American Subjects* (Hanover, NH: University Press of New England, 2000).

Bird, Robert Montgomery, *Nick of the Woods or The Jibbenainosay, A Tale of Kentucky*, ed. Curtis Dahl (Albany, NY: New College and University Press, Inc, 1967).

Bird, Robert Montgomery, *Peter Pilgrim: Or A Rambler's Recollections*, 2 vols (Philadelphia: Lea & Blanchard, 1838).

Bird, Robert Montgomery, *Sheppard Lee: Written by Himself*, introduction by Christopher Looby (New York: New York Review Books, 2008).

Bird, Robert Montgomery, *The Adventures of Robin Day*, 2 vols (Philadelphia: Carey, Lea, & Blanchard, 1839).

Bird, Robert Montgomery, *The City Looking Glass*, ed. Arthur Hobson Quinn (New York: The Colophon, 1933).

Bird, Robert Montgomery, *The Difficulties of Medical Science: An Inaugural Lecture, Introductory to a Course of Lectures* (Philadelphia: Pennsylvania Medical College, 1841).

Black, Alex W., 'Abolitionism's Resonant Bodies: The Realization of African American Performance', *American Quarterly*, 63.3 (2011): 619–39.

Blakely, Robert, and Judith M. Harrington (eds), *Bones in the Basement: Post-mortem Racism in Nineteenth-Century Medical Training* (Washington, DC: Smithsonian Institution Press, 1998).

Blanco, María del Pilar, *Ghost-Watching American Modernity: Haunting, Landscape, and the Hemispheric Imagination* (New York: Fordham University Press, 2012).

Blazan, Sladja, 'Silencing the Dead: Washington Irving's Use of the Supernatural in the Context of Slavery and Genocide', *Arizona Quarterly: A Journal of American Literature, Culture, and Theory*, 69.2 (2013): 1–24.

Blumin, Stuart, *The Emergence of the Middle Class: Social Experience in the American City, 1760–1900* (New York: Cambridge University Press, 1989).

Boardman, Andrew, 'An Essay on the Means of Improving Medical Education and Elevating Medical Character', in Gert H. Brieger (ed.), *Medical America in the Nineteenth Century: Readings from the Literature* (London: The Johns Hopkins Press, 1972), pp. 24–36.

Bonnett, Alastair, *Left in the Past: Radicalism and the Politics of Nostalgia* (New York: Continuum, 2010).

Boym, Svetlana, *The Future of Nostalgia* (New York: Basic Books, 2001).

Brackenridge, Hugh Henry, *Modern Chivalry*, ed. Claude M. Newlin (New York; London: Hafner Publishing Company, 1968).

Bradley, Elizabeth L., *Knickerbocker: The Myth Behind New York* (New Brunswick, NJ: Rutgers University Press, 2009).

Braude, Ann, *Radical Spirits: Spiritualism and Women's Rights in Nineteenth-Century America*, 2nd edn (Bloomington: Indiana University Press, 2001).

Brittan, S. B. (ed.), *Spiritual Telegraph*, 2 vols (New York: Partridge & Brittan, 1853).

Brockden Brown, Charles, *Arthur Mervyn, or, Memoirs of the Year 1793: With Related Texts*, ed. Philip Barnard and Stephen Shapiro (Indianapolis: Hackett Publishing Company, 2008).

Brockden Brown, Charles, *Edgar Huntly, or, Memoirs of a Sleep-Walker: With Related Texts*, ed. Philip Barnard and Stephen Shapiro (Indianapolis: Hackett Publishing Company, 2006).

Brockden Brown, Charles, *Ormond, Or the Secret Witness*, ed. Mary Chapman (Peterborough, ON: Broadview Press, 1999).

Brockden Brown, Charles, 'Somnambulism: A Fragment', in Charles L. Crow (ed.), *American Gothic: An Anthology, 1787–1916* (Malden, MA: Blackwell, 1999), pp. 7–18.

Brockden Brown, Charles, *Wieland; Or the Transformation, and Memoirs of Carwin the Biloquist*, ed. Emory Elliott (Oxford: Oxford World's Classics, 1998).

Brodkin, Karen, *How Jews Became White Folks and What That Says about Race in America* (New Brunswick, NJ: Rutgers University Press, 1998).

Brooks, Daphne, *Bodies in Dissent: Spectacular Performances of Race and Freedom, 1850–1910* (Durham, NC: Duke University Press, 2006).

Brown, William Wells, *Clotel; Or, the President's Daughter: A Narrative of Slave Life in the United States*, ed. Robert Levine (Boston: Bedford Cultural Editions, 2000).

Burrows, Edwin G., and Mike Wallace, *Gotham: A History of New York City to 1898* (New York; Oxford: Oxford University Press, 1999).

Capron, Eliab W., and Henry D. Barron, *Explanation and History of the Mysterious Communion with Spirits: Comprehending the Rise and Progress of the Mysterious Noises in Western New York, Generally Received as Spiritual Communications* (Auburn, NY: Capron and Barron, 1850).

Carlson, Eric T., 'Charles Poyen Brings Mesmerism to America', *Journal of the History of Medicine and Allied Sciences*, 15.2 (1960): 121–32.

Carter, Steve, 'A Possible Source for "The Facts in the Case of M. Valdemar"', *Poe Studies*, 12.2 (1979): 36.

Castiglia, Christopher, *Interior States: Institutional Consciousness and the Inner Life of Democracy in the Antebellum United States* (Durham, NC: Duke University Press, 2008).

Castronovo, Russ, *Necro Citizenship: Death, Eroticism, and the Public Sphere in the Nineteenth-Century United States* (Durham, NC: Duke University Press, 2001).

Chakkalakal, Tess, *Novel Bondage: Slavery, Marriage, and Freedom in Nineteenth-Century America* (Urbana: University of Illinois Press, 2011).

Chiles, Katy L., *Transformable Race: Surprising Metamorphoses in the Literature of Early America* (Oxford: Oxford University Press, 2014).

Clark, Jennifer, *The American Idea of England, 1776–1840: Transatlantic Writing* (Farnham, Surrey: Ashgate, 2013).

Clay, Edward Williams, *Life in Philadelphia*, 1828–30, *Life in Philadelphia Collection*, Library Company of Philadelphia <https://digital.librarycompany. org/islandora/object/Islandora%3ALINP1> (accessed 9 November 2020).

Clemente, Michael, 'A Reassessment of Common Law Protections for "Idiots"', *The Yale Law Journal*, 124.8 (2015): 2746–2803.

Clymer, Jeffory A., *Family Money: Property, Race and Literature in the Nineteenth Century* (Oxford: Oxford University Press, 2013).

Coates, Ta-Nehisi, 'The First White President', *The Atlantic*, October 2017, <https://www.theatlantic.com/magazine/archive/2017/10/the-first-white-president-ta-nehisi-coates/537909/> (accessed 9 November 2020).

Cockrell, Dale, *Demons of Disorder: Early Blackface Minstrels and Their World* (Cambridge: Cambridge University Press, 1997).

Cody, Michael, *Charles Brockden Brown and the Literary Magazine: Cultural Journalism in the Early American Republic* (Jefferson, NC; London: McFarland & Co, Inc., Publishers, 2004).

Coggeshall, William Turner, *The Signs of the Times: Comprising a History of the Spirit-Rappings, in Cincinnati and Other Places: With Notes of Clairvoyant Revealments* (Cincinnati: W. T. Coggeshall, 1851).

Cohen, Lara Langer, *The Fabrication of American Literature: Fraudulence and Antebellum Print Culture* (Philadelphia: University of Pennsylvania Press, 2012).

Cole, Henry, 'To the Editors of the Sun', *New York Sun*, 20 August 1835, *The Lost Museum Archive*, City University of New York, <https://lostmuseum. cuny.edu/archive/joice-heth-new-york-evening-star-and-new-york> (accessed 9 November 2020).

Collins, Julia C., *The Curse of Caste; Or, the Slave Bride: A Rediscovered African American Novel*, ed. William L. Andrews and Mitch Kachum (New York: Oxford University Press, 2006).

Collins, Kris, 'White-Washing the Black-a-Moor: Othello, Negro Minstrelsy and Parodies of Blackness', *Journal of American Culture*, 19.3 (1996): 87–101.

Connor, Steven, *Dumbstruck: A Cultural History of Ventriloquism* (Oxford: Oxford University Press, 2000).

Cooper, James Fenimore, *The Prairie*, ed. Blake Nevius (New York: Penguin Books, 1987).

Coviello, Peter, *Intimacy in America: Dreams of Affiliation in Antebellum Literature* (Minneapolis: University of Minnesota Press, 2005).

Crockett, Rosemary Faye, 'The Garies and Their Friends: A Study of Frank J. Webb and His Novel', PhD dissertation (Harvard University, 1998).

Dain, Bruce R., *A Hideous Monster of the Mind: American Race Theory in the Early Republic* (Cambridge, MA: Harvard University Press, 2002).

Dayan, Colin, *The Law Is a White Dog: How Legal Rituals Make and Unmake Persons* (Princeton; Oxford: Princeton University Press, 2011).

Dayan, Joan, 'Poe, Persons and Property', *American Literary History*, 11.3 (1999): 405–25.

'Death of Joice Heth', *New York Sun*, 24 February 1836, *The Lost Museum Archive*, City University of New York, <https://lostmuseum.cuny.edu/archive/death-of-joice-heth-new-york-sun-february-24> (accessed 9 November 2020).

DeGuzmán, María, *Spain's Long Shadow: The Black Legend, Off-Whiteness, and Anglo-American Empire* (Minneapolis: University of Minnesota Press, 2005).

Deleuze, Gilles, 'Bartleby; or, The Formula', in *Essays Critical and Clinical*, trans. Daniel W. Smith and Michael A. Greco (Minneapolis: University of Minnesota Press, 1997), pp. 68–90.

DeLombard, Jeannine Marie, 'White-Jacket: Telling Who Is – and Aint – a Slave', in Robert S. Levine (ed.), *The New Cambridge Companion to Herman Melville* (Cambridge: Cambridge University Press, 2014), pp. 51–67.

Deloria, Philip J., *Playing Indian* (New Haven, CT; London: Yale University Press, 1998).

DeRewal, Tiffany, 'The Resurrection and the Knife: Protestant Cadavers and the Rise of American Medicine', *Literature and Medicine*, 32.2 (2014): 388–418.

Dillon, Elizabeth Maddock, 'Atlantic Practices: Minding the Gap between Literature and History', *Early American Literature*, 43.1 (2008): 205–10.

'Dissection of Joice Heth – Precious Humbug Exposed', *New York Sun*, 26 February 1836, *The Lost Museum Archive*, City University of New York, <http://lostmuseum.cuny.edu/archive/dissection-of-joice-heth-precious-humbug> (accessed 9 November 2020).

Dixon, George Washington, 'Zip Coon' (New York: Thomas Birch, 1834), *The Library of Congress Music Copyright Database, 1820–1860*, <http://www.loc.gov/item/sm1834.360780> (accessed 9 November 2020).

Dolar, Mladen, 'The Linguistics of the Voice', in Jonathan Sterne (ed.), *The Sound Studies Reader* (Hoboken, NJ: Taylor and Francis, 2012), pp. 539–54.

Doty, Benjamin J., 'Satire, Minstrelsy, and Embodiment in Sheppard Lee', *Early American Literature*, 51.1 (2016): 131–56.

Douglass, Frederick, *My Bondage and My Freedom*, ed. Celeste-Marie Bernier (Oxford: Oxford University Press, 2019).

Downes, Paul, 'Constitutional Secrets: "Memoirs of Carwin" and the Politics of Concealment', *Criticism*, 39.1 (1997): 89–117.

'Dramatic Reading by a Coloured Native of Philadelphia', *The Illustrated London News*, 2 August 1856, pp. 11–12.

DuBois, W. E. B., *Darkwater: Voices from Within the Veil*, introduction by Manning Marable (London: Verso, 2017).

Dunlap, William, *The Life of Charles Brockden Brown: Together with Selections from the Rarest of His Printed Works from His Original Letters, and from His Manuscripts before Unpublished*, 2 vols (Philadelphia: James P. Parke, 1815).

D.W., 'Account of a Singular Change of Colour in a Negro', *The Weekly Magazine of Original Essays, Fugitive Pieces, and Interesting Intelligence*, 1.4 (24 February 1798): 109–11.

Dyer, Richard, *White: Essays on Race and Culture* (Abingdon: Routledge, 1997).

Eaton, Joseph, *The Anglo-American Paper War: Debates about the New Republic, 1800–1825* (Basingstoke: Palgrave Macmillan, 2012).

Engle, Anna, 'Depiction of the Irish in Frank Webb's "The Garies and Their Friends" and Frances E. W. Harper's "Trial and Triumph"', *MELUS*, 26.1 (2001): 151–71.

Ethiop, 'Afric-American Picture Gallery: Third Paper', *Anglo-African Magazine*, 1.6 (April 1859): 173–7.

Etter, William, '"Tawdry Physical Affrightments": The Performance of Normalizing Visions of the Body in Edgar Allan Poe's "Loss of Breath"', *American Transcendental Quarterly*, 17.1 (2003): 5–22.

Faulkner, Howard, 'The Ambiguousnesses: Linguistic Invention in Pierre', *Leviathan: A Journal of Melville Studies*, 12 (2010): 41–50.

Forbes, Erin E., 'From Prison Cell to Slave Ship: Social Death in "The Premature Burial"', *Poe Studies*, 46 (2013): 32–58.

Foucault, Michel, *The Birth of the Clinic: An Archaeology of Medical Perception*, trans. A. M. Sheridan Smith (London: Tavistock Publications, 1973).

Frank, Adam, 'Valdemar's Tongue, Poe's Telegraphy', *English Literary History*, 72.3 (2005): 635–62.

Frankenberg, Ruth, *White Women, Race Matters: The Social Construction of Whiteness* (Minneapolis: University of Minnesota Press, 1993).

Freeburg, Christopher, *Melville and the Idea of Blackness: Race and Imperialism in Nineteenth-Century America* (New York: Cambridge University Press, 2012).

Garcha, Amanpal, *From Sketch to Novel: The Development of Victorian Fiction* (Cambridge: Cambridge University Press, 2009).

Gardner, Jared, 'Edgar Huntly's Savage Awakening', *American Literature*, 66.3 (1994): 429–61.

Garland-Thomson, Rosemarie, *Extraordinary Bodies: Figuring Physical Disability in American Culture and Literature* (New York: Columbia University Press, 1997).

Gilmore, Paul, *Aesthetic Materialism: Electricity and American Romanticism* (Palo Alto: Stanford University Press, 2008).

Goddu, Teresa A., 'Rethinking Race and Slavery in Poe Studies', *Poe Studies*, 33.1–2 (2000): 15–18.

Goldberg, Shari, *Quiet Testimony: A Theory of Witnessing from Nineteenth-Century American Literature* (New York: Fordham University Press, 2013).

Golemba, Henry, 'Frank Webb's The Garies and Their Friends Contextualized within African American Slave Narratives', in Robert D. Habich (ed.), *Lives out of Letters: Essays on American Literary Biography and Documentation in Honor of Robert N. Hudspeth* (Madison, WI; Teaneck, NJ: Farleigh Dickinson University Press, 2004), pp. 114–42.

Halliwell, Martin, *Images of Idiocy: The Idiot Figure in Modern Fiction and Film* (Farnham, Surrey: Ashgate, 2004).

Halttunen, Karen, *Confidence Men and Painted Women: A Study of Middle-Class Culture in America, 1830–1870* (New Haven; London: Yale University Press, 1982).

Handley, Sasha, *Visions of an Unseen World: Ghost Beliefs and Ghost Stories in Eighteenth-Century England* (London; Brookfield, VT: Pickering & Chatto, 2007).

Harris, Cheryl L., 'Whiteness as Property', *Harvard Law Review*, 106.8 (1993): 1707–91.

Hartman, Saidiya V., *Scenes of Subjection: Terror, Slavery, and Self-Making in Nineteenth-Century America* (Oxford: Oxford University Press, 1997).

Hawthorne, Nathaniel, *The Blithedale Romance* (Oxford; New York: Oxford World's Classics; Oxford University Press, 2009).

Hawthorne, Nathaniel, *The House of the Seven Gables* (Oxford: Oxford World's Classics; Oxford University Press, 2009).

Hawthorne, Nathaniel, *The Scarlet Letter* (Oxford: Oxford World's Classics; Oxford University Press, 2007).

Hedges, William L., *Washington Irving: An American Study, 1802–1832* (Baltimore: The Johns Hopkins Press, 1965).

Hofstadter, Richard, *Anti-Intellectualism in American Life* (New York: Vintage, 1962).

hooks, bell, *Black Looks: Race and Representation* (Boston: South End Press, 1992).

Hsu, Hsuan L., 'Democratic Expansionism in "Memoirs of Carwin"', *Early American Literature*, 35.2 (2000): 137–56.

Hughes, Robert, 'Sleepy Hollow: Fearful Pleasures and the Nightmare of History', *Arizona Quarterly: A Journal of American Literature, Culture, and Theory*, 61.3 (2005): 1–26.

Hyde, Carrie, *Civic Longing: The Speculative Origins of U.S. Citizenship* (Cambridge, MA: Harvard University Press, 2018).

Ignatiev, Noel, *How the Irish Became White* (New York: Routledge, 1995).

Irving, Washington, *Bracebridge Hall, Tales of a Traveller, The Alhambra* (New York: Library of America, 1991).

Irving, Washington, *The Complete Works of Washington Irving*, ed. Henry A. Pochmann, Herbert L. Kleinfield, Richard D. Rust, 30 vols (Boston: Twayne Publishers, 1978), vol. 23: *Letters, Volume 1, 1802–1823*, ed. Ralph M. Alderman, Herbert L. Kleinfield and Jennifer S. Banks.

Irving, Washington, *The Sketch Book of Geoffrey Crayon, Gent.*, ed. Malcolm Bradbury (London: Everyman, 1993).

Jacobson, Matthew Frye, *Whiteness of a Different Color: European Immigrants and the Alchemy of Race* (Cambridge, MA; London: Harvard University Press, 1999).

Jones, Douglas A., Jr, *The Captive Stage: Performance and the Proslavery Imagination of the Antebellum North* (Ann Arbor: The University of Michigan Press, 2014).

Jonik, Michael, *Herman Melville and the Politics of the Inhuman* (Cambridge: Cambridge University Press, 2018).

Joyce, Valerie M., 'Creating a Living Historiography: Tracing the Outlines of Philadelphia's Antebellum African American Women and Mapping Memory on to the Body', *Pennsylvania History: A Journal of Mid-Atlantic Studies*, 80.3 (2013): 420–41.

Karcher, Carolyn, *Shadow over the Promised Land: Slavery, Race and Violence in Melville's America* (Baton Rouge: Louisiana State University Press, 1980).

Kennedy, J. P., *Swallow Barn: Or, a Sojourn in the Old Dominion*, 2 vols (Philadelphia: Carey and Lea, 1832).

Kerber, Linda, *Women of the Republic: Intellect and Ideology in Revolutionary America* (Williamsburg, VA; Chapel Hill, NC: Omohundro Institute of Early American History and Culture; University of North Carolina Press, 1980).

Kettner, James H., *The Development of American Citizenship, 1608–1870* (Williamsburg, VA; Chapel Hill, NC: Institute of Early American History and Culture; University of North Carolina Press, 1978).

Knighton, Andrew Lyndon, *Idle Threats: Men and the Limits of Productivity in 19th-Century America* (New York; London: New York University Press, 2012).

Knott, Sarah, *Sensibility and the American Revolution* (Chapel Hill: University of North Carolina Press, 2009).

Kohl, Natasha, 'Frank Webb's "The Garies and Their Friends" and the Struggle over Black Education in the Antebellum North', *MELUS*, 38.4 (2013): 76–102.

Korobkin, Laura, 'Avoiding "Aunt Thomasina": Charles Dickens Responds to Harriet Beecher Stowe's Black American Reader, Mary Webb', *English Literary History*, 82.1 (2015): 115–40.

Lacan, Jacques, 'XVIII – Desire, Life and Death', in *The Seminars of Jacques Lacan: Book II – The Ego in Freud's Theory and in the Technique of Psychoanalysis 1954–1955*, ed. Jacques-Alain Miller, trans. Sylvana Tomaselli (Cambridge: Cambridge University Press, 1988), pp. 221–34.

Ladino, Jennifer K., *Reclaiming Nostalgia: Longing for Nature in American Literature* (Charlottesville; London: University of Virginia Press, 2012).

Lamb, Jonathan, *The Things Things Say* (Princeton: Princeton University Press, 2011).

Lapsansky, Emma Jones, 'Friends, Wives, and Strivings: Networkings and Community Values Among Nineteenth-Century Philadelphia Afroamerican Elites', *The Pennsylvania Magazine of History and Biography*, 108.1 (1984): 3–24.

Levine, Robert S., 'Disturbing Boundaries: Temperance, Black Elevation, and Violence in Frank J. Webb's The Garies and Their Friends', *Prospects*, 19 (1994): 349–74.

Levine, Robert S., 'Pierre's Blackened Hand', *Leviathan: A Journal of Melville Studies*, 1.1 (1999): 23–44.

Levinson, Marjorie, 'What Is New Formalism?', *PMLA*, 122.2 (2007): 558–69.

Lhamon, W. T., Jr, *Jump Jim Crow: Lost Plays, Lyrics, and Street Prose of the First Atlantic Popular Culture* (Cambridge, MA: Harvard University Press, 2003).

Lippard, George, *The Quaker City, or, The Monks of Monk Hall: A Romance of Philadelphia Life, Mystery, and Crime*, ed. David C. Reynolds (Amherst: University of Massachusetts Press, 1995).

Looby, Christopher, *Voicing America: Language, Literary Form, and the Origins of the United States* (Chicago: University of Chicago Press, 1996).

Looby, Christopher, and Cindy Weinstein (eds), *American Literature's Aesthetic Dimensions* (New York: Columbia University Press, 2012).

Lorde, Audre, *Sister Outsider: Essays and Speeches* (Berkeley: The Crossing Press, 1984).

Lott, Eric, *Love and Theft: Blackface Minstrelsy and the American Working Class* (New York; Oxford: Oxford University Press, 1993).

Luciano, Dana, *Arranging Grief: Sacred Time and the Body in Nineteenth-Century America* (New York: NYU Press, 2007).

Luskey, Brian, *On the Make: Clerks and the Quest for Capital in Nineteenth-Century America* (New York: NYU Press, 2010).

Maillard, Mary, '"Faithfully Drawn from Real Life": Autobiographical Elements in Frank J. Webb's The Garies and Their Friends', *The Pennsylvania Magazine of History and Biography*, 137.3 (2013): 261–300.

Martineau, Harriet, *Retrospects of Western Travel*, 2 vols (London: Saunders and Otley, 1838).

McAllister, Marvin, *Whiting Up: Minstrels & Stage Europeans in African American Performance* (Chapel Hill: University of North Carolina Press, 2011).

McGarry, Molly, *Ghosts of Futures Past: Spiritualism and the Cultural Politics of Nineteenth-Century America* (Berkeley: University of California Press, 2008).

McMahon, Lucia, *Mere Equals: The Paradox of Educated Women in the Early American Republic* (Ithaca: Cornell University Press, 2012).

McMillan Cottom, Tressie, 'The Problem with Obama's Faith in White America', *The Atlantic*, 13 December 2016, <https://www.theatlantic.com/

politics/archive/2016/12/obamas-faith-in-white-america/510503/>
(accessed 9 November 2020).

Medina, Louise H., *Nick of the Woods: A Drama in Three Acts* (Boston: William V. Spencer, 1856).

Melville, Herman, *Moby Dick*, ed. Tony Tanner (Oxford: Oxford World's Classics; Oxford University Press, 1998).

Melville, Herman, *Pierre, Or, The Ambiguities: The Kraken Edition*, ed. Hershel Parker (New York: HarperCollins Publishers, 1995).

Melville, Herman, *Pierre: Or The Ambiguities*, introduction and notes by William C. Spengemann (New York: Penguin Books, 1996).

Melville, Herman, *The Complete Shorter Fiction*, introduction by John Updike (London: D. Campbell, 1997).

Melville, Herman, *The Confidence-Man: His Masquerade*, ed. Tony Tanner (Oxford; New York: Oxford University Press, 1991).

Melville, Herman, *White-Jacket or The World in a Man-of-War*, ed. Harrison Hayford, Hershel Parker and G. Thomas Tanselle, *The Writings of Herman Melville* (Evanston; Chicago: Northwestern University Press; The Newberry Library, 1970).

Mielke, Laura L., *Provocative Eloquence: Theatre, Violence, and Antislavery Speech in the Antebellum United States* (Ann Arbor: University of Michigan Press, 2019).

Moreton-Robinson, Aileen, *White Possessive: Property, Power and Indigenous Sovereignty* (Minneapolis: University of Minnesota Press, 2015).

Morrison, Toni, *Playing in the Dark: Whiteness and the Literary Imagination* (Cambridge, MA: Harvard University Press, 1992).

Morton, Samuel George, *Crania Americana: Or a Comparatif View of the Skulls of Various Aboriginal Nations of North and South America* (Philadelphia: J. Dobson, 1839).

'Mr. and Mrs. Webb at Camden House', *The Era*, 31 May 1857: 10.

'Mrs Webb's Reading', *The National Anti-Slavery Standard*, 22 December 1855, <http://utc.iath.virginia.edu/uncletom/xianslav/xsno08ot.html> (accessed 9 November 2020).

Mueller, Monika, *The Infinite Fraternity of Feeling: Gender, Genre and Homoerotic Crisis in Hawthorne's The Blithedale Romance and Melville's Pierre* (Madison, NJ: Farleigh Dickinson University Press, 1996).

Murison, Justine S., 'Hypochondria and Racial Interiority in Robert Montgomery Bird's Sheppard Lee', *Arizona Quarterly: A Journal of American Literature, Culture, and Theory*, 64.1 (2008): 1–25.

Murison, Justine S., 'The Tyranny of Sleep: Somnambulism, Moral Citizenship, and Charles Brockden Brown's "Edgar Huntly"', *Early American Literature*, 44.2 (2009): 243–70.

Murray, Laura J., 'The Aesthetic of Dispossession: Washington Irving and Ideologies of (De)Colonization in the Early Republic', *American Literary History*, 8.2 (1996): 205–31.

*Native and Alien. The Naturalization Laws of the United States: Containing Also the Alien Laws of the State of New York* (Rochester, NY: D. M. Dewey, 1855).

Nelson, Dana D., *National Manhood: Capitalist Citizenship and the Imagined Fraternity of White Men* (Durham, NC: Duke University Press, 1998).

'New Poll: Some Americans Express Troubling Racial Attitudes Even as Majority Oppose White Supremacists', *University of Virginia Center for Politics*, 14 September 2017, <http://centerforpolitics.org/crystalball/articles/new-poll-some-americans-express-troubling-racial-attitudes-even-as-majority-oppose-white-supremacists/> (accessed 19 May 2020).

Nichols, Marcia D., 'Poe's "Some Words with a Mummy" and Blackface Anatomy', *Poe Studies*, 48 (2015): 2–16.

Nielsen, Kim E., *A Disability History of the United States* (Boston: Beacon Press, 2012).

Nord, Deborah Epstein, *Gypsies and the British Imagination, 1807–1930* (New York: Columbia University Press, 2006).

'Notices Concerning the Scottish Gypsies', *Blackwood's Edinburgh Magazine* 1 (April 1817): 43–58.

Nowatzki, Robert, 'Blurring the Color Line: Black Freedom, Passing, Abolitionism, and Irish Ethnicity in Frank J. Webb's The Garies and Their Friends', *Studies in American Fiction*, 33.1 (2005): 29–58.

Nyong'o, Tavia, *The Amalgamation Waltz: Race, Performance, and the Ruses of Memory* (Minneapolis: University of Minnesota Press, 2009).

Ogden, Emily, *Credulity: A Cultural History of US Mesmerism* (Chicago: University of Chicago Press, 2018).

Otter, Samuel, 'An Aesthetics in All Things', *Representations*, 104.1 (2008): 116–25.

Otter, Samuel, *Philadelphia Stories: America's Literature of Race and Freedom* (New York: Oxford University Press, 2010).

Parker, Hershel, *Herman Melville: A Biography*, 2 vols (Baltimore; London: The Johns Hopkins University Press, 2002).

Pease, Donald E. (ed.), *Revisionary Interventions into the Americanist Canon* (Durham, NC: London: Duke University Press, 1994).

Percich, Aaron Matthew, 'Irish Mouths and English Tea-Pots: Orality and Unreason in "The System of Doctor Tarr and Professor Fether"', *Poe Studies*, 47 (2014): 76–99.

Peters, Richard (ed.), *The Public Statutes at Large of The United States of America, from the Organization of the Government in 1789, to March 3, 1845*, 8 vols (Boston: Charles C. Little and James Brown, 1845), vol. 1.

Pethers, Matthew, 'The Secret Witness: Thinking, and Not Thinking, about Servants in the Early American Novel', in Andrew Lawson (ed.), *Class and the Making of American Literature* (New York: Routledge, 2014), pp. 40–55.

Poe, Edgar Allan, *The Collected Works of Edgar Allan Poe*, ed. Thomas Ollive Mabbott, 3 vols (Cambridge, MA; London: Harvard University Press, 1978), vol. 2: *Tales and Sketches, 1831–1842*.

Poe, Edgar Allan, *The Collected Works of Edgar Allan Poe*, ed. Thomas Ollive Mabbott, 3 vols (Cambridge, MA; London: Harvard University Press, 1978), vol. 3: *Tales and Sketches, 1843–1849*.

Poe, Edgar Allan, *The Letters of Edgar Allan Poe*, ed. John Ward Ostrom, 2 vols (Cambridge, MA: Harvard University Press, 1948), vol. 1: *1824–1845*.

Poe, Edgar Allan, 'The Philosophy of Composition', in *Essays and Reviews: Theory of Poetry, Reviews of British and Continental Authors, Reviews of American Authors and American Literature* (New York: Library of America, 1984), pp. 13–25.

Post, Isaac, *Voices from the Spirit World: Being Communications from Many Spirits. By the Hand of Isaac Post, Medium* (Rochester, NY: Charles H. McDonell, 1852).

Pratt, Lloyd, *Archives of American Time: Literature and Modernity in the Nineteenth Century* (Philadelphia: University of Pennsylvania Press, 2009).

Ramsay, David, *A Dissertation on the Manners of Acquiring the Character and Privileges of a Citizen of the United States* (Charleston, SC: n.p., 1789).

Ray, Angela, *The Lyceum and Public Culture in the Nineteenth-Century United States* (East Lansing: Michigan State University Press, 2005).

Rebhorn, Matthew, 'Ontological Drift: Medical Discourse and Racial Embodiment in Robert Montgomery Bird's Sheppard Lee', *ESQ: A Journal of the American Renaissance*, 61.2 (2015): 262–96.

Rebhorn, Matthew, *Pioneer Performances: Staging the Frontier* (Oxford: Oxford University Press, 2012).

Reed, Peter P., *Rogue Performances: Staging the Underclasses in Early American Theatre Culture* (New York: Palgrave Macmillan, 2009).

Reid, Thomas, *An Inquiry into the Human Mind, on the Principles of Common Sense*, 4th edn (London: T. Cadell, 1785).

Reid, Thomas, *Essays on the Intellectual Powers of Man*, 2 vols (Dublin: L. White, 1786).

Reid-Pharr, Robert, *Conjugal Union: The Body, The House, and the Black American* (New York; Oxford: Oxford University Press, 1999).

Reiss, Benjamin, *Showman and the Slave: Race, Death, and Memory in Barnum's America* (Cambridge, MA: Harvard University Press, 2010).

'Review: Bracebridge Hall', *Blackwood's Edinburgh Magazine* 11 (June 1822): 686–92.

'Review: The Garies and Their Friends', *The Morning Post*, 6 October 1857: 7.

Ricci, David M., *Good Citizenship in America* (Cambridge: Cambridge University Press, 2004).

Riga, Kate, 'LePage: Eliminating Electoral College Would Make Whites "A Forgotten People"', *Talking Points Memo*, 28 February 2019, <https://talkingpointsmemo.com/news/lepage-eliminating-electoral-college-whites-forgotten-people> (accessed 9 November 2020).

Ringe, Donald A., 'New York and New England: Irving's Criticism of American Society', *American Literature*, 38.4 (1967): 455–67.

Roach, Joseph, *Cities of the Dead: Circum-Atlantic Performance* (New York: Columbia University Press, 1996).

Robinson, J. H., *Marietta, or the Two Students. A Tale of the Dissecting Room and 'Body Snatchers'* (Boston: Jordan & Wiley, 1846).

Roediger, David R., *The Wages of Whiteness: Race and the Making of the American Working Class* (London: Verso, 1991).

Rosenfeld, Sophia A., *Common Sense: A Political History* (Cambridge, MA: Harvard University Press, 2011).

Rubin-Dorsky, Jeffrey, *Adrift in the Old World: The Psychological Pilgrimage of Washington Irving* (Chicago: University of Chicago Press, 1988).

Rush, Benjamin, *Benjamin Rush's Lectures on the Mind*, ed. Eric T. Carlson, Patricia S. Noel and Jeffrey L. Wollock (Philadelphia: American Philosophical Society, 1981).

Rush, Benjamin, *Essays, Literary, Moral and Philosophical*, 2nd edn (Philadelphia: Thomas and William Bradford, 1806).

Rush, Benjamin, *Medical Inquiries and Observations*, 2nd edn, 4 vols (Philadelphia: J. Conrad & Co., 1805), vol. 1.

Rush, Benjamin, 'Reasons for Ascribing the Colour of Negroes to Leprosy', *The Monthly Magazine and the American Review*, 2.4 (April 1800): 298–301.

Ruttenburg, Nancy, *Democratic Personality: Popular Voice and the Trial of American Authorship* (Stanford: Stanford University Press, 1998).

Ryan, Susan M., *The Grammar of Good Intentions: Race and the Antebellum Culture of Benevolence* (Ithaca; London: Cornell University Press, 2003).

Saint-Rémy, Joseph, *Mémoires du Général Toussaint-L'Ouverture* (Paris: Pagnerre, Libraire-Éditeur, 1853).

Samuels, Shirley, '"Wieland": Alien and Infidel', *Early American Literature*, 25.1 (1990): 46–66.

Sansay, Leonora, *Zelica, the Creole; A Novel, by an American*, 3 vols (London: William Fearman, 1820).

Sappol, Michael, *A Traffic of Dead Bodies: Anatomy and Embodied Social Identity in Nineteenth-Century America* (Princeton: Princeton University Press, 2002).

Sbriglia, Russell, 'Specters of Marxism in Frank J. Webb's The Garies and Their Friends: Class, Race, and the Critique of Ideology', *ESQ: A Journal of Nineteenth-Century American Literature and Culture*, 64.4 (2018): 564–602.

Schmidt, Leigh Eric, *Hearing Things: Religion, Illusion, and the American Enlightenment* (Cambridge, MA: Harvard University Press, 2000).

Sealts, Merton M., 'Melville and the Shakers', *Studies in Bibliography*, 2 (1949): 105–14.

Seltzer, Mark, 'Saying Makes It So: Language and Event in Brown's "Wieland"', *Early American Literature*, 13.1 (1978): 81–91.

Shapiro, Stephen, *The Culture and Commerce of the Early American Novel: Reading the Atlantic World-System* (University Park: The Pennsylvania State University Press, 2008).

Silyn Roberts, Siân, *Gothic Subjects: The Transformation of Individualism in American Fiction, 1790–1861* (Philadelphia: University of Pennsylvania Press, 2014).

'Singular Anecdote Relative to Ventriloquism', *Weekly Magazine, Or Edinburgh Amusements*, 1.25 (25 August 1774): 275–7.

Sizemore, Michelle, *American Enchantment: Rituals of the People in the Post-Revolutionary World* (Oxford: Oxford University Press, 2017).

Sizemore, Michelle, '"Changing by Enchantment": Temporal Convergence, Early National Comparisons, and Washington Irving's Sketchbook', *Studies in American Fiction*, 40.2 (2013): 157–83.

Sklansky, Jeffrey P., *The Soul's Economy: Market Society and Selfhood in American Thought, 1820–1920* (Chapel Hill: University of North Carolina Press, 2002).

Smith, Caleb, *The Oracle and the Curse: A Poetics of Justice from the Revolution to the Civil War* (Cambridge, MA: Harvard University Press, 2013).

Smith, Rogers M., *Civic Ideals: Conflicting Visions of Citizenship in U.S. History* (New Haven; London: Yale University Press, 1997).

Sondey, Walter, 'From Nation of Virtue to Virtual Nation: Washington Irving and American Nationalism', in Jean Pickering and Suzanna Kehde (eds), *Narratives of Nostalgia, Gender and Nationalism* (Basingstoke: Macmillan Press, 1997), pp. 52–73.

Soto, Isabel (ed.), *A Place That Is Not a Place: Essays in Liminality and Text* (Madrid: The Gateway Press, 2000).

Spahn, Hannah, *Thomas Jefferson, Time, and History* (Charlottesville; London: University of Virginia Press, 2011).

'Special Notices', *The New York Times*, 18 December 1855, <http://utc.iath.virginia.edu/uncletom/xianslav/xsno05at.html> (accessed 9 November 2020).

Spires, Derrick R., *The Practice of Citizenship: Black Politics and Print Culture in the Early United States* (Philadelphia: University of Pennsylvania Press, 2019).

Stampone, Christopher, 'A "Spirit of Mistaken Benevolence": Civilizing the Savage in Charles Brockden Brown's Edgar Huntly', *Early American Literature*, 50.2 (2015): 415–48.

Stanhope Smith, Samuel, *An Essay on the Causes of the Variety of Complexion and Figure in the Human Species*, revised edn (New Brunswick, NJ: J. Simpson and Co., 1810).

Stern, Julia A., *Plight of Feeling: Sympathy and Dissent in the Early American Novel* (Chicago: University of Chicago Press, 1997).

Stockton, Elizabeth, 'The Property of Blackness: The Legal Fiction of Frank J. Webb's The Garies and Their Friends', *African American Review*, 43.2–3 (2009): 473–86.

Stowe, Harriet Beecher, *The Christian Slave, A Drama* (Boston: Phillips, Sampson and Company, 1855).

Stowe, Harriet Beecher, *Uncle Tom's Cabin*, ed. Jean Fagan Yellin (Oxford: Oxford World's Classics; Oxford University Press, 1998).

Tamarkin, Elisa, *Anglophilia: Deference, Devotion, and Antebellum America* (Chicago: University of Chicago Press, 2008).

Tavor Bannet, Eve, 'The Constantias of the 1790s: Tales of Constancy and Republican Daughters', *Early American Literature*, 49.2 (2014): 435–66.

Taylor, Charles, *Philosophical Papers*, 2 vols (Cambridge: Cambridge University Press, 1985), vol 1: *Human Agency and Language*.

*The Dred Scott Decision: Opinion of the Chief Justice with An Introduction by Dr. J. H. Van Evrie* (New York: Van Evrie, Horton & Co., 1860).

'The Garies and Their Friends', *The Literary Gazette, and Journal of Archaeology, Science, and Art*, 26 September 1857: 917–19.

*The Life of Joice Heth, the Nurse of Gen. George Washington, (the Father of Our Country,) Now Living at the Astonishing Age of 161 Years, and Weighs Only 46 Pounds* (New York, 1835), <http://docsouth.unc.edu/neh/heth/heth.html> (accessed 9 November 2020).

Thompson, Graham, '"Through Consumptive Pallors of This Blank, Raggy Life": Melville's Not Quite White Working Bodies', *Leviathan: A Journal of Melville Studies*, 14 (2012): 25–43.

Thurman, Judith, 'Philip Roth E-Mails on Trump', *The New Yorker*, 30 January 2017, <https://www.newyorker.com/magazine/2017/01/30/philip-roth-e-mails-on-trump> (accessed 9 November 2020).

Tiffany, Joel, *Lectures on Spiritualism: Being a Series of Lectures on the Phenomena and Philosophy of Development, Individualism, Spirit, Immortality, Mesmerism* (Cleveland: J. Tiffany, 1851).

Tompkins, Jane, *Sensational Designs: The Cultural Work of American Fiction 1790–1860* (New York; Oxford: Oxford University Press, 1985).

Trump, Donald J., 'The forgotten men and women of our country will be forgotten no longer. From this moment on, it's going to be #AmericaFirst' [*Twitter post*] (@realDonaldTrump, 20 January 2017), <https://twitter.com/realdonaldtrump/status/822502450007515137?lang=en> (accessed 9 November 2020).

Trump, Donald J., 'Such a beautiful and important evening! The forgotten man and woman will never be forgotten again. We will all come together as never before' [*Twitter post*] (@realDonaldTrump, 9 November 2016), <https://twitter.com/realdonaldtrump/status/796315640307060738?lang=en> (accessed 9 November 2020).

Tuck, Eve, and K. Wayne Yang, 'Decolonization is Not a Metaphor', *Decolonization: Indigeneity, Education & Society*, 1.1 (2012): 1–40.

Turner, Victor, *Process, Performance and Pilgrimage: A Study in Comparitive Symbology* (New Delhi: Concept Publishing Company, 1979).

Turner, Victor, *The Forest of Symbols: Aspects of Ndembu Ritual* (Ithaca: Cornell University Press, 1967).

Turner, Victor, *The Ritual Process: Structure and Anti-Structure* (New Brunswick, NJ: Transaction Publishers, 2008).

Van Gennep, Arnold, *The Rites of Passage*, ed. Solon T. Kimball, trans. Monika B. Vizedom and Gabrielle L. Caffee (London: Routledge & Kegan Paul, 1965).

Viljoen, Hein, 'A Poetics of Liminality and Hybridity', in Hein Viljoen and Chris N. van der Merwe (eds), *Beyond the Threshold: Explorations of Liminality in Literature* (New York: Peter Lang, 2007), pp. 1–26.

Warner, Michael, 'The Mass Public and the Mass Subject', in Craig Calhoun (ed.), *Habermas and the Public Sphere* (Cambridge, MA: MIT Press, 1991), pp. 377–401.

Watts, Richard J., *Politeness* (Cambridge: Cambridge University Press, 2003).

Watts, Steven, *The Republic Reborn: War and the Making of Liberal America, 1790–1820* (Baltimore; London: The Johns Hopkins University Press, 1987).

Webb, Frank J., 'Biographical Sketch', in *The Christian Slave*, by Harriet Beecher Stowe (London: Sampson, Low, Son, and Co., 1856), <http://utc.iath.virginia.edu/uncletom/xianslav/xsesfjwat.html> (accessed 9 November 2020).

Webb, Frank J., *The Garies and Their Friends*, ed. Megan Walsh and William Huntting Howell (Peterborough, ON: Broadview Press, 2016).

Weinstein, Cindy, *Time, Tense, and American Literature: When Is Now?* (Cambridge: Cambridge University Press, 2015).

Weinstein, Cindy, 'We Are Family: Melville's Pierre', *Leviathan: A Journal of Melville Studies*, 7.1 (2005): 19–40.

Weinstock, Jeffrey Andrew, *Charles Brockden Brown* (Cardiff: University of Wales Press, 2011).

Weld, Theodore Dwight, *American Slavery As It Is: Testimony of a Thousand Witnesses* (New York: The American Anti-Slavery Office, 1839).

Weyler, Karen A., *Intricate Relations: Sexual and Economic Desire in American Fiction, 1789–1814* (Iowa City: University of Iowa Press, 2005).

White, Ed, 'Carwin the Peasant Rebel', in Philip Barnard, Mark L. Kamrath and Stephen Shapiro (eds), *Revising Charles Brockden Brown: Culture, Politics, and Sexuality in the Early Republic* (Knoxville: University of Tennessee Press, 2004), pp. 41–59.

Wills, Gary, *Inventing America: Jefferson's Declaration of Independence* (New York: Vintage Books, 1979).

Wilson, Harriet E., *Our Nig: Or, Sketches from the Life of a Free Black*, ed. P. Gabrielle Foreman and Reginald H. Pitts (London: Penguin Random House, 2004).

Wolfe, Eric A., 'Ventriloquizing Nation: Voice, Identity, and Radical Democracy in Charles Brockden Brown's Wieland', *American Literature*, 78.3 (2006): 431–57.

Woodworth, Samuel, *The Forest Rose, Or, American Farmers* (Boston: William V. Spencer, 1855).

Wray, Matt, *Not Quite White: White Trash and the Boundaries of Whiteness* (Durham, NC: Duke University Press, 2006).

Wright, Tom F., *Lecturing the Atlantic: Speech, Print, and an Anglo-American Commons, 1830–1870* (Oxford: Oxford University Press, 2017).

Yancy, George, *Look, a White!: Philosophical Essays on Whiteness* (Philadelphia: Temple University Press, 2012).

Yerrinton, J. M. W., *The Boston Mob of 'Gentlemen of Property and Standing.': Proceedings of the Anti-Slavery Meeting Held in Stacy Hall, Boston, on the Twentieth Anniversary of the Mob of October 21, 1835* (Boston: R. F. Walcutt, 1855).

Young Welke, Barbara, *Law and the Borders of Belonging in the Long Nineteenth Century United States* (Cambridge: Cambridge University Press, 2010).

Zakim, Michael, 'Producing Capitalism: The Clerk at Work', in Michael Zakim and Gary J. Kornblith (eds), *Capitalism Takes Command: The Social Transformation of Nineteenth-Century America* (Chicago: The University of Chicago Press, 2012), pp. 223–48.

# INDEX